W9-CPN-634

How You Can Help Your Child Learn Best

You, as a parent, can raise your child's lifelong level of intelligence and increase his joy in learning by the ways in which you care for him during the first six years after birth. This easy-to-follow guide, *How to Raise a Brighter Child*, provides the understanding, information and simple activities that will help you nourish your youngster's mind well so he will grow up brighter and happier.

JOAN BECK, journalist and syndicated columnist, explains the important new scientific findings on early learning, and shows you how to apply them to your child's particular personality and needs.

For orders other than by individual consumers, Pocket Books grants a discount on the purchase of 10 or more copies of single titles for special markets or premium use. For further details, please write to the Vice-President of Special Markets, Pocket Books, 1633 Broadway, New York, NY 10019-6785, 8th Floor.

For information on how individual consumers can place orders, please write to Mail Order Department, Simon & Schuster Inc., 200 Old Tappan Road, Old Tappan, NJ 07675.

HOW TO RAISE A BRIGHTER CHILD

The Case for Early Learning

by JOAN BECK

POCKET BOOKS

New York   London   Toronto   Sydney   Tokyo   Singapore

The sale of this book without its cover is unauthorized. If you purchased
this book without a cover, you should be aware that it was reported to
the publisher as "unsold and destroyed." Neither the author nor the
publisher has received payment for the sale of this "stripped book."

A revised and updated edition.

POCKET BOOKS, a division of Simon & Schuster Inc.
1230 Avenue of the Americas, New York, NY 10020

Copyright © 1967, 1975, 1986 by Joan Beck

All rights reserved, including the right to reproduce
this book or portions thereof in any form whatsoever.
For information address Pocket Books, 1230 Avenue
of the Americas, New York, NY 10020

ISBN: 0-671-73999-9

Revised Pocket Books printing September 1986

10 9 8 7

POCKET and colophon are registered trademarks of
Simon & Schuster Inc.

Printed in the U.S.A.

Acknowledgments

Permission to quote from published materials has been obtained from these sources:

The Ronald Press Company for J. McV. Hunt, *Intelligence and Experience.* Copyright © 1961, The Ronald Press Company, New York.

Holt, Rinehart and Winston, Inc. for Benjamin S. Bloom, Allison Davis, and Robert Hess, *Compensatory Education for Cultural Deprivation.* New York, Holt, Rinehart and Winston, Inc., 1965.

National Education Association of the United States for Educational Policies Commission, *Universal Opportunity for Early Childhood Education.* Washington, D.C., National Education Association of the United States.

John Wiley & Sons, Inc. for Benjamin S. Bloom, *Stability and Change in Human Characteristics.* New York, John Wiley & Sons, Inc., 1964.

The Atlantic Monthly and Wilder Penfield for "The Uncommitted Cortex," *The Atlantic Monthly,* Vol. 214, No. 1 (July, 1964). Copyright © 1964, by The Atlantic Monthly Company, Boston, Mass. 02116. Reprinted with permission.

American Montessori Society for George Stevens, "Reading for Young Children," *Building the Foundations for Creative Learning.* New York, American Montessori Society, 1964.

Princeton University Press for Wilder Penfield and Lamar

ACKNOWLEDGMENTS

Roberts, *Speech and Brain-Mechanisms*. Reprinted by permission of the Princeton University Press. Copyright © 1959, by Princeton University Press, Princeton, N.J., 1959.

Teachers College Press for Kenneth D. Wann, Miriam Selchen Dorn, and Elizabeth Ann Liddle, *Fostering Intellectual Development in Young Children*. New York: Teachers College Press, 1962, © 1962 by Teachers College, Columbia University. Reprinted with permission from the publisher.

American Academy of Pediatrics for The Committee on Accident Prevention, "Responsibility Means Safety for Your Child," 1964.

G. P. Putnam's Sons for "Naughty Soap Song," and "About Candy," from Dorothy Aldis, *All Together*. Reprinted by permission of G. P. Putnam's Sons. Copyright 1925–1928, 1934, 1939, 1952 by Dorothy Aldis.

Aileen Fischer for "A Bug," from Aileen Fischer, *Up the Windy Hill*. New York, Abelard-Schuman Limited, 1953. Reprinted with permission of Aileen Fischer.

The National Council of Teachers of English and Arthur I. Gates for "Unsolved Problems in Reading: A Symposium," *Elementary English*, Vol. 31, No. 6 (October, 1954).

McGraw-Hill Book Company, Inc., for Calvin W. Taylor, *Creativity: Progress and Potential*. McGraw-Hill Book Company, Inc., 1964. Used by permission.

Prentice-Hall, Inc. for E. Paul Torrance, *Guiding Creative Talent*, © 1962. Englewood Cliffs, N.J., Prentice-Hall, Inc. Reprinted by permission.

Teachers College Record for Robert J. Havighurst, "Conditions Productive to Superior Children," *Teachers College Record*, Vol. 62 (April, 1961).

The *Chicago Tribune* for permission to use material from my column, "You and Your Child," distributed by the Chicago Tribune-New York News Syndicate, Inc.

To Ernie,
who shares the adventure

Contents

Preface

This is a child-care book about your youngster's mind, not his body. It won't tell you how to feed, burp, diaper, and put your baby back to sleep—but what you can do to stimulate his mind to learn and grow. It concerns the nourishment you should be giving his brain, not his stomach. It is devoted to thinking, not thumb-sucking. It holds that parents should spend more time—and can have far more fun—sharing a youngster's delight in learning than fretting about toilet training.

For we now know that parents can raise a child's useful level of intelligence substantially by the ways in which they care for him during the first six years of his life, long before he begins his formal education. Even the most skilled and loving parents, in the best of homes, have probably been stunting their children's mental development to a degree because they have not known what fast-growing brains need so urgently.

The purpose of this book is to report to parents about new research on the growth of children's intelligence during the first six years of life and to translate this research from scientific journals, professionals' symposiums, and experimental laboratories into a form that will be useful to those who live and work with small children daily. It aims to do for your child's mind what other books do for his physical and emotional growth.

This book was the first ever written to report to parents about the new research on early learning and how the new scientific discoveries could be used to help their children's brains grow better, to their lasting benefit and joy. Since it was first published, hundreds of thousands of parents have tried the ideas in this book. Many have written to say how much their youngsters have profited from this new understanding about their enormous and innate need to learn and how it could best be filled. Many of the letters echoed the key finding in early-learning research: Satisfying a child's mental hunger not only results in his becoming brighter but makes him happier and helps family life to go more smoothly.

Now the book has been updated. Its basic ideas still hold true and are therefore included here. But now there is more research to confirm them, more experience to report on how they can best be used for your child's benefit. Now there is more scientific agreement about the startling successes and loving joys of early learning. The ideas that were so controversial when this book was first published are now becoming an accepted part of child-rearing.

The new research and the years of experience that go into this new edition reconfirm the book's first premise: Parents—instead of being too emotionally involved to teach their own offspring—are the first and most influential teachers a child ever has. The most obvious evidence is, of course, the way in which mothers and fathers help a youngster master the complexities of his native language long before the age of six.

You won't be able to follow all of the suggestions in this book with one individual boy or girl. Children differ too much, one from another. So do homes, parents, circumstances. No child is ever developed, like a recipe, by adding precisely so much of each ingredient. Every youngster comes with different inborn characteristics and temperament and potentialities which a parent must take into consideration in rearing him. Parents also vary in how much time they can spend on child care, what responsibilities they must take on outside the home.

But this book will give you broad guidelines to follow. It will help you see your child in a new light, give you a fresh perspective on what his growing mind needs, and suggest hundreds of specific ways in which you can help to provide for these needs. Once you begin to think of him as an eager, growing, exploring, budding intelligence as well as a small human being with urgent physical and emotional needs, your whole relationship with him will be different—richer, happier, and more satisfying.

In writing this book, I am functioning in my primary role as a journalist—not as an educator or child-care professional. The new research about early learning and the promise it holds for so many young lives is one of the most exciting ideas of the last two decades and one about which I have been fortunate to do considerable reporting. I am deeply grateful to the physicians, educators, psychologists and behavioral scientists who have shared their knowledge and explained their work to me so that I could report it to readers in a form most useful to them in their lives with small children.

I appreciate the encouragement I received from my editors at the *Chicago Tribune* and for permission to include in this book some material from my articles and columns about children published by that newspaper and by the Chicago Tribune-New York News Syndicate, Inc. The information in this book comes from many sources, including research reports, professional journals, government studies, interviews, scientific meetings, physicians, child-care professionals, educators, psychologists, and parents; I am grateful to all of them for sharing their expertise and experience. Leon Shimkin, chairman of the board of Simon & Schuster, played a major role in making this book a best-selling success when it was first published, and I will always be appreciative of his interest and enthusiasm. I wish to thank James Ertel for his advice and help. Norma Howard, of the ERIC Clearinghouse on Early Childhood Education, contributed much by making computer searches for relevant research. The March of Dimes Birth Defects Foundation has provided information and help for the chapter on prenatal care of infants; I have learned much from their experts and, in particular, from Dr. Virginia Apgar when she was the foundation's medical director. Physicians and staff at the American Academy of Pediatrics have been helpful in providing research and insight, as always. Todd Hallenbeck deserves thanks for his generous and cheerful help in setting up my word processor. And so does my father, Roscoe Wagner, for myriad reasons.

My two children, Christopher and Melinda, indelibly shaped my feelings about the satisfactions of being a mother and first taught me unmistakably about the eager insistence with which babies and young children seek to learn. I am grateful to them for what they taught me and for the joys they have given me all of their lives and to my husband, Ernest Beck, for taking such a loving and liberated share in parenting.

The names of parents and children and identifying details used in illustrative examples in this book have been changed, although all of the incidents are factual. For convenience in writing, the pronoun "he" is used to refer to the child, although both girls and boys are obviously intended. And although the book is addressed primarily to mothers, the suggestions also apply to fathers, who should, of course, share the adventure and the joy of helping their children's minds to grow.

HOW TO RAISE
A BRIGHTER CHILD

1. Your Child's First and Best Teacher: You

How much is your child capable of learning before he's six years old and ready for first grade? What happens to his brain during these preschool years when his body is growing and changing so rapidly?

Is your youngster's intelligence level actually fixed for life by the genes he inherits from his parents? Or can it be raised by the way you care for him at home, long before he ever meets a teacher in the classroom?

As a parent, what specifically can you do to give your child ample opportunity to grow in intelligence during these irreplaceable early years of life?

New research about learning and brain development in preschool youngsters has reached the stage where exciting and rewarding answers to these questions are available to parents. These answers add up to a larger, happier, and most important role for parents in fostering the mental development of their children before school age and to the promise of a lifelong higher intelligence for these youngsters.

In the past, child-care books have concentrated on helping parents learn how to raise children who are physically healthy and emotionally well adjusted. They have detailed directions about how to become a competent diaper-changer, tantrum-stopper, rash-identifier, bathroom attendant, and referee between rival siblings. But parents have received almost no help or information or credit for their role as teacher and nurturer of their offspring's developing

1

intelligence. Much more has been written about what should go into a baby's stomach than what should go into his growing mind. More emphasis has been put on teaching a child to use the bathroom than to use his brain.

Today, knowledge about the development of intelligence in small children is increasing rapidly. Neurophysiologists, neurobiologists, and psychologists are beginning to learn more about the biology of the mind, to understand what happens to the brain of a child as he grows. There is now major evidence that the optimum time for many kinds of learning and for the stimulation of basic learning abilities in a child is already largely past before he reaches age six and enters first grade. Given some understanding and information about early learning, a parent can substantially increase his youngster's intelligence and joy in learning for the rest of his life.

You, as a parent, are of necessity the first and most important teacher your child ever has. You have the unique opportunity to boost your youngster's intelligence when it is most subject to change, to teach him individually, at his own rate and when and by what means he is most likely to learn, to shape your relationship with him in ways that can actually help him become brighter. It's time you got more help in this vital role. That is the purpose of this book.

Parents who have tried using early-learning techniques with preschool children often report delightedly about the results. Some cases in point:

In a small town in Indiana, Jeanne Jenkins is giving a birthday party for her four-year-old daughter, Emily, and six small friends. Toward the end of the party comes the crucial five minutes when Emily's mother has to leave the four-year-old guests alone in the living room while she goes into the kitchen to dip up the ice cream and light the candles on the birthday cake.

From the kitchen Mrs. Jenkins hears nothing but a worrisome quiet. Anxiously, she peeks into the living room and sees that one of the guests has pulled a "Smokey the Bear" book from the shelf and is reading with great delight to the other children, who are fascinated by the story.

After the party, Mrs. Jenkins telephones the small guest's

mother. "Oh, yes, Martha learned to read last summer," replies the four-year-old's parent. "No, she'd never read a 'Smokey the Bear' book before. But she does read everything she can get her hands on."

In Washington, D.C., Patrick, age five, pesters his father for time on the family's home computer. When it is his turn, Patrick begins using a program called LOGO, figuring out how to command a "turtle" to draw geometric shapes on the screen in front of him and to arrange them into designs.

In Ann Arbor, Michigan, a third-generation Armenian couple—she a grade-school teacher on extended maternity leave and he a teaching assistant finishing work on his Ph.D.—want their son to appreciate and profit from his Armenian heritage. So they have spoken only Armenian to him since his birth. Outside of his home, he hears, and of course learns, English. Now, at age four, he is happily fluent in both languages and effortlessly switches from one to the other when it is appropriate.

In a Chicago apartment, a young father holds up cards with printed words for his son, Jonathan, age twenty-one months, to read. By acting out what the words say, Jon demonstrates that he has a reading vocabulary of 160 words—larger than his speaking vocabulary.

In a nursery school in a Manhattan skyscraper, Danny, four, walks purposefully over to a supply cupboard and pulls out a big box of beads and numbered cards. Sprawling on a little rug on the floor, he begins to work. First, he arranges a set of the numbers in order from 0 to 9. Beside each he places a little glass dish and into each dish he drops the corresponding number of beads.

Next, Danny puts another set of numbers in "tens place," making his figures read 11 to 99. With ready-made chains of 10 beads each, he lays out matching rows of 10 to 90 beads beside the tiny dishes. Then he adds a third set of numbers in "hundreds place" and the right number of 100-bead units. When he finishes, he has correctly created and labeled rows of 111, 222, 333, 444, 555, 666, 777, 888, and 999 beads—and with obvious satisfaction, taught himself a major lesson in number concepts.

None of these children was born a genius. But because someone who loved each youngster knew about new theories of early learning and brain development, each had the opportunity to learn more than most children usually do at the age when their fast-growing brain could absorb knowledge readily. All of them appear to be developing above-average intelligence and a joyous love of learning as a result.

Martha's mother taught her to read for fun, using a series of phonetic games and cartoons published by a Chicago newspaper. "We had no idea a four-year-old could learn so fast or enjoy reading so much," she wrote to the newspaper's editor. Patrick's father simply enjoyed sharing his own enthusiasm about computers with his son.

The Ann Arbor parents are deliberately using early-learning principles to preserve an ethnic heritage that is important in their own lives and that they want to pass on, with all its cultural richness, to their offspring. Jonathan's father has been casually exposing him to printed words as a game they both enjoy since the boy was sixteen months old. Danny attends a Montessori school, where he can choose freely from a wealth of early-learning materials.

Interest in early learning and research about it are coming from many different scientific fields. Neurologists, neurophysiologists, and pediatricians are trying to determine precisely what happens to the brain during its fastest growing stages. Psychologists are learning more about the biological and biochemical basis of behavior and are including in their research about the mind a consideration of the brain, which is the organ of the mind. Biologists are conducting thousands of experiments probing the effects of early stimulation on the brains of young animals, and neurobiologists are studying how cells in the brain grow, "talk" to one another, and change and learning about the complex chemistry of brain development and functioning.

Sociologists and teachers are urgently searching for ways to help disadvantaged and minority children, many of whom reach first grade with learning abilities already stunted for lack of adequate stimulation during the first six years of life.

4

Educators are turning to research about the preschool years as the most likely way to raise intelligence levels. Many intelligent, well-educated parents are discovering upon thoughtful observation of their own small children that they are ready and eager for learning previously assigned only to first grade level or beyond.

Computer experts are looking with fresh excitement at the potential that computers offer young children for unprecedented kinds of learning opportunities.

"It is possible to design computers so that learning to communicate with them can be a natural process, more like learning French by living in France than like trying to learn it through the unnatural process of American foreign-language instruction in classrooms," said Seymour Papert, professor of mathematics and professor of education at the Massachusetts Institute of Technology and developer of LOGO, a computer programming language.[1]

Research about early learning emerging from all of these sources, from the fields of neurology, physiology, psychology, biology, and education, from specialists working from many divergent points of view, can be summed up like this:

(1) We have greatly underestimated what children under age six can and should be learning.

(2) It is possible, by changing our methods of child-rearing, to raise the level of intelligence of all children and to have happier, more enthusiastic youngsters as a result.

"To get to the heart of the matter, it appears that a first-rate educational experience during the first three years of life is required if a person is to develop to his or her full potential," said Dr. Burton White, who founded and directed the Harvard Preschool Project.[2]

Early learning doesn't mean that you should try to teach your three-year-old to read to make him a status symbol or because your neighbor's four-year-old can read or because you want to be sure he gets into Harvard fifteen years from now. You aren't trying to make a six-year-old out of a four-year-old or turn a nursery school into a first grade or deprive your youngster of the chance to be a child.

Early learning does mean that you try to understand your youngster's innate drive to learn, to explore, to fill his developing brain's urgent needs for sensory stimuli and

5

satisfying learning experiences, just as you try to understand and fill the needs of his body for nourishing foods. You aren't stuffing his brain with facts so he'll make Phi Beta Kappa at Yale any more than you give him vitamins to force his growth so he'll make the Chicago Bears' backfield.

Early learning simply means using new knowledge about what your youngster's brain needs during the crucial first years of life so that his mental development will come nearer to reaching its potential and your child will be brighter and happier for it.

Research is showing that traditionally accepted child-care practices may even be inadvertently curtailing children's mental development in some ways. Parents may leave an infant alone and crying with boredom in his crib or playpen, in an attempt to train him to be "good" and undemanding. Yet the baby's needs for sensory stimuli and motor activity—to look at a variety of things, to listen to myriad sounds and voices, to move and be moved about, to touch, to hold—are as great as his hunger for food and for love.

Parents may spank the hands of a toddler who is not trying to be destructive, but merely trying to satisfy some of his insatiable desire to explore, to climb, to push, to pull, to take apart, to taste, to experiment.

"Curtailing the explorations of toddlers between nine and eighteen months may hamper the children's rate of development and even lower the final level of intelligence they can achieve," wrote Dr. Joseph McVicker Hunt, professor emeritus of psychology at the University of Illinois.[3]

Researchers have discovered that even well-read, educated, and intelligent parents have probably handicapped their children in the past because of child-rearing practices which ignored the needs of the developing brain. These are the parents who were most aware of prevailing child-care theories, who heeded the warnings about not "overstimulating" a child and who read the books which said a youngster would develop "readiness" for learning on his own inner timetable regardless of the amount of stimuli in his environment. Many of these parents feared to stimulate their children intellectually for fear of "pushing" or "pressuring" them and because they had heard that fathers and mothers are "too emotionally involved" with their youngsters to do an adequate job of teaching.

Much new research now shows that the idea of "readiness" has been overrated and that a child's ability to acquire many skills depends on the stimulation and opportunity in his environment as well as his inner schedule of growth. In fact, some kinds of brain development may actually be dependent on a child's having certain kinds of environmental stimulation, some researchers now say. Most of the experimental programs concerned with early learning have been deliberately designed to remove any kinds of pressures—or even extrinsic rewards—from the learning activities and have been set up so that the young children participate only if they wish and stop whenever they choose and are never praised or criticized for what they do or do not do. Yet even under these circumstances, children of three and four eagerly teach themselves such intellectual activities as reading and writing.

Observers in almost all early-learning research projects comment on the joy and happiness and enthusiasm of the children involved. And the most careful follow-up studies do not detect any ill effects on these youngsters' personality, emotional well-being, behavior, eyesight, or general health.

When Dr. Dolores Durkin, professor of education at the University of Illinois, made studies of children who learned to read before they entered first grade, she was surprised to find that few of them came from professional or upper middle-class families. In fact, more than half of the early readers in her California study had parents she classified as being lower socioeconomic class. One-fourth more she identified as lower middle-class.[4]

Studies of the home backgrounds of these early readers—and of a control group with similar I.Q. who could not read before first grade—pointed up an important difference. The better-educated parents in higher socioeconomic groups knew the theories that reading should be taught only by trained teachers and that parents should keep hands off the whole process.

Families less informed about these traditional concepts had happily and enthusiastically welcomed their children's questions about words, answered them, helped them, and accepted their preschoolers' ability to read. None of these parents felt guilty about their youngster's reading skill, as did two or three of the parents with professional backgrounds.

Dr. Durkin's research showed that the early readers consistently outscored the control group with equal I.Q. in the elementary grades. (But part of the careful, scientific design of the research—which intended to keep each early reader matched with a nonreader of equal I.Q. as they advanced through several grades—was upset because many of the early readers were double-promoted.)

The widely accepted idea that a preschooler's only occupation should be "play" and the attitude that play is the direct opposite of learning have also tended to deprive youngsters of desirable mental stimulation. Small children love to learn. They are born with an innate hunger for learning. And they keep on having an insatiable desire to learn—unless you bore, spank, train, or discourage it out of them.

If you think carefully about what most interests your baby or your toddler, you'll observe that it is seldom "play," as adults use the word. It's much more apt to be learning. In fact, sometimes you can't seem to stop your baby from working hard at learning in order to persuade him to play or eat or rest, no matter how hard you try.

A four-month-old baby, for example, who is just learning to roll from his stomach onto his back works harder at pushing himself up and over than a runner trying to shave seconds off a marathon time. Once he manages to flop over, he usually screams until you put him back on his stomach so he can try again. If you offer him a rattle or a cuddly animal so he will quiet down and play and you can get back to your own work, he usually bats it away in his eagerness to resume his difficult learning activity. No one is forcing him or pressuring him or hurrying him or grading him or making him compete or threatening not to love him unless he learns to roll over. He wants to learn, urgently, on his own.

You can see this same phenomenon clearly when your baby is trying to pull himself up on his feet. He grunts and grimaces and struggles and works harder than a weight lifter.

At first, when he finally does pull himself up on his feet, he doesn't know how to let go and sit down. So he screams. You lower him gently to the floor and give him a toy to play with. But he doesn't want to play. He wants to stand up. He wants to learn.

How long does a baby practice vowel sounds and consonant noises, stringing them together in delightful nonsense before he hits on a single word that brings recognition from his mother? No one pressures him into that concentrated practice which typically goes unrewarded for months. Yet this is what babies and toddlers do endlessly, of their own free choice.

How many questions do two- and three-year-olds ask in a single day? They're trying to find out all they can about the world around them, about cause and effect and all the fascinations of existence. This is not what an adult considers play. Yet a busy, impatient, tired mother can't turn off the torrent of "Whys" even for an hour.

Three- and four-year-olds love what preschool educators call "imitative play"—pretending to be grown-up. But they seldom copy grown-ups at play. They imitate adults at work: washing dishes, caring for babies, going off to work, driving a truck, as doctor, nurse, soldier, mother, grocer, fireman, policeman, teacher.

You can think more objectively about this entire question of preschoolers' play if you keep track of your child's activities for just one day. What makes him happiest? What stimulates him to the greatest concentration? What holds his interest longest? Almost always, it's an activity in which he is learning something which increases his competency or satisfies his curiosity—especially if his mother or his father is right beside him sharing his excitement about learning.

It's an insult to a preschooler and a mistake to write off his urgent and intense learning efforts as play, unless you want to define any absorbing adult occupation as play. And it's an injury to his developing intellect to deprive him of profitable learning experiences on the assumption that all he should be doing before age six is playing.

This play-oriented attitude toward preschool children in the past has had many unfortunate results. The most important: For decades it put a damper on research about ways in which youngsters younger than six can learn best. And it has influenced parents—who had the best intentions in the world—to dull the learning instincts which are an innate part of all small children.

Since new theories about the importance and excitement of early learning were first developed in the mid-1960s (and the first version of this book was first written), they have had several important impacts.

Educators, psychologists, sociologists, and even politicians have come to see in these theories a way to help disadvantaged children get off to a better start in life and in school. It had long been clear to researchers that many youngsters from poor and what were called "culturally deprived" homes began first grade with built-in handicaps. They lacked the learning experiences and mental stimulation during the earliest years of their lives that help prepare middle-class children to succeed in school. They had trouble learning in kindergarten and first grade and limped along academically all through the rest of their schooling until they dropped out, handicapped for life by inadequate education and unable to succeed in most jobs.

"All later learning is likely to be influenced by the very basic learning which has taken place by the age of five or six," emphasized one of the influential reports dealing with this problem which was published by the University of Chicago. It pointed out that unless a youngster has had adequate mental stimulation during the preschool years, the work of the school for the next ten years will be largely wasted. "Ideally, the early intellectual development of the child should take place in the home."[5]

Very early in a youngster's life, he begins to learn about the world via his five senses: vision, hearing, touch, taste, and smell. An environment rich in games, toys, and other objects a baby can handle helps stimulate his perceptual growth. So does a wide range of experiences and contacts with adults at meals, playtimes, and throughout the day. There are large, measurable differences in perceptual development, the report noted, between youngsters who have had great opportunity to explore, to touch, to handle, to try, to play, to learn, and to be with interested adults and those who have not.

The opportunity to learn language skills also separates children who start school ready to succeed and those who seem marked for failure, even at age six. A child's language development depends to a great extent on the adults about him in his earliest years of life. Parents who are aware of a child's learning needs encourage him to say words. They surround him with talk, used freely and naturally. They cheer on his efforts to say the correct words, respond to him when he tries and when he succeeds, read to him, and provide him with what educators call "corrective feedback."

In this kind of rich, verbal environment a child's vocabulary grows and his ability to use sentences develops. As he becomes more skilled with words, he learns to put his emotions and intentions into language. He begins to compare and to differentiate and to express abstract ideas. He uses words as tools of thought.

The report went on:

> The child in many middle-class homes is given a great deal of instruction about the world in which he lives, to use language to fix aspects of this world in his memory, and to think about similarities, differences, and relationships in this very complex environment. Such instruction is individual and is timed in relation to the experiences, actions, and questions of the child.
>
> Parents make great efforts to motivate the child, to reward him, and to reinforce desired responses. The child is read to, spoken to, and is constantly subjected to a stimulating set of experiences in a very complex environment. In short, he "learns to learn" very early. He comes to view the world as something he can master through a relatively enjoyable type of activity, a sort of game, which is learning. In fact, much of the approval he gets is because of his rapid and accurate response to his informal instruction in the home.
>
> Learning to learn includes motivating the child to find pleasure in learning. It involves developing the child's ability to attend to others and to engage in purposive action. It includes training the child to delay

11

the gratification of his desires and wishes and to work for rewards and goals which are more distant. It includes developing the child's view of adults as sources of information and ideas and also as sources of approval and reward.

If the home does not and cannot provide these basic developments, the child is likely to be handicapped in much of his later learning and the prognosis of his educational development is very poor.

Because the mounting evidence about the urgent importance of early learning was so compelling, a wide variety of programs were begun by local, state, and federal governments, by public and private agencies, by universities, foundations, and churches to make learning opportunities available to young children from homes that appeared to be disadvantaged. Best known are the enormous collection of programs receiving federal money through Head Start.

Unfortunately, the kinds of learning opportunities many Head Start programs offer young children are too little and too late. A large percentage of them pay little attention to using new theories about how to foster intelligence. Most are modeled on traditional social-adjustment nursery schools, with an emphasis on group games and social activities. Many have to be so concerned about the youngsters' physical health and nutrition and about helping their families find essential social and community services that they cannot concentrate on encouraging mental development. And the children usually attend such nursery schools at the age of three or four for only two to three hours a day—sometimes only for a single summer. Often these programs are able to offer only a little compensation for an unstimulating home environment, where the youngsters still spend most of their time.

Nevertheless, research shows that even a little attention to children's learning needs during the preschool years can help. Several dozen, scientifically sound, long-term studies have now been completed that trace the results of Head Start and similar preschool learning programs over many years. Almost uniformly, they document significant gains for

12

children in Head Start and other early-learning programs, especially when measured over several years.

The general pattern of such results is that the children show an immediate gain in achievement that usually persists through the first two or three years of elementary school. Then the academic differences between the children who have had the advantage of being in a Head Start program gradually diminish and the gap between them and other youngsters gradually narrows. But subsequent testing at the junior high and high school levels once again shows considerable advantage for the Head Start children in terms of school grades and other measures of mental development.

Compilations of studies on Head Start children, for example, show that they had higher I.Q. scores than comparison youngsters—ranging from 7 to 10 points in several studies to as much as 30 points in one report. Far more of them were scoring at grade level in reading and math. Fewer had been flunked and had to repeat a grade.

The greatest successes, moreover, were chalked up by the Home Start programs, which aim to reach disadvantaged youngsters earlier than age three or four and to work with mothers to increase the learning stimulation the youngsters receive in their own homes. In some of these experimental plans, a visiting teacher—much like a visiting nurse—makes regular calls at a home to show the mother how to play learning games with a baby or toddler and often to give or lend a learning toy or two. Often a parent-child center operates in connection with such a home-visiting program, giving mothers a place where they can go with their offspring to learn more about child care and to find out about community services.

Because Home Start programs reach youngsters at an earlier age than Head Start and because they have an impact on the quality of the child's home itself, they have consistently shown the most success in raising children's I.Q.'s over both immediate and long-term timespans, according to dozens of follow-up reports.

One long-term study even offers evidence that preschool education can also pay off in terms of lower costs to taxpayers in dealing with social problems. During the 1960s, the

Ypsilanti Perry Preschool Project conducted by the High/Scope Educational Research Foundation of Ypsilanti, Michigan, began a study of 123 youngsters born into poor black families and considered to be at high risk of school failure. Few of their parents had finished high school. Half were on welfare and almost as many were single parents.[6]

The children were randomly divided into two groups. One attended a high-quality preschool program five mornings a week, either for one year at age four or for two years when they were three and four. And a teacher came to each child's home for ninety minutes a week to work with a parent on early learning. The other group had no preschool experience and no efforts were made to help parents increase learning stimuli in the home.

Both groups have been followed and tested ever since. And even at the age of nineteen, the differences between them were striking. Those who had preschool experience were much more likely to have been graduated from high school, to score average or above on competency tests, and to be enrolled in post–high school educational programs or have a job. They were less likely to have been pregnant, been arrested, or be on welfare.

Earlier reports showed that those who had preschool experience had better grades, fewer failing marks, and less absenteeism from class. They needed fewer special education services and had a better attitude toward school.

Taxpayers benefit considerably by paying for a high-quality preschool program for such youngsters, the Perry Preschool Program makes clear. Just in terms of reduced crime rates, the program had already saved taxpayers $3,100 per child by the time the group had reached age nineteen. There were other substantial savings from reduced need for special education services in school and from lower welfare dependency and increased employment later on.

Preschool early learning starts a "chain of cause and effect," the researchers suggested. Because they are more intellectually and socially competent, the youngsters do better in school. So they are more likely to be graduated from high school, less likely to be involved in crime, and more likely to get a job. "These factors weave a pattern of life success that not only is more productive for children and

14

their families but also produces substantial benefits to the society at large through reduction in taxpayer burden and improvement in the quality of community life," the report concluded.

Evidence is overwhelming that opportunities for early learning are critical and that how a child's home and parents encourage his mental development makes the most important difference in the growth of his intelligence. But most mothers and fathers still get almost no help or guidance in this matter. That is why this book was first written—and why it is now being revised and updated.

By now, however, a substantial number of research projects have shown that young children can profit enormously when their parents are given some information and encouragement about early learning. For example, a Massachusetts local school district enlisted the help of Harvard University educators in setting up the Brookline Early Education Project (BEEP) to offer the parents of all children in the community help with early learning. Parents had access to a community early-learning center, classes in early learning, learning toys, and the expertise of educators with special interest and experience in fostering intelligence in young children.

The BEEP program has turned out to be highly successful and cost effective. Similar programs could someday become widespread as a tax-supported extension of public schooling, so that all parents could have expert, personal guidance in providing an optimum environment for their children's mental development during the most critical years of their lives.

How successful that can be is clearly shown in the New Parents as Teacher's Project conducted by four Missouri school districts in the St. Louis area and involving 380 families from a broad cross section of socioeconomic backgrounds. Beginning even before the birth of the first child in each family, specially trained educators made regular visits to each home, teaching parents how to help their offspring develop well. Mothers—and fathers—also met periodically in small groups at a nearby school.

Parents were given packets of learning materials, directions for simple learning games they could individualize for their own offspring, and detailed kits of information about every short phase of a child's development from birth to age three. They also got lots of encouragement ("This one will take an extra dose of patience on your part, but it's definitely worth it") and happy suggestions for ways to have fun in making learning a natural part of their home environment.

At age three, the youngsters—and a comparison group whose parents had not received training—were tested by independent evaluators. (Outside evaluators are rare in child care research and give added substantiation to the findings.)[7]

"Children of parents participating in the New Parents as Teacher's Project consistently scored significantly higher on all measures of intelligence, achievement, auditory comprehension, verbal ability and language ability than did comparison children," the report noted.

"These three-year-olds look woderful," said Dr. White, the senior consultant to the Missouri project. "Hard data show that these kids are way ahead on intelligence and language, two key indicators. No matter what kind of parents these children had, the project helped all of them.

"Our educational system should get children to their third birthday as beautifully developed as possible," Dr. White emphasized. That makes more sense, he said, than waiting until they start school at age five or trying a Head Start program if they are showing deficits at age three.

In the Missouri program, gains were chalked up by youngsters from homes with well-educated parents and above-average resources, as well as high-risk youngsters from poor families. Only about 10 percent of American families manage to give their children enough learning opportunities to get them by age three as well educated and developed as they should be, according to Dr. White.

It is now clear that there are no practical substitutes for involving parents in providing the kind of home life and stimulating experiences that encourage a child's mind to grow. Home and parents are so pervasive, so dominating in a child's life that parental participation in and understanding of early-learning techniques is essential—even when toddlers and preschoolers spend much of their time in day-care centers.

We now know that informed, caring parents—using many loving, happy, and easy ways—can do much to raise the level of intellectual functioning in their children and to help them realize to a greater extent their true intellectual potential. In fact, such stimulation may be necessary for the development of a "bright" or "gifted" young person, regardless of his innate potential.

"In no instance (where documentation exists) have I found any individual of high ability who did not experience intensive early stimulation as a central component of his development," pointed out Dr. William Fowler, professor of applied psychology at the Ontario Institute for Studies in Education and a former director of the Laboratory Nursery School at the University of Chicago. "The unvarying coincidence of extensive early stimulation with cognitive precocity and subsequent superior competence in adulthood suggests that stimulation is a necessary if not sufficient condition for the development of high abilities."[8]

"Deprivation is a relative concept which should be measured relative to ultimate potential," emphasized Dr. Fowler. "Deprivation may be just as extreme for the potentially bright who must endure average conditions as for the potentially average to live through conditions below the stimulation 'norms' of the affluent half of our society."

Large numbers of potentially superior, as well as average, achievers are probably lost to our society because of a lack of sufficient early stimulation, said Dr. Fowler.

The 1980s have seen a new and growing interest in children who are identified as "bright" or "gifted," probably for several reasons. Educators and parents are less reluctant to speak out for the needs of these exceptional youngsters, now that special programs are largely in place for children who need extra help. Research has shown conclusively that most bright children are emotionally healthy, socially adept, and usually delightful to know.

It has also become increasingly obvious that the nation's position in the free world depends on maintaining its leadership in the sciences and in technology and production. Yet evidence is growing that young people in other countries, particularly the Japanese, are ahead of American students academically.

For example, the I.Q. of the Japanese has been rising sharply for years and is now the highest in the world, according to a compilation of I.Q. studies made by British psychologist Dr. Richard Lynn. In one generation, the mean I.Q. of the Japanese has jumped 7 points and is now 11 points higher than the mean for the United States and other advanced Western nations.[9]

Among Americans and Europeans, said Dr. Lynn, only about 2 percent of the population have an I.Q. higher than 130. But 10 percent of the Japanese do. And 77 percent of Japanese do better on I.Q. tests than the average for Americans or Europeans.

I.Q. tests, of course, are a limited and controversial way to measure intelligence. There are many hazards to drawing conclusions from them about the comparative intelligence of different races and nationalities. But the tests used in these studies were designed to be culture-free. Testing samples were carefully chosen to measure the same socioeconomic cross-sections of population as in the United States.

It's probably not heredity that accounts for this difference in intelligence, said Dr. Lynn, because the increase has been too rapid to reflect a change in the genetic makeup of the population. Because the increase in I.Q. can be found even among six-year-old Japanese, it's also not likely that what is boosting the I.Q. is the stiffly competitive atmosphere and rigorous workloads of Japanese schools. Instead, Dr. Lynn suggests, improvements in health and nutrition may be in part responsible.

But what almost certainly accounts, at least in part, for the fact that I.Q. is so much higher in Japan than elsewhere in the world by age six is probably the kinds of early-learning experiences that the Japanese are giving very young children. Japanese mothers are intensely involved in their children's education; in fact, they are often called *kyoiku-mama*, a name that translates as "education mama."

A major cross-cultural study made by the University of Michigan's Center for Human Growth also found that American children lag behind Japanese and Taiwanese youngsters in reading and math right from the beginning of first grade—and they stay behind, especially in math. Japanese children work much harder in school and spend much more time in class than American children. But what accounts for the differences at age six is that Japanese and Taiwanese mothers and fathers use more of their time with their children for informal education, for providing opportunities to learn that are fun, and for showing enthusiasm about their offspring's achievements, according to Dr. Harold Stevenson, professor of psychology at the University of Michigan, who directed the study.[10]

The problem with American youngsters isn't working mothers, said Dr. Stevenson. Even employed parents have time in the evening and on weekends to be with their children. The critical element, he said, is that the time together be used for direct interaction.

It's one thing for the Japanese to build better cars and cameras and TVs. Or for the Taiwanese to make products for American markets more efficiently than American manufacturers can. But it's much more worrisome to educators and political leaders when the Japanese and Taiwanese seem to be building better brains—and making children's learning more successful.

There is also increasing public awareness that bright children are a major national asset and that they should be encouraged and cherished and their intellectual development fostered not only for their own benefit but for the public good as well. Another concern is the long, gradual slippage in scores high school students make on the Scholastic Aptitude Test and the fact that far fewer students now score in the SAT's highest ranges than did in the early 1970s.

Along with the new interest in the brightest children has come an enormous increase in special programs to identify them and provide them special educational opportunities. These now include everything from special summer camps to early admission to universities, Saturday programs in colleges for young teenagers, enrichment classes, honors academic tracks, individual tutorials, mentors, individualized learning, and many other strategies. (Chapter 13 has more information about bright and talented children.)

If you fill your child's life full of stimulation all of his early years, if you make your home what scientists call an enriched, "culturally abundant environment," if you use early-learning techniques we now know, you can do much to raise your youngster's intelligence. In such a home a child who would have grown up to be "average" will almost certainly become an "above-average" individual. And a youngster who would have been "above average" in normal circumstances will probably grow up to be "bright" or "gifted."

This doesn't mean that you must set up a school in your family room and proceed to hold formal lessons for your three-year-old. It doesn't mean substituting the alphabet song for your baby's evening lullaby. It doesn't mean drilling a four-year-old in number facts or showing flashcards with the names of dinosaurs to your 12-month-old baby, as one highly promoted "superbaby" program advocates. It doesn't mean pushing your three-year-old aggressively to get him into a particular nursery school that is reported to be a pipeline to Ivy League colleges. It doesn't even mean you must buy your child toys that are labeled "educational" or send him to a day-care center or nursery school that is promoted as "educational."

Your role may, indeed, occasionally be to teach your child directly, especially if he's asking questions or trying to master a task you can break down into small steps for him. But more often you should function more as a scene setter who provides a loving atmosphere full of learning experiences your child can choose for himself and as a coach who cheers him on and shares the exhilaration of his accomplishments with him.

You can guard against any possibility you may be pushing your child undesirably by monitoring his reactions to the learning stimuli you give him. If he's not interested, there is no reason to push a learning activity on him. You should not insist that he stick to a task you have chosen if it's too difficult or he doesn't want to. You should never let him get the idea that you won't love him if he can't succeed in a task you've set. And you should remember that a major purpose of early learning is to make your child happy by fulfilling his brain's need for stimuli and to help him learn at his own individual pace and in his own individual way, as he will not be able to do once he enters school.

Using early-learning techniques with a young child can be just as simple and easy as this incident that occurred in a restaurant. A young couple brought their baby girl, about nine months old, with them and plopped her into a high chair at the table to wait for her dinner.

Looking around for something to do, the baby reached out and grasped a goblet with a single ice cube from the table and put it on the high chair tray. Her mother glanced at her, then resumed talking to the baby's father, but kept her hand near enough to the tray to catch the goblet if necessary.

For ten quiet, fascinated minutes, the baby was seriously absorbed in experimenting with the ice cube. She slipped it in and out of the goblet. She slid it around the tray. She tasted it, rubbed her nose with it, passed it from hand to hand. As it melted she repeated the activity with the ice water.

Until her dinner came, the baby continued to fill her brain with information and stimuli. And because this filled a basic—although often unrecognized—need, she was happy and absorbed. As a fringe benefit, the baby's father and mother were free to talk together at an adult level, without constantly saying "No" and fussing at the youngster to "be good." It was far easier for them to use the early-learning technique of letting the baby explore a tiny portion of her environment, using every possible sensory organ, than it would have been had they acted as most parents, taking the goblet away and then having to cope with the crying of a bored and frustrated child.

Fathers and mothers who have tried using early-learning principles with their offspring are delighted not only with the intellectual progress of their children, but also with the new and happy relationship that follows.

"I had no idea my daughter would be so interesting to me," commented a mother who had been teaching her four-year-old to read. "It's just like the way I felt the day she took her first steps toward me, only better." And because her four-year-old is seldom bored, she is seldom fussy, unhappy, angry, or defiant, like many four-year-olds.

You can help your child to become brighter, more intelligent, happier. There is no doubt about it. And in the process your offspring will have a more satisfying childhood, and you will enjoy him more. You don't have to pressure or push your child, and your efforts to help him learn will not hurt him in any way, unless you make your love for him contingent on his performance.

This is not just another job you have to do. It is a whole,

new, exciting, wonderful way of looking at your child and your relationship with him during the first six years of his life.

Chapter 2 will explain the new psychological, neurological, and physiological concepts and research behind early learning. Succeeding chapters will give you more precise information about how and what you can do to foster the development of your child's intelligence.

2. Why You Can Raise a Brighter Child

The excitement about early learning—with its promise that children of every level of ability, from every kind of background, can learn more and become more intelligent—is based on several important theories emerging from a new convergence of research in the fields of education, medicine, the behavioral sciences, and new specialties of neurobiology, neuropsychology, and cognitive neurophysiology that are now being integrated into what is called the neurosciences.

Scientists studying the brain from several specialist viewpoints are finding new evidence in brain structures and brain chemistry that give neurological credibility to the new understandings of children's behavior being developed by psychologists and educators. Together, all of this new evidence and information confirms the basic premise of this book: Parents can make a substantial difference in their child's mental ability by the kind of stimulating environment they provide during the earliest years of his life.

Several important concepts provide the "why" for the suggestions made in later chapters of this book, showing specific ways in which you can help raise the level of intellectual and creative abilities of your own youngster. By adding another dimension to the standard child-care books about physical and emotional development, they will also help you understand your child better.

Not all of these important theories have as yet been completely proven in statistically sound, controlled research. (For that matter, very few of the traditional ideas about how children should be raised are validated by this kind of scientific data, either.) Some of these theories still must be more thoroughly tested by research involving children from every type of social, economic, and educational background, with every level of genetic endowment and over long periods of their lives.

But thousands of scientific studies—many of them made since this book was first written—do back up these concepts, and together they add up to a new philosophy of child-rearing which is rapidly being put into practice.

A knowledge of these basic theories will help you in thinking about and planning for and living with your child. And these concepts will give you a better understanding of the changes in child care which are occurring in this country as a result of research.

The major theories behind the emphasis on early learning include these:

1. Your child does not have a fixed intelligence or a predetermined rate of intellectual growth, contrary to much widespread opinion in the past. His level of intelligence can be changed—for better or worse—by his environment and especially during the earliest years of his life.[1]

It used to be assumed that every child had a specific level of intelligence which remained the same all of his life and which grew and unfolded automatically at various stages of his development. This intelligence supposedly could be measured with reasonable accuracy by an I.Q. test. Such an I.Q. level was thought to remain stable during an individual's lifetime, regardless of how much education he received or what kind of environment he lived in.

It is true that for large groups of school-age children, I.Q.s seem to stay relatively constant—if for no other reason than that I.Q. tests are constructed to yield such scores with large groups. But we now know that scores for some individuals can vary tremendously, particularly during the preschool years. Most research shows only a small relationship between a toddler's I.Q. at age two and the same child's score

24

at age five. There is almost no relationship at all between the scores a child makes as a preschooler and again as a teenager.

Why does the I.Q. change? And why does it sometimes change so greatly? Some researchers attribute it to inadequacies in I.Q. tests themselves. (It is true that such examinations measure only a few of the many factors that are part of what we usually call "intelligence" and fail to take into consideration such qualities as creativity, imagination, and motivation.) Others point out that the I.Q. tests for infants and toddlers rely heavily on motor abilities which may or may not be directly related to later intelligence. Emotional factors have also been suggested as triggering I.Q. ups and downs.

But it is now also considered likely that the I.Q. changes simply because a child's actual intelligence also changes. And these increases or decreases are largely caused by stimulation, or lack of stimulation, in the environment.

For example, if you put a normal, healthy youngster of average intelligence into an institution such as a hospital or orphanage where he gets adequate physical care but little mental stimulation, he will become mentally duller in as short a time as three months. The longer he stays in a deprived environment, the greater will be the decline in his intelligence. Some of this loss is reversible; much is not. This concept has long been accepted in the United States and is one reason why foster homes have been substituted for orphanages for children whose parents could not care for them.

Usually, this retardation is blamed on a lack of a mother's love and is termed "maternal deprivation." But new research—both with infants and animals—indicates that a contributing factor is also a lack of all sorts of sensory stimulation.

One classic study that shows vividly what can happen to institutionalized children was made more than two decades ago by Dr. Wayne Dennis, then professor of psychology at Brooklyn College of the City University of New York, in three orphanages in Tehran.[2]

In the first institution, where most of the youngsters were admitted before the age of one month, the infants were kept almost continuously in individual cribs. They lay on their backs on soft mattresses and were never propped up or even turned over until they learned how to do so by themselves. Their milk was given them in propped-up bottles, although they were occasionally fed semisolid food by an attendant. These babies had no toys. They were changed when necessary and bathed every other day. Four poorly-paid attendants cared for a room of thirty-two infants, and Dr. Dennis noted that the supervisors cared more about the neatness of the room than the development of the babies.

When a baby did manage to learn to sit up by himself and was in danger of tumbling out of his shallow crib, he was placed on a strip of linoleum on the floor during his waking hours. Dr. Dennis also described seeing rows of children, who were able to sit up, seated on a bench with a bar across the front to prevent them from falling. They had nothing to do.

When these youngsters were about three years old, they were transferred to a second orphanage, where the same type of care and conditions, or worse, prevailed. In studying these children, Dr. Dennis found that of those between the ages of one and two, fewer than half could sit up and one could walk—although almost all normal, noninstitutionalized American children sit alone by the age of nine months. Only one in every six could creep or scoot on the floor. Of the two-year-olds in this institution, fewer than half could stand, holding on to a hand or a chair. Fewer than 10 percent could walk alone.

Dr. Dennis reported that most of the three-year-olds in the second orphanage could sit up by themselves, but only 15 percent had learned to walk alone.

Children in the third Tehran orphanage provided a dramatic contrast. Most of them had originally been assigned to the first institution, but were transferred because they seemed to be more retarded than the other youngsters. But in the third orphanage, they began to flourish. They had more contact with attendants, who were encouraged to mother them whenever possible. They were held during feedings, occasionally propped up in a sitting position, and given toys to play with. As a result, most of these supposedly retarded children between the ages of one and two had progressed more than the supposedly normal babies. Most of the one-year-olds could sit alone and a few could walk by themselves. All of the two-year-olds could sit up, creep, and walk, holding on to a hand or chair.

In a later study in an orphanage in Beirut, Lebanon, Dr. Dennis demonstrated how even a little added sensory stimulation could produce great gains in the development of babies. An experimental group of foundlings between the ages of seven months and one year, none of whom could sit up, were taken from their cribs into an adjoining room for an hour a day. Here they were propped up in low chairs or on a foam-rubber pad and given a variety of objects to look at and handle: fresh flowers, paper bags, pieces of colored sponge, plastic flyswatters, metal box tops, bright jelly molds, multicolored plastic dishes, small plastic medicine bottles, metal ashtrays. No adults worked with the youngsters or helped them play with the objects.[3]

All of the babies quickly learned to sit up independently, and after considerable hesitation by some, all delighted in playing with the objects. Dr. Dennis reported that during the experiment, these infants made four times the average gain in development, just as a result of the daily hour of stimulation.

Once you accept the theory that a child's intelligence can change and that it can be lowered by lack of stimulation during the earliest years of life, the next obvious question is: What happens if you deliberately enrich a youngster's environment with intriguing, loving stimulation from birth on?

Some behavioral scientists and many delighted parents and happy children have already demonstrated the answer: The child becomes brighter. It's even quite likely that we may eventually be able to raise the level of intelligence of our whole population as we understand better how to stimulate the learning abilities of small children.

Dr. Hunt commented, "In the light of the evidence now available, it is not unreasonable to entertain the hypothesis that, with a sound scientific educational psychology of early experience, it might become feasible to raise the average level of intelligence as now measured by a substantial degree. In order to be explicit, it is conceivable that this 'substantial degree' might be of the order of 30 points of I.Q. In a technological culture which is requiring more and more people with a high level of intelligence, this is an important challenge."[4]

Because behavioral scientists assumed in the past that intelligence is a fixed, genetically based quality, they were not searching for ways to increase the intellectual abilities of children, Dr. Hunt noted. But now that the nature and development of intelligence are better understood, we are finding many ways of increasing learning abilities. More such intelligence-boosting techniques of rearing and educating youngsters will undoubtedly be developed in the coming years.

2. *Early stimulation can actually produce changes in the size, structure, and chemical functioning of the brain.*

Thousands of experiments with dogs, cats, rats, mice, monkeys, guinea pigs—and even with chickens and fish— show that when these animals are given stimulation in infancy, they develop at a more rapid rate and become more intelligent than others which are not stimulated. A rat, for example, which comes from a strain known to be dull, will outperform a rat of similar age from a genetically bright strain if he is given extra stimulation as a baby while the supposedly born-bright rat is not. It even makes a demonstrable difference whether the early stimulation comes before or after weaning. The more stimulation and the earlier the rats receive it, the brighter they become.

Very young laboratory animals which are handled and stimulated as babies develop at a more rapid rate than those which are not. They open their eyes at an earlier age and show better motor coordination. They gain weight faster than other animals in the same litter which are not stimulated—not because they eat more food, but apparently because their bodies make more efficient use of what they do consume. They also seem more resistant to disease.

An enriched environment actually produces changes in the anatomy and chemical characteristics of rats' brains, according to Dr. Mark R. Rosenzweig, of the University of California's psychology department. Dr. Rosenzweig and his colleagues divided litters of baby rats into two groups.

One group received early stimulation; the other did not. Tests showed that the rats which received the early stimulation were more intelligent and could solve problems better than the nonstimulated litter mates.[5]

Then the rats' brains were studied closely. The brains of the early-stimulated rats were found to have a heavier cortex, with an increased number of a certain type of brain cells and more branching between cells than the brains of the unstimulated rats. Greater amounts of two important chemicals were also found in the brains of the stimulated rats than in their unstimulated brothers and sisters.

These same types of differences in brain weight and brain chemistry were also found when the scientists compared the brains of rats from bright and dull strains.

We can't assume, of course, that the results of experiments with animals apply in toto to human infants, too. And of course it's impossible to make the same type of controlled laboratory experiments with human babies. But because so many animal tests have been made with approximately the same results and because the more intelligent the animal the more difference early stimulation makes in its adult intelligence, researchers are increasingly sure the same answers hold for human beings, too.

"Evidence exists that some features of sensory-neural mechanisms do require experience for their full development and that brain growth sometimes *depends upon* behavioral development," explained Dr. Lewis P. Lipsitt, director of the Child Study Center at Brown University, and his colleague Dr. John S. Werner. "Nervous system tissue change is sometimes *attributable* to environmental stimulation."[6]

We cannot say any more that learning must wait until the neurological system has reached certain milestones of maturation, Dr. Lipsitt pointed out. Recent studies, he noted, show that brain growth itself depends on inputs of experience and stimulation. Specific neurons in the brain are now known to acquire specific functions as a result of specific experiences the infant has. Brain development and individual experiences interact with each other, he pointed out. Some brain development depends on an infant's having certain crucial experiences, just as certain kinds of brain development are essential for some kinds of behavior.

Dr. Peter Huttenlocher, a pediatric neurologist at the University of Chicago, has contributed another kind of evidence for the importance of early learning because of its effect on the structure of the brain. Dr. Huttenlocher has found that the nerve cells in the cortex of the brain of newborn infants have about the same number of branches (called dendrites and axons) and interconnecting links (synapses) as adult brains. But their structure is immature. During infancy, the number of synapses increases rapidly. By the time a child is twelve to twenty-four months old, his brain has about 50 percent more synapses than the average for an adult brain. But gradually, over the years of childhood, those synapses that are not being used begin to atrophy and disappear. After about age sixteen, the density of synapses in the brain stays about the same until the mid-seventies, when the number again begins to drop slightly. This great number of synapses may be one reason why young children learn so easily during the first years of their life and why, when a child suffers a brain injury, he is likely to recover more mental functions than an adult who had similar damage.

3. Heredity does put an upper limit on your child's intellectual capacity. But this ceiling is so high that many scientists believe no human has as yet even approached it.

You will never be able to separate completely the effects of heredity and the influence of environment on your child. Countless research projects have been undertaken to answer this age-old question of nature versus nurture. But no one can even come close to controlling all of the complex factors involved in human intelligence. No completely satisfactory measurements of environment exist, for example, although researchers are developing some useful models. And so many complicated and interrelated factors are involved in heredity that it is virtually impossible to isolate even a few of them and separate them from environmental influences for study.

Is Mark doing well in school because he inherited his father's intelligence? Or because his father's interest in books rubbed off on him as a small child? Was Mozart born to be great? Or did his genius flower because his father began giving him lessons at the age of three and because his childhood was spent in a world of music and musicians who stimulated and encouraged each other?

The more scientists study the question, the more complex and subtle the relationship between heredity and environment is shown to be. For example, there is evidence that heredity can play a role in human emotions, which was not suspected before. And we are finding many ways in which environment can alter constitutional factors which we had believed were fixed for life.

The genes that your youngster inherits certainly lay the groundwork for his intelligence. They determine the basic quality of his brain. Clusters of genes probably give rise to special talents, particularly those like musical and mathematical abilities, which can be traced through families for generations. And genes help determine your offspring's basic bodily constitution.

But it is your child's environment which determines how much of his genetic potential will be realized. Even an Einstein, born with the intellectual capacity for genius, might have been classified as mentally retarded all of his life if he had been reared in an atmosphere like that of the Tehran orphanage.

You can't do anything to change your child's heredity, of course. His brain has basic qualities, not yet understood by scientists, which help determine how much and how quickly he learns from his environment and by means of which sensory organs he learns most easily. He may have been born with a good quality brain or a poor one—just as he may have been born with a strong bodily constitution or a relatively weak one.

But you can alter your offspring's environment in many ways, which will affect the development of his inherited potentialities—just as you can help your child develop the physique he inherits.

"It is highly unlikely that any society has developed a system of child-rearing and education that maximizes the potential of the individuals which compose it," Dr. Hunt emphasized. "Probably no individual has ever lived whose

31

full potential for happy intellectual interest and growth has been achieved."[7]

Is it possible to push a child too hard in hopes of raising his I.Q. to its maximum? At least one aggressively promoted program of baby stimulation has raised that question in the minds of some parents and early-childhood educators. But young children seem to have considerable built-in protection that should prevent mental overloading: They fuss, they turn off, they go to sleep, they run off, or they simply say "no more book" or refuse to cooperate.

The best gauge for using any early-learning ideas and stimulation with your child is simply to monitor his reactions. If he's interested, if he enjoys learning, if he's responsive, and if he seems generally happy, you are doing him good. But if he resists your efforts, squirms away, or won't pay attention for even a few seconds, you should reconsider whether the learning opportunities you are offering him are pushing him too fast—or, perhaps, if they may not be stimulating enough.

4. *Changes in mental capacity are greatest during the period when the brain is growing most rapidly. And the brain grows at a decelerating rate from birth on.*[8]

The younger your child is, the greater the influence his environment has on him and the more his characteristics—including his level of intelligence—can be changed. So the stimuli you add to your youngster's environment will have the greatest results in raising his intelligence during the earliest years of his life. The same amount of change and stimulus during his elementary or high school years won't result in nearly such large gains.

More than one thousand research studies carried out during the last half-century support this concept and its far-reaching implications. These findings were summed up in a scholarly volume, *Stability and Change in Human Characteristics,* by Dr. Benjamin Bloom, professor of education at the University of Chicago and a former president of the American Educational Research Association. The book has had tremendous influence on educators, pediatricians, administrators of antipoverty programs and other professionals concerned with child care. Because parents have the chief responsibility for managing the lives of children under age six—the years when their intelligence is changing most rapidly—it is important that you be informed about these findings, too.

We've tended to overlook the importance of intellectual development during the preschool years for many reasons, said Dr. Bloom. One reason is that education in our society lasts so long. Young people stay in school for a minimum of ten or eleven years. Many take for granted seventeen years of schooling, including college. An increasing number are seeking graduate training, upping their school years to twenty or more. What difference could a more or less wasted year at age three or five matter?

We now know that intellectual development doesn't proceed at a uniform rate, but at a decreasing rate. What is missed in the preschool years can be difficult or impossible to make up later on—as experience with disadvantaged children has demonstrated.

Future learning, inevitably, rests on the basis of past learning, Dr. Bloom pointed out. If your child has learned to learn and to enjoy the process, if he has sharpened his intellectual curiosity and found pleasure in using it, he will be a far different type of student in school than the youngster whose learning drives have been thwarted and dulled by his environment.

Six-year-old Todd, son of a lawyer father and a journalist mother who spend much time with him in stimulating activities, learns far more in first grade than Carl. Carl's home is a dark, crowded apartment containing no books, no records, few toys, and a weary mother who is too preoccupied with the problems of being a single parent to answer Carl with more than a shake of her head. Yet both Todd and Carl are exposed to the same teachers and the same teaching every day.

Four-year-old Kathy, who can read at second grade level, learns far more about her everyday environment than does Barbara, who lives next door in a home of the same size with parents of similar educational and social background.

What a child learns early in life has a powerful, persistent quality that makes unlearning difficult, noted Dr. Bloom. We don't know enough yet about the neurophysiology of the learning process to understand precisely why this is so. But we do know that early learning differs from later learning in its effectiveness. This is another reason why parents urgently need more information and help in guiding their children through these vital years.

During the years of rapid learning, an environment extremely lacking or abundant in intellectual stimuli can change a child's I.Q. as much as 20 points, Dr. Bloom estimated. (Other researchers put this figure somewhat higher.)

"This could mean the difference between a life in an institution for the feebleminded or a productive life in society," Dr. Bloom said. "It could mean the difference between a professional career and an occupation which is at the semiskilled or unskilled level."

Dr. Bloom, too, holds out the hope that through a better understanding of early-learning processes and by changes in child-care practices "we can drastically reduce the incidence of low levels of intelligence and increase the proportion of individuals reaching high levels of measured intelligence," and that a general gain in intelligence in our country can be achieved.

5. *Your child has already developed half of his total adult intellectual capacity by the time he is four years old and 80 percent of it by age eight. After age eight, regardless of what type of schooling and environment your child has, his mental abilities can only be altered by about 20 percent.*[9]

An individual's I.Q. seems to stabilize at its adult level by about age seventeen, most research indicates, although some studies show slight increases or decreases during the college-age years and afterward. But adult intelligence is generally considered to be a stable characteristic, just as adult height is.

Your youngster will continue to learn, of course, after age seventeen. He will be able to use his intellectual abilities in many different ways. But the opportunity of increasing his basic intelligence will be almost completely gone by the time he is old enough to be graduated from high school.

These findings, also from Dr. Bloom's important book, do not mean that your child accumulates half of all the facts he'll ever know by age four, or that by age seventeen he has filled his brain with all the knowledge he's ever going to have. They do mean that his level of intelligence is fixed by about age 17—whether he is brilliant or above average, whether he is trainable or educable, mentally handicapped, average, or dull-normal, whether his I.Q. is 120 or 150, 50 or 70. He may use his mental capacity to a high degree in obtaining further knowledge and in productive work. Or he may waste it. But after age seventeen, he can't change it to any significant degree.

As much of your child's intelligence develops in the first four years of his life as in the next thirteen years. This really isn't surprising in view of the rapid growth of your youngster's brain these early years. You can see clear evidence of this same, fast growth in other areas of his development. Your baby increases in height, for example, as much in the nine-month period from conception to birth as he does in the nine-year period from ages three to 12. And if he kept on gaining weight all during his childhood at the same rate as in the first year of his life, he'd be too big to fit into your house by the time he became a teenager.

These findings about intellectual growth put enormous responsibility upon parents. "Although there must be some genetic potential for learning, the direction the learning takes is most powerfully determined by the environment," Dr. Bloom pointed out. "Home environment is very significant not only because of the large amount of educational growth which has already taken place before the child enters the first grade, but also because of the influence of the home during the elementary school period."

6. The cortex of your child's brain can be roughly compared to a computer, which must be programmed before it can operate effectively. Your child "programs" his brain by means of sensory stimuli he sends to it along the nerve pathways from his eyes, ears, nose, mouth, and tactile and kinesthetic senses. The more sensory stimuli with which he activates his brain, the greater will be the capacity of his brain to function intelligently.

The cortex is the thick layer of gray matter that forms the outer surface of the brain. It contains billions of nerve cells which can receive and send messages via chemicals called neurotransmitters. Human brains contain much more cortex than do the brains of animals. Parts of the human cortex, like other portions of the brain, have a fixed function, even at birth. But parts of it do not. They are "uncommitted," explained Dr. Wilder Penfield, a neurosurgeon and for 25 years the director of the Montreal Neurological Institute of McGill University.[10]

"This uncommitted cortex is the part of the human brain that makes man teachable and thus lifts him above all other species," explained Dr. Penfield, a pioneering brain scientist who mapped out different areas of brain function during the course of many long neurosurgical operations. Neurochemical impulses generated by the sensory organs and transmitted by the nerve cells pass through this cortex, making pathways and activating cells which process and store information, in ways which are not yet completely clear to scientists.

These uncommitted areas of the brain are used chiefly for the memory and use of words and for the memory and interpretation of experience, according to Dr. Penfield. The dominant area concerned with speech and with written language usually develops in the hemisphere of the brain opposite from the child's dominant hand: in the left half of the brain if your child is right-handed and in the right half if he is left-handed.

Part of the information an individual stores in his cortex isn't available for his conscious recall. But neurosurgeons are able to demonstrate that these "forgotten" experiences and feelings and learnings are still filed away in the brain. For example, during the course of an operation on the brain of a patient who is conscious (but free of pain), when the surgeon touches various areas of the cortex with a mild electrical stimulus, the patient suddenly remembers long-forgotten scenes and emotions.

The information stored in the cortex is used by the brain—somewhat as a complex computer utilizes programmed material—in the process of thought. The precise kind of neurochemical activity which takes place when the brain "thinks" is not yet understood. Several dozen different neurotransmitters have already been discovered, and neuroscientists assume there are many more. But there is little doubt that the quantity and quality of information cached in an individual's cortex determines to a great extent the level of his intelligence.

"What the brain is allowed to record, how and when it is conditioned, these things prepare it for great achievement, or limit it to mediocrity," commented Dr. Penfield.

7. *But there is a time limit to when these brain cells can be activated easily.*

"The human brain is a living, growing organ," explained Dr. Penfield. "But it is bound by the inexorable evolution of its functional aptitudes and no one can alter this, not even an educator or a psychiatrist. One can draw up a functional timetable for the brain of a child. One might well say there is a built-in biological clock that tells the passing time of educational opportunity."

We know, for example, that when a small child injures the area of his brain used in speech and cannot talk, he is usually able, after many months, to create a new speech center in another part of his brain, using cells which were "uncommitted" previously. But an adult in whom this vital area of brain is hurt has enormous difficulty building a new speech area. His brain no longer possesses its earlier plasticity.

Because of this changing plasticity of the brain, learning acquired early in life—even if it can't be recalled consciously—is almost impossible to erase. It is doubly important because it also influences future learning and behavior.

A simple case in point: A mother was driving a car pool home from school one day. Betsy, age nine, announced to the group, "My speech teacher said I would have to work on saying 's' better this whole semester."

"That's nothing," replied an 11-year-old. "I worked on 's' for two years."

Yet parents take it for granted that their youngster will learn "s" and all the other sounds of the English language correctly, without undue effort and without formal teaching before they are three or four years old. Every speech teacher knows how difficult it is to change even one of these sounds at third or fourth or fifth grade level if it is learned incorrectly at the preschool age.

8. *Sensitive periods exist in the life of every child for specific types of learning. These sensitive periods are the stages in development when the physiological state of the growing brain makes certain kinds of learning most easy to acquire. After these sensitive periods, it is difficult to acquire these kinds of learning.*

Occasionally, on a college campus, you can encounter a student walking about followed by a half-grown duck or chicken which has been conditioned to think of that human as its mother. This phenomenon is called "imprinting," and it is the subject of much study in university psychology departments.

Experiments with geese, ducks, fish, sheep, deer, buffalo, monkeys, dogs, cats, guinea pigs, mice, and chickens have repeatedly shown that for an extremely short time after birth, these animals can be conditioned, or imprinted, by special types of learning situations—and this learning is almost impossible to change or erase afterward. In the most common experiments of this kind, a baby duckling is encouraged to follow a moving wooden decoy for a short period after hatching. The duckling thereafter regards the decoy as its mother and remains attached to it, ignoring other female ducks and ducklings.

Imprinting with a duckling can be done most successfully when it is between thirteen and sixteen hours old and rarely succeeds after twenty-four hours. The physiological condition of the duckling's brain that makes this particular type of learning possible at this specific age has changed beyond recall. Some research suggests that in the brains of children as well as animals there may be mechanisms which can be activated only during a certain period of life or that make certain kinds of learning particularly easy. If these are not triggered at the right time by stimuli in the environment, they cannot be activated later, even by the same stimuli. Such animals or children may suffer from lifelong disabilities as a result.

A baby lamb, separated from its mother after birth for a few days, never learns to follow the flock, no matter how many years it is kept with other sheep. Some birds which are isolated from bird song during the early weeks of life never sing well, regardless of how much they are exposed to singing birds the rest of their lives.

"Like the duck, we, too, begin to learn very early in life, maybe in part by imprinting, but certainly in many other ways as well," commented Dr. George W. Beadle, Nobel prize–winning geneticist, when he was president of the University of Chicago. "It has recently become increasingly clear that early learning is much more significant than we have previously thought."

The development of language suggests how this mechanism may work to a degree in human children. Babies make all of the sounds of all of the languages on earth during the early months of their lives when they are babbling and playing with sounds. But after they learn to talk, they gradually lose the ability to pronounce sounds that are not part of their native language and that they do not hear daily in the talk around them. Japanese people (but not Japanese-Americans), for example, have great difficulty distinguishing between the "r" and "l" sounds that are so familiar to those who speak English. Yet Japanese babies can tell the difference and use both in their babbling. But like the birds who cannot sing, they lose the ability to say these sounds easily if they are not exposed to them during the sensitive period for the development of language.

What other sensitive periods exist in the life of very young children? Much research is now underway to map out these periods more precisely and to help parents learn how to take advantage of these special learning opportunities.

The sensitive period for learning to read and to understand numbers is between the ages of four and five, according to Dr. Maria Montessori, the first woman ever to be graduated from a medical school in Italy and the founder of the Montessori method of teaching. (Chapter 9 describes Montessori ideas about preschool learning.) Dr. Montessori discovered that four- and five-year-olds learn to read with great enthusiasm, ease, and joy when given the opportunity.[11]

A child between the ages of three and one-half and four and one-half can learn to write more easily than he can at six or seven, Dr. Montessori also concluded. The disadvantaged, slum-area children she taught in Italy wrote beautiful script before they were five years old. Today, many four- and five-year-olds in Montessori schools learn both reading and writing as a free-choice activity, with great enthusiasm.

The muscular control in hand and fingers needed to produce written symbols is far less difficult to acquire than the complicated coordination of lips, tongue, throat, and breathing apparatus necessary to produce spoken symbols, Dr. Montessori explained. Furthermore, it's much easier to help a child learn to control his hand and fingers than it is his speech mechanism.

You may see evidence of interest and readiness for reading and writing in your own three- or four-year-old. He may identify labels on cereal boxes in the supermarket because he has seen them on television. He may read gasoline station signs while you're driving, again because he's heard and seen the words on TV. Your child may pester you to teach him how to write his name, your name, the names of his favorite toy animals. He may memorize the books you read him before you've gone through them three times and be able to recite them word for word to you.

In the past, parents have been told to ignore such signs, and advised to tell a youngster who asks questions about words that "you will learn all about that when you get to first grade." They have been warned not to teach a child alphabetical letters, because they will probably do it all wrong, or because home learning will confuse the child when he gets to first grade, or because the youngster will be ahead of the group.

But research shows these important signs of special sensitivity to learning should not be ignored, but observed and encouraged. The child who is eager and interested in reading and writing at four may already be almost past his optimum period for developing these skills by the time the school is ready to teach him at age six or six and one-half.

The sensitive period for helping a child develop a sense of order is when he is between the ages of two and one-half and three and one-half, Dr. Montessori concluded. This is the age when your toddler insists on routine. He wants his teddy bear put precisely in place before he's willing to go to bed and only then provided the door is open just so many degrees, the usual lullaby has been sung and the blankets adjusted just right. He insists on having the red boat, the blue submarine, the yellow bar of soap, and the white washcloth in his bathtub, or he refuses to get in. He demands his milk be served only in his special glass (and he can tell one glass from another, even if you can't). Jamie fumes at dinner if his string beans aren't all the same length. Ann fusses until her mother finds the "fuzzy" corner of her baby blanket to put nearest her face, although her mother can't tell the difference. Colin gets upset if his mother tries to put on his left sock before the right one, when he's accustomed to right before left.

Most parents consider this stage a dreadful nuisance and talk about the "terrible twos." But some of the researchers interested in early learning see this typical two and one-half behavior as evidence of a special period of sensitivity. This is the age when the growing brain of the child is trying to form generalizations from observations, to draw conclusions, to formulate concepts from perceptions. That's why children of this age are so insistent upon routine and ritual. It gives them a sense of order and continuity from which they can draw valid and workable conclusions.

You can use this special period to teach your child orderliness and good working habits, according to Dr. Montessori. Children in Montessori schools are taught to put away every item of equipment they use before starting a new activity. They are encouraged to see every task or game as having a beginning, a middle, and an end and to finish each cycle before starting another. These youngsters take great pleasure in being able to control their environment by ordering it precisely and show great satisfaction in completing self-chosen projects before beginning new ones.

More research needs to be done about sensitive periods in children so that parents can learn how to recognize these stages in their offspring and provide optimum learning opportunities. If you watch your child closely, you can probably see clear indications of some of these sensitive periods when he is eager for particular kinds of learning.

9. *In appraising the intellectual development of small children, we have failed to take into consideration the*

evidence of intelligence provided by the development of speech. Learning to speak the English language is probably the most complex intellectual task any individual of any age ever undertakes in this country—and our children master it as a matter of course before age five.

"Grandma is coming to visit; Mommy telled me so," shouts Brian, three, to his father. Daddy smiles indulgently at Mommy over his son's head and then explains to Brian that he should say "told." It is just another charming, childish mistake, his parents assume, and think no more about it.

But "telled" is probably better proof of Brian's developing mental powers than "told" would have been. Brian didn't say "telled" because he was parroting an adult. What Brian did—although he was probably not aware of it—was to observe that the way in which we usually make a past tense in English is to add "ed" to a verb, and then he applied this general rule to the word "tell." In this case, the English language makes an exception, of which Brian was not yet aware.

Your child may say "mouses" instead of "mice"—not because he is slow or stupid, but because he is highly intelligent. He has observed for himself that we usually form plurals by adding "s" to root words, and he has applied this conclusion to a word which doesn't follow this general rule. "Mice" he could have learned by imitation or repetition. "Mouses" is evidence of important conceptual learning.

It's curious that young children seem to have no difficulty sorting out which words are verbs and which are nouns. They don't, generally, add "ed" to anything except verbs. Yet when they are ten years older and learning grammar in school, many of them will have considerable trouble identifying the parts of speech.

It is this complex ability to observe abstract language forms, draw conclusions from countless observations, and apply them to the construction of new sentences that makes it possible for small children to speak sentences they have never heard before. It also makes it possible for youngsters to use correctly all of the complicated parts of speech in the English language before they are old enough to go to school—without the help of teachers or textbooks and without the pressures of report cards or homework assignments or fear of punishment or failure.

David, in seventh grade, is having difficulty with homework in grammar. He can't seem to remember the rules about complex-compound sentences, past perfect participles, gerunds, and adverbial clauses. Yet he can use all of these forms correctly in sentences, and he can tell what is correct and incorrect "by the way it sounds." All this he learned for himself, without formal help, at the age of three or four. Yet now, at twelve, he can't understand the rules in school.

David's parents try to help him with the homework. But they have the same difficulty. They can use all the grammar rules correctly—because they learned to do so on their own as preschoolers. But they can't remember the rules, either—which they were taught formally in junior high.

"In ignoring the implications of the mastery of language in the child, we are missing a fundamental aspect of human development," commented reading expert George L. Stevens. "If we regard the preschool period as essentially one of physical and emotional development, how are we to explain the miracle of speech? It has been this failure to recognize the implications of language development in the young child and an overemphasis on emotional adjustment that has dominated the educational theory of the past forty years.

"Between the ages of three and six, a period during which all normal children are completing their mastery of a complex system of symbols and completing it with little apparent effort and no formal assistance, our educational theorists consider the child capable of only finger painting and playing musical chairs. By failing to understand the intellectual aspects of child development, the educational theorists have unwittingly retarded our progress in learning theory and educational practice. By not realizing that the very young child has the drive and the capacity for knowledge, educators have delayed the development of new and improved educational methods.

"The most damaging consequence of this educational philosophy has been the ruling idea that reading should not be taught to the very young child. This is the concept—taught in all schools of education—that reading instruction of any kind should be delayed until the age of six or over. This notion has been one of the most disastrous blunders in the history of education."[12]

10. Because of the brain's special physiological characteristics, a child has the ability to acquire a second or third language more easily during the first years of his life than he will ever have again.

"A child's brain has a specialized capacity for learning languages—a capacity that decreases with the passage of years," emphasized Dr. Penfield, who studied the bilingual children of Canada extensively. "The brain of the child is plastic. The brain of the adult, however effective it may be in other directions, is usually inferior to that of the child as far as language is concerned."[13]

If you know any family with young children which has immigrated to the United States, you have probably seen examples of this early-language ability. Typically, the youngsters in such a family pick up English almost automatically, without formal lessons or obvious effort. But their parents, who may be highly intelligent, strongly motivated, and well instructed, learn English only with great difficulty and never speak it without at least a trace of foreign accent.

Dr. Penfield explained why. During the first few years of a child's life, his brain develops "language units," complex neuronal records of what he hears and repeats. These units interconnect with other nerve cells concerned with motor activity, thinking, and other intellectual functions. After about age six and increasingly after age nine, a child uses these language units in his brain as the basis for rapid expansion of his vocabulary. But these new words are built of the same basic units and sounds he has already recorded in his brain.

If, after the age of ten or twelve, the youngster begins studying a second language, he must use the same well-learned language units.

"Instead of imitating the sounds of the new language, he tries to employ his own verbal units—his mother-tongue units—and so speaks with an accent and even rearranges the new words into a construction that is wrong," said Dr. Penfield. "This is a common enough experience. Even though they travel over the world, the Cockney and the Scot and the Irishman betray their origins all through life by a turn of the tongue learned in childhood, to say nothing of the Canadian and the American."

The teenager or the adult trying to learn a foreign language, using the units already fixed in his brain since childhood, must go through the mental process of translation, a neurophysiological process Dr. Penfield called "indirect language-learning." Younger children who are taught by this same method—as, for example, by a teacher who uses English to explain French—must also use this translation process.

But children who learn a second or third language from a teacher who speaks to them in that language only—by what Dr. Penfield called the direct, or "mother's method"—can actually establish language units for the second language in their brains.

"A child who is exposed to two or three languages during the ideal period for language beginning pronounces each with the accent of his teacher," explained Dr. Penfield. "If he hears one language at home, another at school, and a third perhaps with a governess in the nursery, he is not aware that he is learning three languages at all. He is aware of the fact that to get what he wants with the governess he must speak one way and with his teacher he must speak in another way.

"Although the cortico-thalamic speech mechanism serves all three languages, and there is no evidence of anatomical separation, nevertheless, there is a curiously effective switch that allows each individual to turn from one language to another," said Dr. Penfield. "What I have referred to as a 'switch' would be called, by experimental physiologists, a conditioned reflex. When a child or an adult turns to an individual who speaks only English, he speaks English, and turning to a man who speaks French and hearing a word of French, the conditioning signal turns the switch over and only French words come to mind."

By the time a child is ten or twelve, it's too late for his brain to develop the switch mechanism, said Dr. Penfield. Unless he has acquired some language units of a foreign tongue by this age, he is forced to learn a second language by the difficult and relatively unsuccessful translation process.

It is often argued that it is useless to expose a small child to a second language if he lives in an English-speaking community and will not continually hear and use these foreign words all during the time he is growing up. Dr. Penfield disagreed. He said that it is true that such a youngster will forget the foreign words he has learned. But as a teenager or as an adult, if he studies that language or visits a country where it is spoken, he will discover an unsuspected gift of language-learning because the basic units of that speech are still stored in his brain.

Dr. Penfield studied for a time in Madrid during the period when his older son was five years old. For three months, the boy attended a Spanish school, where he played games and listened to other children speak but was not taught Spanish in any formal way. It was assumed that if the boy had learned any Spanish, it was soon forgotten when the Penfields left Spain.[14]

But twenty-five years later, it was necessary for Dr. Penfield's son to learn Spanish for business reasons. To his surprise, he discovered that he made very rapid progress, that forgotten pronunciations came flooding back, and that he was able to speak excellent Spanish without the expected Canadian accent. Dr. Penfield explained that units of understanding and pronunciation were hidden away in his son's brain, but not completely lost.

Europeans seem to find it easier to learn foreign languages than do English-speaking Americans, noted Dr. Penfield. He attributed this special aptitude to the fact that European children are accustomed to hearing second and third languages routinely, during the first decade of their lives, while most youngsters growing up in the United States do not.

11. The interaction of young children with computers offers fresh evidence of their unique ability to learn, given nonpressuring opportunities in their environment. As young-

sters learn to communicate with computers, the way they go about other kinds of learning may change.

"It is generally assumed that children cannot learn formal geometry until well into their school years and that most cannot learn it too well even then," pointed out Dr. Papert, the MIT mathematician and computer expert. "But we can quickly see that these assumptions are based on extremely weak evidence by asking analogous questions about the ability of children to learn French. If we had to base our opinions on observations of how poorly children learned French in American schools, we would have to conclude that most people were incapable of mastering it. But we know that all normal children would learn it very easily if they lived in France."[15]

If young children had the opportunity to interact freely with computers, they would learn to program them and to work comfortably with fundamental mathematical ideas as naturally and easily as they learn English, Dr. Papert argued.

"Very powerful kinds of learning are taking place" when children discover how to program a computer, said Dr. Papert. For example, he pointed out, "Children working with an electronic sketchpad are learning a language for talking about shapes and fluxes of shapes, about velocities and rates of change, about processes and procedures. They are learning to speak mathematics and acquiring a new image of themselves as mathematicians."

A child need not be exceptionally bright to learn to program a computer, according to Dr. Papert. "All children will, under the right conditions, acquire a proficiency with programming that will make it one of their more advanced intellectual accomplishments," he said.

The point here is not that computers are an educational gimmick that intrigue youngsters—but that the brains of young children are quite capable of learning in unexpected and unprecedented ways when they are given the opportunity in an unpressuring environment.

12. A child has a built-in drive to explore, to investigate, to try, to seek excitement and novelty, to learn by using every one of his senses, to satisfy his boundless curiosity.

And this drive is just as innate as hunger, thirst, the avoidance of pain, and other drives previously identified by psychologists as "primary."[16]

Because of failure to recognize curiosity as a basic drive, much behavior among small children has been misinterpreted and labeled "naughtiness." Toddlers and preschoolers are frequently punished for "getting into everything" because their urgent need for mental stimulation isn't recognized and they aren't helped to find outlets for this basic drive that are better than emptying dresser drawers or seeing what happens when a box of detergent is flushed down the toilet.

Bright youngsters with an abundance of curiosity are often considered troublemakers in schools which fail to understand their great need for learning stimulation.

"Most of us have the spirit of scientific inquiry spanked out of us by the time we are twelve years old," a research chemist commented.

Today, however, psychologists and biologists are finding ample evidence of curiosity as a basic drive—not only in children, but also in laboratory animals. Monkeys, for example, will work for long periods of time on mechanical puzzles, even when there is no reward involved—apparently just out of curiosity. Rats prefer to take a long but interesting route to reach their food rather than a short, quick one. Many laboratory animals can be motivated to perform tasks by the reward of a view out an open window, from which they can see activity outside their cage.

Even in newborn infants, behavior can be triggered by what psychologists call "perceptual novelty." For example, when researchers show a two- or three-day-old baby in a hospital nursery a simple, bright-colored object, such as a red ball or a red circle on a white card, his eyes can be seen to focus on it and his whole body seems to become alert. The next time he sees the same object, the infant pays the same alert, interested attention. But the novelty begins to wear off. And the baby will give more attention to a second, different object or shape than he will to the first one.

Much behavior which we have considered childish or immature may actually be a sign of this primary drive in operation. For example, we know that a small child has a very short attention span and have assumed it was because his brain was capable of learning only in small amounts. However, it is more likely, in view of new research, that a youngster can concentrate on one thing for only a brief span because of his brain's urgent need for more stimulation—because of his great drive to pay attention to many things.

When parents find better means of helping a youngster satisfy his urgent need to explore, to look, to experiment, to try, to experience a variety of sensory stimuli, he will not only learn, but he will be much happier and much more content. The baby who is dry, fed, neither too hot nor too cold nor ill, and who is still fussing in his crib or playpen, has an unsatisfied basic need—the need for new sensory stimuli.

13. Your child has a built-in drive for competency, an inborn desire to do and to learn how to do. He manipulates, handles, tries, repeats, investigates, and seeks to master as much of his environment as he can, primarily for the pleasure of such activity.

If you observe your baby's actions closely, as Swiss epistemologist Dr. Jean Piaget did his own youngsters, you can see this basic drive at work quite clearly. Dr. Piaget, for example, described his own son Laurent, at the age of three months and ten days, lying in a bassinet. Over the baby, Dr. Piaget hung a rattle with a string attached. One end of the string he placed in Laurent's hand. Soon, by a chance movement, Laurent pulled the string to produce a noise. For the next fifteen minutes, the baby delighted in tugging the string and listening to the rattle, laughing with obvious joy.

Three days later, Laurent again by chance pulled the string and set off the rattle. This time he obviously experimented with the effects of pulling the string. He swung it gently, tugged at it, shook it, listening to the different sounds produced from the rattle and laughing exuberantly.[17]

Your baby may drop his rattle over the side of his high chair and howl for you to retrieve it. Then he drops it again. And again. And again, as long as you are willing to fetch it for him. If you see his actions as purposeless behavior, or as an attempt by your baby to control you, you'll probably become annoyed and cross with him. But if you understand that your youngster is trying to learn all he can about grasping and releasing, about falling objects, gravity, and impact noises, you'll find it much easier to be patient and understanding and to help him with his enormous learning task. The perceptual observations your baby gains from this repeated experiment are nothing he can put into words. But they will be stored away in his brain, where they can help him later in forming concepts and in developing intelligent behavior.

This drive for competency is easier to see in somewhat older youngsters. A toddler will often delight in spending half an hour climbing up and down the same three front steps. A three-year-old discovering how to zip her jacket will insist on zipping it and unzipping it a dozen times before she is willing to hang it away in the closet. A five-year-old will draw the same picture of a ship again and again for days.

Just how strong this drive is, any parent knows who has tried to do something for a child that the youngster is determined to do all by himself. No matter how difficult the task or how frustrating the failure, a two- or three-year-old will often persist to the point of exhaustion in his efforts to master his self-selected task.

All of this seemingly random "play" has a great underlying purpose in human development, suggested psychologist Dr. Robert W. White. He said that all human beings have an innate, biological need for myriad perceptual and motor experiences to fill up the large, underdeveloped cortex area of the brain. A human infant is born so ill-equipped to function in the world and has so much to learn before he is able to care for himself that this drive for learning—for competency—is essential to his survival. He has to spend the earliest years of his life filling his brain with information and perceptions or he will not be able to act intelligently when he is older.[18]

Once a baby has had the opportunity to store up in his brain all of these many perceptions and experiences—to program his brain with information—then subsequent learning can be swift and complex, Dr. White pointed out. This conclusion, although it comes from psychological theory and research, is quite similar to that reached by Dr. Penfield, whose work was based on neurological findings.

This same need of a small child to develop competence was also observed by Dr. Montessori in her studies of preschool youngsters. She deliberately designed learning frames to help her tiny pupils develop competency in buttoning, buckling, tying, and lacing, for example. And she demonstrated how a young child can be helped to learn how to carry out many of the simple operations of a household if taught in very simple, logical, programmed ways. The great joy this feeling of competency, or control over the environment, gives to children is a basis of her teaching methods.

14. Learning can be intrinsically enjoyable, and small children learn voluntarily when their efforts are not distorted by pressure, competition, extrinsic rewards, punishments, or fear.

Long before a child is ready for first grade, he's well aware that you don't go to school for fun. He knows you have to go. He hears older boys and girls talking about the strict teacher or the hard assignments or the confining rules. His mother tells him that he has to do what the teacher tells him. He learns to stand in line, to keep quiet, to do what the group does, no matter how much it bores him.

By the time he's in high school, his interest in learning is so distorted by worry about grades, by competition, by the need to win the teacher's approval, by homework assignments, and by pressures that he has almost given up expecting learning to be a joy. Even if he is lucky enough to encounter a class or a textbook or a teacher he finds fascinating, he knows it isn't socially acceptable to admit it.

But in his beginning, it was not so. Because of his innate drive toward competency, because of his inborn curiosity, learning was originally a pleasure. He worked almost constantly at learning during his waking hours—by looking intently at everything around him, by touching, tasting, listening, practicing sounds, exploring, trying, falling down, trying again. He enjoyed the process of learning and he enjoyed practicing again and again what he had learned.

Montessori schools, for example, show clearly that when given free choice, three- and four- and five-year-olds will choose learning activities and enjoy them enormously.

A parent who remembers that learning should be intrinsically pleasurable for a small child has a good guide in planning mentally stimulating activities that aren't too immature or too advanced, too easy or too difficult. The purpose of these learning activities isn't to push the youngster or pressure him or make him compete with a neighbor's child or perform like a puppet to show off—but to make the youngster himself happy.

15. *The more new things your child has seen and heard, the more new things he wants to experience. The greater the variety of environmental stimuli with which your child has coped, the greater is his capacity for coping.*

Among the great mass of theories and observations by Dr. Piaget regarding intelligence in children, this concept is one of the most useful for parents. By it, Dr. Piaget meant, roughly, that stimulating changes in a youngster's environment trigger changes in the organization and functioning of his basic biological structures—in other words, they further the development of his brain. The more differentiated and flexible these structures become, the more capable the child is of reacting intelligently and appropriately to future stimuli from the environment.[19]

At every stage in a youngster's life, moreover, his environment should supply him opportunity to use the range of mental abilities he has acquired. He also needs enough challenge and stimuli in his surroundings to trigger additional development of his potentialities.

If your youngster doesn't get enough stimuli to make effective use of what he can do, he suffers from boredom and his development is curtailed because of lack of challenge and learning opportunity. This can happen, for example, when a kindergartener, who has already had two years of nursery school, is forced to sit through another year of group-singing games and coloring exercises, without any intellectual challenges. On the other hand, the child who isn't mature enough to cope with challenges in his environment suffers if he is pressured.

It is an art basic to both parenthood and education to match the stimuli and challenges in a child's environment with his growing abilities to learn. In the past we have greatly underestimated the learning capacities of our children. New research is now suggesting many practical ways in which you can help your child develop a high degree of his potential intelligence. These will be detailed for you in following chapters.

3. How the Atmosphere in Your Home Can Foster Intelligence

The emotional climate you create in your home can do much to stimulate your child to learn, to foster his growing mental abilities. Or it can stunt his developing mind and dull his innate creative feelings. Your relationship with him as a parent, coupled with his inborn traits and temperament, will largely determine how he goes about learning for the rest of his life.

It's impossible to blueprint precisely the ideal home in which maximum learning can take place—and have it fit every individual youngster. Children differ too much. So do parents and family circumstances. But recent research suggests many important guidelines you can use to make your home a creative, stimulating environment for your child.

Many long-term research projects show that your youngster's intelligence will develop to a higher degree if the attitude in your home toward him is warm and democratic, rather than cold and authoritarian. In one study, for example, the I.Q. of small children living in homes where parents were neglectful or hostile or restrictive actually decreased slightly over a three-year period. But in homes where parents were warm and loving, where they took time to explain their actions, let children participate in decisions, tried to answer questions, and were concerned about excellence of performance, there was an average increase in I.Q. of about 8 points.

This doesn't mean that you should be completely permissive or let your youngster run wild or interfere with the rights and possessions of others. It doesn't mean giving him a vote equal to his father's in a council that makes all the family decisions. Nor does it mean that your home must be child-centered.

It does mean that you should love your child wholeheartedly and enthusiastically and be sure that he knows it. (If a youngster thinks his own parents don't love him or approve of him, how can he face his teacher or his friends with self-confidence enough to keep trying?)

Sometimes it even helps to point out to a three- or four- or five-year-old just how many different ways you do show your love for him, especially if you work full-time away from home or if you have a younger baby. Often an older child, who equates love only with hugging and cuddling, may think that the baby is getting the bigger share.

"I show my love for Lisa by cuddling her and rocking her and changing her diapers," you can tell your firstborn. "But you certainly don't want diapers anymore, and you only like to be rocked just once in a while, when you've hurt yourself or you are very tired. So I show my love for you in ways you enjoy better now—like inviting Michael to go to the beach with us and reading to you and fixing the pedal on your trike and taking you to the park to swing. I even show my love for you by not letting you play in the street, because I don't want you to get hurt."

A warm and democratic home also means that you plan your family's activities to take into consideration your child's needs to grow and develop as an individual and that you give him as much voice in decisions involving him as he can handle. Your goal is to develop a thinking individual who can evaluate a situation and act appropriately—not a trained animal who obeys without question.

Even a two-year-old can be given choices, when you intend to abide by what he decides: "Do you want to wear the blue shirt or the green one today?" "Would you like to have your milk warm or cold this morning?" "Shall we have peas or carrots for dinner this evening?" "It's almost bedtime; shall we finish the puzzle or shall we stop now so there will be time for a story?"

It helps, too, if you explain the why behind the rules you set up and the decisions you enforce on your child—not in tiresome detail, not as an apology, not at a level above his understanding, but as a teaching device. Your child will learn, gradually, to evaluate alternatives. He will slowly begin to accumulate information upon which he can make good decisions. And he will realize, increasingly, that the rules you set up and the discipline you enforce are based on reasons and love and wisdom—not caprice or arbitrary or dictatorial power that he will sometimes feel compelled to challenge.

There is a happy by-product of this strategy, too. A two-year-old who is permitted some choices of his own isn't quite so negativistic and zealous of his independence as a child who is struggling for some beginning recognition of his developing self. An older child, who has learned that his parents only set up rules and make decisions for him when it is necessary, isn't nearly so apt to rebel as a youngster whose mother or father expects him to obey "because I say so."

"The intellectual tasks involved in the process of socialization are formidable," pointed out Dr. Kenneth Wann and his associates at Teachers College, Columbia University. "It is all too easy to come to see only the overtly behavioral aspect of social development. When this happens, then the job of the child is seen as simply that of conforming to the dos and don'ts of behavior codes. The role of the adult, then, is viewed as primarily that of restraining the changing, overt behavior. This, of course, is not an adequate concept of the child's task or the adult's role. Such activity is part of the socialization process, but only a small part. The major task is intellectual. It consists of understanding and conceptualizing the demands of social living so that one can respond to the complex stimuli of continually varying situations with appropriate, adequate behavior. This is a giant of a task. And young children work hard at it."[1]

Parents, said Dr. Wann, should do whatever they can to help children with this intellectual task of learning how to get along in the world. Within a warm and understanding home, you should see yourself not only as a parent, but also as your child's first, best, and most successful teacher.

"Teacher" doesn't imply that you help your child by means of structured, formal lessons. Your role is much more informal: to teach by example, by creating a stimulating environment, by talking to your youngster, by listening to him seriously, by loving him, by letting him teach himself with your guidance, by introducing him to the fascinations of the world you know, by taking advantage of every opportunity for learning in your life with him.

Just as you are not a formal teacher, so your preschooler is not a pupil in the sit-down-and-be-still-while-you-learn image of the word. Most youngsters can't sit quietly for very long before the age of six; that's one reason why it's often been assumed they aren't ready to learn. Most preschool learning takes place on the go, along with much motor activity.

Many factors interlace to make most homes a good place to learn and most parents ideal teachers. At home, a youngster can learn at his own pace. He needn't wait in fidgety boredom for two dozen other pupils to catch up, or he needn't continually drag behind because he can't maintain a grade-level pace or has somehow missed out on grasping some essentials. He faces no competition. No academic pressures. No formal timetable for learning. No tests. No fear of humiliating public mistakes. At home, a youngster can receive immediate feedback of praise or correction, which is considered by many researchers to be of major importance in the learning process and which is difficult for a teacher to provide for large groups of children.

At home, before age six, a youngster's growing brain makes him hungry for learning and uniquely easy to teach. During the preschool years, too, most children are eager to imitate and emulate their parents—to a degree seldom experienced by teachers or by parents themselves at other stages in their offspring's life.

These are positive strengths and great advantages which a parent possesses in his role as a teacher. Almost always they outweigh a parent's lack of special training and formal educational skills in dealing with his own youngster.

"But I have a job and a house and a whole family to take care of; I haven't time to be a teacher, too," some mothers object. Yet it takes no longer to think of your child in terms of helping him learn than it does to function chiefly as his caretaker, and it certainly makes both of you happier in your relationship.

A case in point: A trip to the shoe store. Often you see a mother with her fidgety preschooler waiting for a salesperson. The mother is bored, cross, impatient. The youngster is bored, restless, whining. He begins pulling shoes off of a display counter. The mother watches him idly for a few minutes, then scolds him to stop. He doesn't. She jerks him away. He pulls back. She hoists him back on his chair, scolding, "No, no, no." As soon as she lets go of his arm, he goes back to messing up the shoes. This time she yanks him away and spanks him. He cries. She slams him down on the seat in exasperation. He slides off defiantly and sits on the floor.

It's so easy to do it differently. The mother might have anticipated a wait in the store and brought along a book to read to her youngster. Then she'd have found ten bonus minutes the two of them could have enjoyed together. They could have played a beginning reading game or a guessing game. The mother might have a small pad of paper in her purse so she and her son could have drawn pictures for each other. They could have walked about the store together, talking quietly about the kinds of shoes they saw and guessing what kind of people would buy them or how women's shoes differ from those for men. The mother might have shown the youngster how shoe sizes are marked or how laces go.

Almost anything the mother wanted to do to help the youngster learn or satisfy his curiosity or direct his restless energy toward acquiring information or sensory experiences would have kept him intrigued, interested—and better behaved—for the waiting period. The mother had to spend the time with the child anyway and whatever effort she put into reading or talking would have been less than the strain of scolding him or trying to deal with his unpleasant behavior in public.

A child's attention span is usually short. You needn't hunt for big blocks of time in your day to help him learn. You can play word games with a child while you are doing almost every kind of housework, for example. You can count red cars or white trucks or out-of-state license plates while you're driving. You can keep a mental file of ideas handy for all the times you wait with your child—for the doctor, the barber, the salesperson, the bus, or the checker in the supermarket. Even if you invest only the usual quota of scolding-whining-fussing time in learning, it will pay dividends for your child later on and make your relationship much happier now.

As a parent, you have the time and the opportunity to study your child as an individual, not just as a member of a class or an age-stage group. Better than any teacher ever could, you know how he learns best, what encourages him to try, when he needs a touch of humor and when a bit of firmness, how much challenge spurs him on and how much blunts his interest. You can observe his responses and understand his feelings and shape the learning environment in your home so it is uniquely right for your child.

Another way to foster your child's mental development is to make encouragement, love, and praise your chief methods of discipline. For these techniques work most effectively in helping your child grow not only socially and emotionally, but intellectually, too.

Christopher, five, attended a four-family picnic one evening and was introduced to the architect husband of one of his mother's friends. Although he had not yet been taught to do so, Christopher happened to stick out his hand for the man to shake at the introduction. Later that evening, the architect remarked to Christopher's mother what a fine impression the boy had created with this simple courtesy and how well the gesture reflected on the whole family.

That night, when his mother tucked Christopher into bed, she repeated what the architect had said, and she thanked him for helping to make a friend for all the family. Christopher glowed at her praise. Never once afterward has he failed to offer his hand promptly, courteously, confidently, and without a reminder, when he is introduced to an adult.

It isn't always so easy to reinforce a desirable response in a small child, of course. But it does help to be alert to opportunities to give your youngster legitimate praise. False compliments ring phony even to a small child. But no matter how dull or slow or troublesome a child, you can always find a few opportune moments to praise him justly for something he is doing right or well or thoughtfully. If you emphasize what he has done right, rather than scold him for what he has done wrong, you'll teach him to work from strength, not from weakness and discouragement.

Sometimes you can even create situations which will give your child small successes and you opportunities for praise. Some parents set their standards so high, in an attempt to keep their child striving toward major goals, that he never can satisfy them. But it's much more likely that the youngster will become discouraged, feel inadequate, and stop trying if you continually point out where he has fallen short.

It helps if you let your child know that you have confidence in his abilities so he will have enough self-confidence in himself to keep trying. Your youngster has enormous respect for your judgment. If you tell him he's "stupid" or "never will amount to anything" or that he's the "naughtiest boy in the neighborhood" or that he "won't get into college the way he's doing now," he's almost certain to believe you and quite likely to give up trying.

Because a child does believe almost any label a parent hangs on him, you can use this technique to foster a self-image that will enable the youngster to learn easily and without dragging self-doubts. You might tell him, for example, "This is hard, but you are the kind of boy who enjoys tackling difficult things. I can remember how hard you worked at learning to walk, how you never stopped trying, no matter how many times you fell down or how many black and blue bruises you got."

"I enjoy reading to you because you always listen so closely," you could tell a child. Or "It makes me feel proud to take you to the supermarket with me because you behave so well and you help me find the groceries I need." Or "I know I can always count on you to be gentle with your baby sister; it's no wonder she loves you so."

Don't use fear—of failure, of scolding, of disappointing you, of physical punishment, of the withdrawal of your love, of ridicule, or of unmentioned consequences in the future— to motivate your child. Most parents do use fear of one kind or another as a handle to control a youngster, without intending to, or even being aware that they are doing it. It may take time and practice to get out of the habit—but your child will learn more readily if you do, and your relationship with him will be more pleasant and comfortable.

Do encourage your child to feel that it's all right to try, that failure isn't a crime, and that a mistake can be one way of learning. Many youngsters spend so much energy worrying and trying to keep out of trouble and avoiding mistakes that their abilities to learn are stifled.

Your child will make mistakes, of course. Everyone does. It will encourage him to keep on learning if you teach him how to handle his mistakes. Spilled milk, for example, is just that, not evidence that your offspring is hopelessly clumsy or naughty. All you need to do is show your youngster how to wipe it up and get himself another glass. If he accidentally breaks another child's toy, help him to apologize, work with him to make a plan for seeing that the toy is replaced, and then talk with him a bit about why some toys break and how they can be safeguarded.

This doesn't mean, of course, that you immediately absolve your youngster of responsibility when accidents or mistakes occur. You should help him try to understand what went wrong and how it can be prevented. But you can do it in an objective way that promotes learning, rather than discourages your youngster from trying.

Every child develops a "life style" or "learning style" that determines how he reacts to his environment, to people he encounters, to new experiences like school. "Learning style is the way individuals concentrate on, absorb, and retain new or difficult information or skills," explained Dr. Rita Dunn, professor at the Center for the Study of Learning and Teaching Styles at St. Johns University. "It is not the materials, methods, or strategies that people use to learn; those are the resources that complement each person's style. Style comprises a combination of environmental, emotional, sociological, physical, and psychological elements that permit individuals to receive, store, and use knowledge or abilities."[2]

This learning style is shaped in part by constitutional factors with which he was born and to a larger extent by his experiences from infancy on. The older a child grows, the harder it is to change his learning style.

Many parents, inadvertently, encourage a child to develop a life style that hampers learning. For example, Jeremy's parents seem to show their love for him only when he is quiet, clean, and undemanding. Their house is full of "no-no's" that Jeremy mustn't touch. His mother insists on feeding him, because "he makes such a mess of things if he holds the spoon." She runs to catch him every time he tries to take a step on his own, because he might fall. And she keeps him in the playpen most of the day so he won't be spoiled by too much attention and get into everything.

Jill's mother is making exciting progress in her career in business management. She is efficient, hard-working, well paid, and so busy and highly organized that she tries to schedule her time with her daughter down to the minute. Jill has learned that her mother seems to love her best when she plays by herself, never asks questions, and keeps out of the way. Jill's mother assures everyone it's easy to juggle both parenthood and career. But the sitter who is with Jill all day while her mother is away also makes it clear she likes Jill best when she's undemanding and quiet. Eventually, the behavior style Jill is being pressured to develop will hamper her learning and perhaps her eventual level of intelligence.

When both parents work full-time, or in a single-parent home, it's particularly important that whoever takes care of the child during the day—sitter or staffer in a day-care center or mother who runs a day-care home—understands the importance of encouraging the child's mental ability and won't insist on behavior that hampers learning and the development of an effective learning style.

Sometimes the youngest child in a family finds it rewarding to develop a life style of being babyish and depending on others. Or a boy may discover he gets more of the attention he needs by clowning than by serious achievement. Or a little girl may be subtly encouraged to smile and wheedle, rather than to put forth learning effort. Parents must be alert to such situations and make sure their offspring gets attention when he is behaving constructively in ways that foster learning, rather than by being a problem.

One major way in which you shape your child's learning style is by your use of language with him, noted Dr. Robert H. Hess, professor of psychology and education at Stanford University. How you talk to your preschool child and the verbal method you use to control him have an enormous effect on encouraging—or discouraging—the growth of his intelligence, explained Dr. Hess.[3]

After studying groups of mothers and children from different social, economic, and occupational backgrounds, Dr. Hess and his associates concluded that a major difference between disadvantaged youngsters and others is not basic intelligence or emotional relationships or pressures to achieve—but the way in which mothers use language with the youngsters.

Language largely determines what and how a child learns from his environment, and it sets limits within which future learning may take place, Dr. Hess pointed out. It can encourage, or discourage, thinking.

For example, a small child is playing noisily with pots and pans in the kitchen. The telephone rings. In one type of home, the mother says, "Be quiet" or "Shut up." In another, the mother tells the youngster, "Would you keep quiet for a minute? I want to talk on the phone."

In the first instance, explained Dr. Hess, the child has only to obey a command. In the second, the youngster has to follow two or three ideas. He has to relate his behavior to a time dimension. He must think of the effect of his actions on another person. His mind receives more stimulation from the more elaborate and complex verbal communication.

The command "Be quiet" cuts off thought and offers little opportunity for the child to relate information to the context in which behavior occurs, said Dr. Hess. The second type of communication helps the child to link his behavior to his environment and may encourage him to seek the whys in future situations.

If incidents like this continue to occur during the early years in the lives of the two children and if they continue to receive quite different learning stimuli, their verbal and intellectual abilities will be significantly different by the time they are ready for school, Dr. Hess observed.

In studying "mother-child communication systems," Dr. Hess found that middle-class mothers elaborate on what they say, use more complex and explanatory sentences, and give their child more information than do lower-class mothers. They use language to encourage a youngster to reflect, to anticipate the consequences of his actions, to avoid error, to weigh decisions, and to choose among alternatives.

Communication from mother to child that is stereotyped, limited, and lacking in specific information curtails a youngster's learning, emphasized Dr. Hess. Such language patterns are characterized by short, simple, and often unfinished sentences, clichés, and generalities, such as "You must do this because I say so" and "Girls don't act like that."

But the mother who uses words to relate a child's behavior to his surroundings, to the future, and to possible consequences is teaching her youngster problem-solving strategies which will be useful in other situations, suggested Dr. Hess. She is encouraging a wider and more complex range of thought. She is stimulating her child to learn, and she is laying the foundation for learning in the future.

Dr. Ellen Sheiner Moss of McGill University, Montreal, found the same sort of differences in teaching style between mothers of gifted preschoolers and mothers of children of the same age who were tested as average. She videotaped the interactions of the mothers and children as each parent helped her preschooler with three different problem-solving activities: a puzzle, a peg game, and a block design task. And she found that the mothers of the gifted youngsters spent more time helping their youngsters understand the goal of each activity, gave them more cues as to the concepts involved, and offered them more encouraging feedback. They did more to suggest that the children anticipate the consequences of the actions they were planning and encouraged them to monitor their own thinking processes than the mothers whose youngsters tested out as average.[4]

Everyone learns by all of the sensory pathways that relay information to the brain. But almost everyone—children as well as adults—learns more easily and efficiently by some sensory pathways than others. Some adults know, for example, that they grasp material better if they hear it in a lecture or a conversation than if they read it. Others learn better by reading. Some adults know that if they want to remember, say, a telephone number or a name, they must write it down and read it so they can learn it visually. Others learn just as easily by hearing it.

These physically based learning abilities vary at different stages of life, said Dr. Dunn, and are still developing during the preschool years. Kindergarteners, for example, don't have as much ability to learn by either auditory or visual means as older school children, several studies show. But preschoolers are strongly tactile and kinesthetic in style, she pointed out, and "they find it easiest to learn by manipulating resources and actually experiencing through activities." She suggested helping young children find as many ways as possible to learn through their sense of touch and by means of physical games, acting out situations and real-life experiences. She also emphasized that young children cannot sit still for more than a short period, if that long, and need opportunities to learn on the move.

In assessing how much your child is interested in learning and knowing about before he's old enough to start first grade, you're much more likely to err by underestimating than overestimating. Almost everyone does—including educators.

For example, three members of a research team from Teachers College, Columbia University, along with the staffs of five schools for three-, four-, and five-year-olds in the New York City area, made a detailed study of preschoolers' learning activities. The 319 youngsters observed came from a wide range of home backgrounds—poor, immigrant, middle class, upper-income, foreign-language speaking, city, and suburbs.

At the beginning of the study, reported Dr. Wann and his associate, "No one would have denied that young children know and think. We had worked with children too long to be that naive. We also had the benefit of the work of other people before us who have studied young children. None of us, not even the most sophisticated of our group, however, was prepared for what was found. The depth and extent of the information and understanding of three-, four-, and five-year-old children was much greater than we had anticipated."[5]

For a brief time, the team kept anecdotal records of the children's activities and comments. In the first 600 such notes, the youngsters covered a total of 609 topics.

Dr. Wann commented:

> Impressive as was the extent of the knowledge of the young children, even more impressive were the ways in which they were using and testing their knowledge. Information became for these children the raw material for thinking and reasoning . . . The children repeatedly sought more and more information and they consciously tried to relate and test one bit of information against another. Their capacity for remembering a great range of information was remarkable. They employed all the essential elements of conceptualization in their efforts to make sense of the information they were collecting. They used and tested their information in many ways. They associated ideas. They sought to understand cause-and-effect relationships. They classified objects and phenomena they observed. And they attempted to make generalizations from their experiences.

Children are far more interested in questions of "how" and "why" than merely "what," observed Dr. Wann. He suggested that parents and preschool teachers should do more to make this type of information available to young children.

> It is clear that the interests of these young children were global, even universal, in scope. We found children attempting to understand people, places, and events remote in time and space from their own immediate surroundings. We found children struggling to understand phenomena in their environment. We found children developing confused and inaccurate concepts. We found children indulging in animism and the enjoyment of fantasy as they viewed their immediate world. More frequently, however, we found them

seeking to understand the causes of the phenomena they observed and to test their own thinking about these phenomena. We also found children concerned about the demands of social living and struggling to understand the very complex symbol system of their social world.

Parents and teachers need to realize that children not only crave great amounts of knowledge, but they also enjoy having information and using it, said Dr. Wann. They often relay facts to another child, starting out, "Guess what!" And they frequently make a game out of testing their own or other children's information.

Adults—both parents and teachers—must find ways to encourage small children in their great efforts and desire to learn, emphasized Dr. Wann. "Probably the greatest resource for young children, in this respect, is adults who listen to children, who talk with them about their ideas and who provide experiences for developing further understanding."

He suggested that adults should take preschoolers on more trips—to museums, zoos, and other places of interest and to visit people working at interesting occupations. They can tactfully and encouragingly help children correct some of their misconceptions. They can not only furnish them with stimulating sensory material, but they can assist them in sorting it out and making sense out of their observations. One of the happiest and most successful ways to stimulate your child's mental development is to let him share your own interests and activities.

In studying the home backgrounds and child-rearing practices which produced famous twentieth-century men and women, Victor and Mildred Goertzel observed that parents who raise distinguished offspring themselves tend to be curious, experimental, restless, and seeking. The common ground for the highly diverse types of families which produce outstanding sons and daughters—as well as many other highly competent and successful children not quite so famous—is a driving need to be going, doing, learning, striving, involved in activities and concerned about ideas.[6]

Family value systems have the strongest impact on these

children, rather than schools or teachers, reported the Goertzels. Parents help their children build on personal strengths, talents, and aims. They are usually so interested and interesting themselves that their youngsters eagerly tag along to share the excitement.

Parents who set high standards of excellence for their children and who are warm and positive about their abilities and accomplishments usually find that their youngsters live up to their expectations, researchers who have studied gifted preschoolers have found.

"Parents who explain their requests, consult with their children, and give reasons for discipline have higher achievers," noted Dr. Merle B. Karnes, who, with associates, has studied gifted and talented preschoolers attending a special program at the University of Illinois. "In general, the attitudes, values, and expectations of the parents influenced the child's behavior and aspirations. Finally, the parents' acceptance of the child had a definite effect on the child's self-concept. In other words, children who perceive that their parents think highly of them are likely to feel good about themselves.[7]

"If the child is not challenged and if expectations are not compatible with his or her abilities, motivation to learn may be dulled and the child may join the ranks of the under-achievers," continued Dr. Karnes. Preventing gifted youngsters from becoming underachievers and wasting their abilities and talent is a strong argument for the involvement of parents in early learning.

In an unusual kind of investigation into the environment in which great talent and ability develop, Dr. Bloom and a team of researchers picked out twenty-five individuals who had made world-class achievements before the age of thirty-five in each of six fields: research mathematics, research neurology, concert piano, sculpture, Olympic swimming, and tennis. Then they interviewed these outstanding individuals, their parents, and some of their teachers to learn more about their characteristics, the influences in their environment, motivation, training, and learning stages.[8]

What Dr. Bloom called "the most striking finding" is the "very active role" of the family, selected teachers, and sometimes a peer group in helping these young people develop into world-class stars. "The old saw that 'genius will out' in spite of circumstances is not supported by this study of talent development," said Dr. Bloom. "Whatever the individuals' original 'gifts' or special early abilities, skill, and achievements, without extremely favorable supporting and teaching circumstances over more than a decade, they would not have been likely to reach the levels of attainment for which they were selected in this study."

Dr. Bloom and the researchers had expected to find that these outstanding individuals showed extraordinary gifts and abilities early in life and as a result were given special instruction, attention, and encouragement. But instead, they discovered that the encouragement and instruction came first, and then later on, the youngsters were identified as being unusual.

Typically, these children grew up in homes where their parents were keenly interested in the field in which they later excelled, although the mothers and fathers themselves were usually not outstanding. The pianists, for example, were surrounded by music from babyhood on. The swimmers were at ease in the water and enjoyed water activities as early as the age of three or four. The mathematicians were remembered as asking questions and trying to sort the answers out into logical relationships.

But these characteristics aren't extraordinary in young children, Dr. Bloom noted. When they are introduced to water and to swimming by a good teacher, almost all preschoolers enjoy the experience and learn to swim quite quickly. "Under the proper circumstances virtually all children should quickly become at ease in the water, learn to swim in a very natural way, and enjoy swimming and play in the water," he said. "Ideally, all humans should possess this 'gift,' were it not for poor instruction, inept teachers of swimming, and very late introduction to swimming."

Similarly, parents of the world-class pianists recalled that as babies, their offspring had appeared to be listening to music that was being played in their hearing and that they moved in rhythm to the sounds. But "child specialists as well as musical specialists note that some early sensitivity to music is displayed by virtually all children in most cultures of the world," pointed out Dr. Bloom. "Responses by infants to music, rhythms, and other sound patterns are universal, even though what is responded to and found to be pleasant differs from culture to culture."

Most three- and four-year-olds ask questions by the dozens, although the future mathematicians may have done so with more purposefulness than other youngsters. "Whether most children would ask such questions if encouraged by adults is not clear," said Dr. Bloom. "Perhaps the important point is that the curiosity represented by this questioning was taken seriously by the parents, who took the time to answer these questions in a truthful and relatively sophisticated way. Such responses by the parents encouraged the child to ask further questions as the need arose. This type of question-raising in other forms characterized these individuals over the years and eventually became central in their field of interest—research mathematics."

Whether or not the highly talented adults studied by Dr. Bloom and his researchers really had unusual aptitudes, traits, or other qualities as young children isn't at all clear, he pointed out. What is important is that their parents thought that they did and treated them as having great potential, providing them with an unusual amount of learning opportunities and making clear they appreciated and valued the early signs of talent.

"Thus, the child's response to marked rhythm of music at an early age may be characteristic of most children at that age," explained Dr. Bloom, "but parents with only one or two children may regard it as unusual. The point is that the parents place a greater premium on this as a marker of musical talent than a well-trained expert in the field would. If the parent is convinced that this is a sign of great musical talent and acts upon this faith, it may be as effective for the child's musical development as if it were in fact a sign of great musical gifts."

Dr. Bloom added, "It should be noted that children have many qualities and characteristics which may or may not be special and distinctive. It is in part the values and interests of the parents which determine which qualities they will or will not note and mark as special and worthy of further attention and cultivation. Girls were, in the past, rarely noted as having special gifts in mathematics and science by parents, while a boy with similar attributes and interests might be much encouraged. Similarly, in the musicians' homes, athletic abilities and interests were rarely noted or encouraged . . . The values and interests of the parents determine which traits and qualities will be given great encouragement and further cultivation and which traits and qualities will be ignored."

Because parents thought these youngsters had special abilities, they encouraged them, provided them with opportunities to learn and often, special teachers. They helped their youngsters practice for lessons, paid attention to them and led them to understand that they were expected to work hard and to achieve. When the children did work hard and perform well, their teachers began to give them extra attention and praise and they soon became "star pupils," winning prizes and still more attention and praise.

As the children's abilities continued to develop, parents invested even more in their training, with special equipment, special schools, special summer experiences, advanced teachers—even freedom from the usual chores and duties expected of other youngsters. The children enjoyed the rewards of their talent as well as the activity itself, liked to please their parents and teachers with their successes, and flourished in the close attention their families gave them.

The continued development of great talent in older children and adolescents is beyond the age limits of this book. But briefly, the cycle of special attention, special teaching, high achievement, and resulting praise and rewards goes on. At a point somewhere between the ages of ten and early adolescence, it becomes evident that these young people do, indeed, have extraordinary potential. By their own choice, they begin devoting more time and effort to their training, even at the cost of slighting other areas in their lives. The commitment of family resources to the pursuit of high achievement becomes greater. And as a final stage, a master teacher or coach is found who spurs the teenagers to outstanding achievement and opens the way into the top ranks in their field.

The point of citing Dr. Bloom's research here is not to

advocate that parents set out to develop future Olympians or scientific geniuses. But it's to demonstrate once again the enormous influence parents and the home environment they create have on young children. And it's to remind parents that the mothers and fathers of these extraordinarily talented young adults motivated them to learn as children, not by pressure or fear, but by sharing their own interests and by praise and attention.

It's estimated that the average young person has watched television and listened to the radio and to records for a total of almost twenty thousand hours by the time he reaches age eighteen—probably twice as much time as he spends in school. Some of these hours yield high dividends in terms of learning. Much more of it is wasted on mindless programs, irrelevant commercials, and brain-numbing time-passing.

One of the greatest gifts you can give your child is the habit of watching television wisely. You should help him learn to choose what he sees deliberately, not merely look at whatever is on the screen. You should encourage him to evaluate his choices in comparison with other uses he could make of the time. And you should reinforce what he does learn from television with books, discussions, and other activities.

Television programs can be marvelous aids for children who are just learning to read. ("Sesame Street" does it deliberately, for example. Commercials, by showing a few words clearly on the screen while they are being spoken, often teaches reading inadvertently.) TV shows can expose young children to wonders and places and ideas and events impossible for them to experience otherwise. But because they have no background for understanding what they see or for putting it into realistic perspective, they need a great amount of parental help.

It's also essential that parents realize they are setting a powerful example for their children in the use of television. Those who keep a TV set turned on regardless of what's in view or who watch randomly or excessively have little chance of teaching their offspring to do otherwise. Those who demonstrate that they often prefer to read a book or pursue a hobby or enjoy an in-depth conversation have at least a chance of convincing their children that there may be better uses for at least some of those twenty thousand hours.

As you begin to understand and better satisfy your child's urgent need to learn, to experiment, to try, to explore, to handle, to touch, to see, to understand, you'll find he is much happier. He is easier to manage. He presents fewer discipline problems because his inner needs come closer to being fulfilled and he has an outlet for his restless curiosity.

Much of the typical preschooler's time is spent in activities which bore him and his parents and in matters of discipline. Parents who use early-learning principles with their youngsters report they cut down drastically on the frequency with which they say "Don't!" and "No!" and on the amount of "What-can-I-do-now?" whining.

There is much to be said for considering your preschooler as a gifted child, even though there is little reason to have him formally tested and labeled and most tests for giftedness are designed for school-age youngsters. But if you see your child as needing special and ample opportunities to learn, you'll be more likely to fulfill his needs and to appreciate his accomplishments more. Many of the signs of giftedness are quite similar to characteristics of young children who haven't yet been pushed into learning conformity. And if you cherish these traits and help your youngsters to develop them, chances are good he will be considered "gifted" when he's older.

For example, one list of the behaviors of a young child who could be considered "gifted," which was compiled by Dr. Margie Kitano, an early-childhood education specialist at New Mexico State University, included the following:[9]

- has a high level of curiosity
- is alert and attentive
- learns rapidly
- shows early interest in books and reading
- retains information
- has a large vocabulary for his age
- likes new and challenging experiences

73

- enjoys being with older children
- asks many questions
- experiments with materials around him
- produces original ideas
- likes to do things in his own way
- adapts easily to new situations
- may prefer to work alone
- has a good imagination
- may give unexpected, smart-aleck answers

Dr. Kitano made several suggestions for fostering the development of bright children that are useful for parents, although they are intended primarily for teachers in pre-school programs where there are gifted youngsters. For example:

—Give your youngster opportunities to think creatively. You can make a game of asking him questions that have many possible answers instead of only one correct response. For example, "How many ways can you use a wagon?" (There are many more examples of this strategy in Chapter 8.)

—Plan activities that encourage him to stretch his mind and to do some in-depth thinking. For example, instead of just letting your youngster scribble with a crayon or splash paint on poster paper, talk with him about colors, how they can be mixed to form other hues, what emotions his artworks suggest, why he made the artistic choices that he did.

—Involve your child in planning and decision-making and encourage him to talk about his ideas, feelings, and thinking processes.

—Provide things he can do that encourage the orderly process of scientific thinking. (Chapter 6 explains this strategy in detail.)

—Help your child to develop moral concepts and apply them to specific situations. (Chapter 6 also details how parents can help in this regard.)

Whether or not your youngster is formally identified as a gifted child isn't important at this age. What is essential is that you make sure he has enough mental challenge and stimulation in his life and the kind of atmosphere in his home that encourages mental development. Not only will your child be happier if the needs of his fast-growing brain are satisfied, but you will enjoy your youngster more. Parents can't help enjoying their offspring's excitement and delight in learning, just as they shared the joy of his beginning to walk and talk.

That early learning should be a happy experience for a child needs to be emphasized again. New research about the marvelous abilities of very young children to absorb new information and about brain growth during these early years has tempted a few teachers and parents to subject toddlers and preschoolers to intensive, rigid programs that bombard them with unrelated facts. These programs have once again aroused some opposition to early learning, on the grounds that it creates undesirable pressures on youngsters and may turn them off from learning in the future.

This kind of mental force-feeding is not at all what this book advocates. There are three ways to make sure you are not "pushing" your youngster in a harmful way, even inadvertently. First, you should not suggest in any way to your child that your love for him is contingent on his intellectual performance, that you are disappointed in him, for example, if he forgets a word you are trying to teach him to read or isn't using a grammatical form correctly.

Second, you should let his reactions to the early-learning experiences you give him be your guide in helping him learn. If he seems interested and eager most of the time, you are on the right track; if he balks, refuses to pay attention, or indicates in other ways he doesn't want to do what you are suggesting, don't try to force him.

And third, if what you are doing seems to make your child happy, then you almost certainly are not pushing him. Your purpose is to provide the nourishment his brain needs, not to force-feed his mind.

An emotional relationship between you and your child in which you act as guide and teacher and fellow explorer in a fascinating world—rather than as judge, jury, examiner, therapist, or boss—is one that grows well with time. Your child will feel less need to rebel against you when he is an adolescent and less of a sense that he must make a clean break with you in order to be independent when he is a young adult.

4. How to Raise a Brighter Baby: The First Year of Life

When you bring a newborn baby home from the hospital, many of his needs are obvious. He must be fed, burped, changed, bathed, protected, loved. Dozens of pamphlets, hundreds of baby books, and millions of grandmothers can tell you precisely how. But because the needs of a baby's fast-growing brain are not so obvious, they have usually been overlooked or misinterpreted or left to chance. Many of the ways in which we usually go about caring for babies may actually be limiting the growth of their intelligence.

During the first few years of his life, your baby's brain will triple in size. Even before he is ready to be born, all of the approximately 50 billion nerve cells he will ever possess have already been formed. But the connecting links between these special cells grow at a tremendous rate during early childhood, and their growth appears to be stimulated, at least in part, by the activity of the nerve pathways leading to the brain.

"The brain's growth spurt of the last fetal trimester and the first three months postnatally will never be matched again in the child's life," noted Dr. Lipsitt. "We cannot help being awestruck by the phenomenon.[1]

"Normal infants are born with all sensory systems functioning," Dr. Lipsitt said. And like the growth of the brain itself, the rate at which babies learn is also "phenomenal," he pointed out.

"The most important aspect of infant development in the first months, however, is the capacity for learning," he said. "All of the developmental milestones involve an immense input and appreciation by the baby of sensory stimulation, the registration of that stimulation in memory and the alteration of behavior style as a function of that experimental input; this is the stuff of which learning is made."

Thus, in a very real physical sense, your baby's early environment and the amount of sensory stimulus he receives can actually cause physical changes in his brain and foster the growth of his mental capacity.

This "developmental explosion" in the early years of your baby's life does not happen by chance or by a predetermined process, noted Dr. Leon Eisenberg, of Harvard Medical School. "How fast it happens and how far it goes are, within limits, a direct function of the amount and variety of patterned stimulation supplied by the environment."[2]

Your infant's brain is actively learning from the very first hours of his life, chiefly by means of sensory stimulation and motor activity. But because he has such limited means of communication, because he can't talk or walk, the importance of early input into his brain has been largely overlooked.

An enormous amount of sensory stimulation is necessary to give a baby's brain basic information to use in functioning and in forming concepts. It is during the earliest years of life that the brain is best able to record sensory experiences, researchers have discovered. That's why parents should give a baby all possible opportunities, within the limits of safety and common sense, to learn through a wide variety of sensory stimuli. Your baby needs vast experience in hearing, seeing, touching, moving—and to a lesser extent, in tasting and smelling.

But your newborn's brain isn't just a blank computer disk on which you can write any program or store any data that you choose. The genes he has inherited and the experiences of his prenatal life interact even before his birth to form the basis of an innate temperament and personality that will, in part, determine how and how well he will learn. Part of the art and science of parenting is to shape learning opportunities so they work best for your individual child.

Just how much difference the environment you create for your baby does make can be seen from research Dr. Burton White and his colleagues did years ago at Harvard University's Laboratory of Human Development.

Dr. White and his associates made intensive studies of babies between birth and the age of six months, trying to pinpoint how much of their development is an automatic result of age and growth, how much can be changed by the way in which they are handled, and how much they are influenced by their surroundings.

Because home environments vary so much and are difficult to measure precisely, Dr. White did his research in a Massachusetts hospital, where infants awaiting adoption lived in a special wing for several weeks or months (a practice that, fortunately, has since been replaced by speeding up adoption procedures or by placing babies in individual foster homes within a few days of their birth). At that time, all of the babies were exposed to the same environment, which the researchers then enriched in different, but measurable, ways.

First, the researchers observed a control group of infants carefully, for long periods of time, charting what the babies did every minute they were awake. They developed complicated devices for measuring the infants' abilities to focus their eyes and to follow moving objects visually and for recording blink reactions to approaching objects.

All of the babies in Dr. White's studies were physically and mentally normal. Like infants in some private homes, those in the control group were kept in cribs lined with solid white bumpers. They lay on their backs; they were changed when necessary, picked up for feedings at four-hour intervals, and bathed daily by nurses who were devoted and kind—but very busy.

As newborns, these infants were visually alert—that is, paying obvious attention with their eyes—only about 3 percent of the daylight hours, Dr. White discovered. Gradually, during the first few weeks of life, they began to pay more attention to the world around them with their eyes. At an average of fifty days of age, they discovered their hands with their eyes. Fascinated by their fingers, they increased their visual attention sharply, to about 35 percent of daylight hours by the age of sixty days. For the next few weeks, these babies spent much of their waking time watching what their fists and fingers were doing.

Hand-watching tapered off a little between the ages of thirteen and fifteen weeks for the babies in Dr. White's control group. But another spurt in visual activity occurred at one hundred five days to one hundred twenty days, when the infants were put into open-sided cribs where they had more chance to look out. About this time, their visual attention jumped to 50 percent of daytime hours.

Dr. White also studied the abilities of infants to follow an object with their eyes as it approached or receded. Until the babies were about thirty days old, Dr. White found, they could focus on and track a moving target only at one specific distance—usually about seven and a half inches from their eyes. But by the time they were forty-five days old, their visual accommodation had improved. At four months, the babies had visual accommodation skills comparable to those of normal adults.

The precise steps by which an infant learns to coordinate the movements of his hands and eyes, so that he can reach out accurately and grasp what his eyes are seeing, were also studied.

Typically, at about the age of two months, the babies in Dr. White's control group began to swipe haphazardly at objects with their hands. By about seventy-eight days, they could raise one hand deliberately and a few days later, both hands. Soon after they were three months old, they could bring both hands together in front of them to clasp an object they were offered.

At fifteen weeks of age, these babies learned to turn toward an object they could see. At eighteen weeks, they could grasp by moving one hand toward the object, glancing back and forth from the object to the approaching hand before making contact. What Dr. White calls "top level reach," or skilled one-handed grasping directed by the eyes, was achieved at about one hundred fifty days of age.

Yet this normal pattern of eye-hand development, so enormously important between the ages of forty-five days and five months, is "remarkably plastic," according to Dr.

White. It can be speeded up considerably by enriching the baby's environment.

For example, after he had recorded developmental data for babies as they were normally cared for in the hospital, Dr. White began to change and enrich their surroundings. First, he arranged for nurses to have time to give one group of babies twenty minutes of extra handling every day when they were between the ages of six and thirty-six days. After this period, these babies were more visually active than the control group—but their developmental timetable stayed about the same.

Next, Dr. White added more stimuli to the environment of another group of infants. The white padded bumpers on their cribs were replaced by bumpers and sheets with a multicolored, printed design, starting when the babies were thirty-seven days old. After each daytime feeding, the bumpers were removed from the cribs and the babies were placed on their stomachs so they could see the activities of the hospital ward around them. A special stabile was erected over each crib to give the babies something colorful to look at.

The stabile, which Dr. White designed, contained a small mirror in which the baby could see his face, two rattles low enough for him to grasp, a rubber squeeze toy that made a noise, and a gaily colored paper decoration at the top. These objects were mounted on a red and white checkered pole at various distances from the infant's eyes and the entire stabile was suspended above his head, where he could easily see it.

The babies in this enriched environment were a few days slower in beginning to observe the motions of their own hands and not quite so visually alert at the start of the experimental period. But soon they became much more attentive and active than the control babies. In less than one month, they learned how to reach out and grasp accurately—a skill that took the control babies three months to develop. They reached the stage of top-level grasping at about ninety-eight days of age—about two months sooner than the infants in the standard environment.

For a third group of infants Dr. White tried a modified environment. This time, instead of adding the bright stabile to the crib on the thirty-seventh day of each baby's life, he mounted a pacifier against a red and white patterned background on each side of the crib rails at an easy distance from the infant's eyes. Then, on the sixty-eighth day of life, he replaced these with the stabile.

These infants made the fastest gains of all, apparently because the stimuli in their environment were better matched to their basic needs. They were much more visually alert and active than the other groups of babies. They began swiping at objects several days earlier than control babies. They started guiding their hand visually toward an object at about the sixty-fifth day of life—twenty days earlier than babies in the normal environment. They reached top-level grasping at the eighty-ninth day of life, in contrast to one hundred fifty days for the infants in the standard environment.

Dr. White's experiments showed to what a great extent "developmental landmarks" in early childhood can be speeded up by changes in the environment. And they demonstrated what major gains can be achieved by relatively small changes in an infant's surroundings.

Dr. White called these changes "of striking magnitude." For when an infant is able to reach and grasp and learn from his sense of touch at the age of three months, he can learn more—and wants to learn more—from his environment than a baby who doesn't develop this skill until he is six months old. The infant who is paying attention visually 45 percent of the day learns more than the one who is attentive only 20 percent of the time.

You will see a great variety of learning activities occurring in your own infant, if you watch for them—and if you give him enough learning opportunities. Following are guidelines suggesting what you can expect as your baby grows and how you can foster his learning. But your best guide will be the reactions of your child. Watch him. Observe him carefully. Learn from him, even as he is learning from you.

(These age-level divisions aren't sharply defined stages. Some babies develop more quickly. Some go more slowly. Most grow and learn unevenly, by jumps and spurts, with plateaus and even some backtracking. If you begin providing your child with extra stimulation early in his life, you'll probably need to read ahead of these general age classifications to find ideas for him.)

Birth to Six Months

The moment of birth thrusts your baby out of a warm, watery, sheltering, dark, cramped environment into a new world of lights, sounds, smells, human contact, and somewhat frightening freedom to move about. He may be exhausted and a bit battered by the long process of birth, and he must cope with the instant need to breathe and survive on his own, separated for the first time from the support system of his mother's body.

Yet he is already learning—from the moment he is gently laid on his mother's abdomen and nuzzles his way to her breast, where he may begin nursing with a little help. If researchers test him during the first day of his life, or the next few days following, he will show them that he can focus his eyes on shapes and patterns and register obvious enjoyment at looking at them. He will prove that he is learning by beginning to act bored after he has looked awhile and by showing preference for more complicated patterns over simple shapes and by paying more attention to a new design than one he has been shown repeatedly.

Babies as young as twelve hours can detect differences in odors and will indicate by their facial expressions which ones they like and which ones they don't. Newborns not even a full day old generally indicate that they enjoy the smells of banana, vanilla, and strawberry. But they dislike the artificial odors of rotten eggs and fish, experimenters have found. By the time they are one to six days old, infants are able to determine where an unpleasant odor is coming from and will turn away from it.

Infants will pucker up their lips if a drop of lemon juice is placed on their tongue, but will indicate an obvious liking for a drop of sugar water. Given different concentrations of sugar water, they show they can tell the difference by sucking the hardest when offered the sweetest liquid. By the age of twelve days, babies are able to do something as complicated as imitate an adult sticking out his tongue; if a baby has a pacifier in his mouth so he can't stick out his tongue, he can remember what he wants to do and will stick it out when an adult removes the pacifier.

Newborns also show emotional feelings from the minute they are born, researchers point out. And they are capable of forming give-and-take relationships with other people from the first day of their life. They have been practicing their hearing skills before birth and, after they are born, will move their eyes in a way that indicates they can tell where sound is coming from. They also make it clear that they prefer the human voice to any other sound.

In fact, the more researchers study newborn babies, the more competent they turn out to be. In the past, scientists have grossly underestimated newborn competence, Dr. Lipsitt said. He described a newborn as a "complex biological system, shaped by its evolutionary history to solve problems in a complex environment."

It's easy to forget your baby's need for sensory stimulation when you first begin taking care of him after his birth. You're tired. He is still recovering from the trauma of birth. His sleep patterns don't match yours. Just the unfamiliar actions of handling him still make you feel awkward and anxious. His breathing patterns may seem irregular and worrisome. And even the healthiest infants with the most experienced mothers can still scream with colic for hours a day until they outgrow it at about the age of three months.

But it's worth the effort to be sure your infant is getting at least adequate sensory stimulation right from the beginning—because like satisfying his intense need for food, satisfying your baby's mental hunger will make him happier and easier to care for.

It isn't as difficult to begin filling your infant's life with appropriate sensory stimulation as it may sound. You can easily tell when a stimulus is effective, or when your infant is too sleepy or too hungry to care, or whether he's just not interested. Your baby will concentrate intently on sights and sounds and movements that interest him. And he'll fuss and cry when he's bored. When he's fed, changed, burped, and not too hot or too cold but is still crying, you can often quiet him by giving him something fascinating to look at, to feel, or to hear, or by rhythmic motor activity.

As you come to know him better, you can also tell by his reactions the infrequent times when he's had enough stimulation—it's usually when he's been tickled or jiggled—and needs to be rocked or nursed or back-rubbed or soothed to sleep. But too much stimulation is comparatively rare and almost all babies don't receive nearly enough.

From the first day of his life, your baby will enjoy having something interesting to look at. You can hang a bright shape or colorful mobile over his bed, make it move whenever you are in the room, and get him a new one every few days. (They are easy to construct yourself.) You can use bright colors in his room wherever possible, instead of hospital white or wishy-washy pink. You can tack or tape bright pictures on his wall. You can carry him from room to room with you and encourage him to look at objects in your home and outside of the window. You can put him in a safe, padded spot in the kitchen where he can watch you preparing meals and listen while you talk to him.

During the first few weeks of life, if your infant is crying and you pick him up and put him on your shoulder, he will usually stop crying and start looking around—at least for a short time. This visual alertness can be of major importance in your baby's very early learning, research at Stanford University School of Medicine suggests. This particular combination of a parent's soothing along with an opportunity to look about seems to be ideal for learning in very young infants, according to the Stanford study.[3]

Toting your baby with you in a canvas sling that holds him cuddled against your chest or, when he can manage his head better, lets him ride on your back, gives him a wealth of sensory stimulation. It's effective even if you just pack him around the house with you occasionally, but even better when you can take him outside for a fresh rush of stimuli.

A playpen and an infant's seat make more sense during the first few months of your baby's life than they do later on. At this age, your aim should be to give your baby a wider view of his world, and both playpen and seat are better than bassinet, crib, or baby carriage for this purpose. It's when a playpen is used to restrain a crawling child from physically exploring his environment that it begins to limit development.

The foundation of language is laid during the earliest weeks of life, too. You should begin talking to your baby from the very first time you hold him. You should vary your tone of voice as you greet him in the morning, change him, feed him, put him to bed. Take his attempts to communicate with you seriously and respond—for even in the first weeks of life he'll learn how to tell you by his cry when he is hungry, hurt, colicky, or bored.

Soon, your baby will begin babbling, practicing vowels, consonants, syllables, sounds of every type. Linguists say that a baby makes all the basic units of sound in every language on earth during the first year of his life. But eventually, he will discard those which are not part of the language he hears in his home. As an adult, he'll never again be able to make some of these sounds, even if he studies a language in which they are used.

Do listen interestedly when your baby babbles at you. When he stops, talk back to him. This will help him get the idea of what language is all about. When he makes the same sound consistently and deliberately, you can repeat it to him. But generally, you should avoid baby talk because your infant needs your example to learn correctly. Sing to your baby, too, and play records and tapes for him.

Physical movement is another major way in which your baby develops his intelligence. There is considerable evidence that the tactile-kinesthetic sense is the basic avenue of very early learning. Movements generate a great number and variety of sensory stimuli and sensory information, which is stored in the brain, accumulating and becoming interrelated until the baby has an organized body of information learned from movement exploration.

To this basic tactile-kinesthetic information, a baby then relates the stimuli he gains through his eyes and his ears, his nose and his taste buds. A newborn probably learns to recognize his mother by the sensory stimulus of being cuddled close against her and to anticipate feeding by the bodily position in which he is being held and the feeling of the nipple against his lips. But soon, he will associate the visual stimuli of seeing his mother and hearing her voice with the tactile-kinesthetic information he has already acquired.

Later on, as his brain accumulates more information gained from movement and touch and he has had a chance to receive much more visual stimuli, your baby will begin to rely more on seeing than on touching. Eventually, he will learn primarily by means of his eyes. But even as a two- or three-year-old, he will still feel a great need to touch new objects, to verify the visual stimuli, to learn through more than one sensory route. Adults do the same thing when they finger a fabric they consider buying or handle a dish as they browse around a china shop.

To build up this basic body of sensory information obtained from movement, your baby needs great freedom and opportunity to touch, to move about, to manipulate objects, to reach, to grasp, to learn to release. He also should have as much freedom as possible—consistent with his safety and health—from constricting clothing and from a confining bassinet.

How a baby's environment can inadvertently retard development is illustrated by an observation Dr. Piaget related about his three youngsters. Both Laurent and Lucienne reached the stage at which they could follow the movements of their hands with their eyes shortly after they were two months old. But Jacqueline didn't until the age of six months. The reason for the delay in development, suggested Dr. Piaget, was that she was born in the winter. So that she could be kept outside in the sun as much as possible, which her parents thought desirable at the time, her hands were usually mittened and her arms tucked under blankets.

During the first months of your baby's life, you can help him pour tactile-kinesthetic stimuli into his growing brain in many ways. You can give him opportunity during his waking hours to lie on a pad on the floor, where he can move his arms and legs freely without hitting the sides of a bassinet. You can put him on his stomach on a hard surface so he can eventually learn to roll himself over. You can hang a plastic ball or bell on the side of his crib for him to bat. You can suspend a simple toy from a piece of elastic so he can watch it move and learn to pull on it.

Most important, you can remember that your baby isn't an invalid who needs to live in bed and to be quiet almost all of the time, but a living, growing child who needs activity, exercise, and stimulation.

You can give your infant interesting textures to grasp: swatches of material like velvet, silk, wool, burlap, and satin; small blocks of foam rubber; a piece of sponge; tissue paper that crinkles with a fascinating sound; simple wooden toys. (Do remember that he'll try to put almost everything in his mouth, so make sure that the materials are too big to swallow and watch him carefully.) You can touch his fingers gently with an ice cube and with a just-warm trickle of water. You can play nursery rhyme games which involve counting fingers and toes or touching eyelids, ears, nose, and mouth.

As your infant begins to coordinate his hands and eye muscles, you can encourage him to reach out for objects, and when he has grasped them, let him experiment freely in banging, testing, shaking, and using them in any exploratory way that is safe. Peekaboo, with a man's handkerchief laid across your baby's eyes, makes a delightful game as soon as you are sure that your baby can grasp the cloth and pull it away.

If you observe closely during the third, fourth, and fifth months of your baby's life, you'll probably notice that he likes repetition. He makes the same movements again and again. He may spend a surprising amount of time handling and looking at an object that intrigues him or repeating the motions of his hands. If you rock him or bounce him on your knee and then stop, he'll often try to imitate the motion to get you to repeat your activity. If you do, he'll smile and laugh delightedly.

This experimentation with familiar activity is based on preliminary months of absorbing a great variety of sensory stimulation, both Dr. Piaget and Dr. Hunt have noted. In turn, repetition of familiar patterns leads into the next stage—that of fascination and curiosity in exploring new objects and activities. Dr. Hunt said that "the more different visual and auditory changes the child encounters during the first stage, the more of these will he recognize with interest during the second stage. The more he recognizes during the second stage, the more of these will provide novel features to attract him during the third stage."[4]

These changes in your baby's basic motivation for learning, Dr. Hunt suggested, explain what Dr. Piaget meant by his statement that the more a child has seen and heard, the more he wants to see and hear.

As Dr. Lipsitt put it, a baby is born with sensory systems immediately ready for learning. At the same time, these systems are immature and that tends to canalize infant experiences in particular directions and to put some limitations on what he can learn. As a result of this sensory learning made possible by his environment, his brain continues to develop and to become more capable, and he becomes better prepared to cope with the development tasks of later childhood.

It's also critical that you develop a warm, loving, personal relationship with your baby, in which you learn from each other and each of you shapes the other's behavior. Your baby learns much by discovering how to please you and how to fit into the environment you have created for him. And you learn from his responses and actions how best to be his parent.

As you get to know your baby better during these early months of his life, you can begin to shape his learning experiences to take into account his innate temperament. As child psychologists use the term, temperament includes such characteristics as your youngster's general level of activity (Is he constantly busy, restless even in his sleep?); his sociability (Does he smile and laugh easily and seem to enjoy being with people?); the ease with which he fits into a daily rhythm of activities; soothability (Is he easy to comfort when he's unhappy and irritable?); ability to concentrate; and the way he deals with frustration (Does he persist or shift his attention to something else?).

If you understand, for example, that your child is slow to warm up to new stimuli and often reacts first with fear instead of interest, you can plan to give him extra emotional support until he's comfortable in new situations. If you know that your youngster gets frustrated and angry when he can't master a new challenge quickly, you can figure out how to break the activity into smaller steps which make quick success much more likely.

Your child also needs some basic sense of order and consistency in your parenting, so he can build up what psychologists call "cognitive operating systems." He needs to know what kind of behavior you will allow, what makes you respond happily to him, that his home life is stable and predictable enough so that he can draw reliable conclusions from what he is experiencing.

Six to Twelve Months

By the time your baby can sit up by himself, he'll be enormously fascinated with looking at and handling objects of every kind, and he needs great opportunity to do so. By this age, too, he's ready to do more than just look and touch and record these sensory stimuli in his brain. He's beginning to make some primitive experiments with cause and effect. He'll pick up a small block and drop it again, testing repeatedly just what relationship there is between the movement of his fingers and the bang on the floor.

In fact, the force of gravity is the one constant point around which a baby systematizes all the spatial relationships he is working out for himself during his early sensory-motor stage of life, suggested Dr. Newell C. Kephart, when he was director of the Achievement Center for Children, Purdue University.[5] (This *may* make you feel a little bit better about picking up your baby's toys for the eighty-seventh time in a morning.)

At this stage, you can stimulate your baby's mental development by providing him with a changing variety of objects to touch, taste, bang, throw, grasp, and shake. Toys with safe, moving parts that can be attached to playpen bars and plastic blocks with bells inside make stimulating toys. So does an unbreakable mirror with hard-rubber edging. Sponge toys, floating animals, boats, and pouring utensils encourage him to experiment with water in his bathtub. He'll want one or two cuddly, stuffed animals with interesting textures, especially for going to sleep.

But you needn't spend much money to buy toys for your

baby. He can find great delight and learning stimuli in a block put into a small kettle, in a nest of lightweight plastic bowls, in a small cardboard box with a piece of tissue paper inside and in scores of simple objects already in your home.

As soon as your baby is ready to begin moving forward with a crawling motion, he needs to be taken out of the playpen and put on a clean floor where he can propel himself along. You can encourage him to start crawling by putting toys just out of his reach and by cheering him on.

The best learning stimuli you can provide for a crawling baby is a big room with a clean floor, where he is free to move about safely and freely for a large part of his waking hours. The room should be kept warm enough for your baby to be barefoot, and he should be dressed in overalls with padded knees, if possible. Everything that can be broken, toppled, swallowed, pulled over, or tripped on should be removed from the room, and all exits and stairs gated and locked. Electrical outlets should be capped, and electrical cords should be put well out of reach, where your baby can't pull or chew on them.

The point is that your baby should be free to explore and manipulate without discouraging and frustrating "Nos" and "Don'ts" from adults—although he does need your watchful, interested supervision. If you continually snatch objects out of his hands, slap his fingers, and scold him, he'll be apt to get the idea that it's wrong to be curious and naughty to investigate.

You will, of course, eventually need to teach your youngster not to touch objects which don't belong to him and to have respect for the property of others. But he is too young now for you to be sure he will heed and remember your prohibitions, although he will sometimes. Your baby will learn more easily and obey with less fuss in a few more months if he is getting ample sensory stimuli and your "Nos" don't frustrate his learning attempts completely.

The room in which your baby does his crawling should contain at least one low shelf of toys and objects your baby can handle. A shallow box can also be used, but the usual toy box is too deep to be effective and produces only confusing clutter. A pot and pan cupboard offers delightful sight, sound, and touch stimuli for a crawling baby, if you can arrange your kitchen so he can explore safely. But he shouldn't be permitted in the kitchen unsupervised, particularly after he is able to pull himself up on his feet.

If the weather is suitable and you can supervise him closely, you can let your baby crawl outdoors on the grass. Opportunity to crawl on carpet, on wooden floors, and on linoleum and vinyl flooring can also vary the stimuli your baby's physical activity is sending to his brain.

The first day your baby crawls an inch, you need to safety-check every place in your house your baby can possibly go. It's almost impossible to overestimate the speed with which a crawling baby can pull a tablecloth off a just-set table. Or reach a hand up to pat a hot electric burner. Or locate a poisonous household cleaner under your kitchen sink and swallow a dangerous dose. Or pick up a pin or a button you had no idea had fallen on the rug.

It's estimated that there are well over a quarter of a million household products on the market today which could kill a baby if swallowed. Some of these carry a poison warning. Most do not. No cleaning agent of any kind, no detergent, furniture polish, or bleach should be kept where a baby could possibly get it. If you've been in the habit of leaving medicine on a night table or on a kitchen counter, change now. Many drugs can be lethal to a baby. Aspirin is the greatest single cause of death by poison in small children and even the pleasant-flavored baby aspirin can be fatal in large enough quantities. Babies can even die from drinking whiskey or other liquor stored where they can reach it.

You will, of course, have to put your baby in a playpen at times to keep him safe when you can't supervise him closely. But you shouldn't keep him there as a matter of course during most of his waking hours. A baby howling in a playpen from boredom has just as urgent a need for mental stimulation as a baby crying from hunger has a need to be fed. You aren't spoiling him or giving in to him or entertaining him when you help him learn, any more than you are when you feed him.

It will disrupt your household considerably more to construct a home environment that gives a crawling baby optimum opportunity for learning, rather than one designed primarily for the convenience of adults and the protection of their possessions. But it is tremendously important for your baby during this early sensory-motor period.

During the second half of his first year of life, your baby will be making greater progress in matching up stimuli from all his senses. He can now anticipate your coming by the sound of your footsteps—and differentiate between those of his father and his mother. He may discover how to make the television louder by twisting a little knob. And he will start crawling toward the cookie box if you mention the word.

He'll also be learning more about space and time, about cause and effect, and about the sequence of activities. He'll scream now when you take him into the pediatrician's waiting room because he can remember that the last visit included an injection. He may cry when he sees a baby-sitter coming into the house, not because he dislikes her, but because he knows that her presence means his parents will go away.

Your baby is now beginning to associate words with objects, although he won't be able to form most of the words himself for several more months. You can encourage his development of language by naming an object he is looking at or holding: "cup," "cookie," "toast," "block." You can put his actions into words for him: "Now we're putting on your shirt" and "Sit on my lap and we'll rock." In addition to this simple labeling, you should continue to talk with him conversationally whenever you are with him and, in turn, listen seriously to his vocalizations.

When your baby makes a sound like "Mama" or "Dada" by accident, you can react with obvious delight; you'll want to, anyway, and it will help your baby understand that he can make noises which have meaning. At this age, it can be helpful if you recognize and use his first few approximations of words—perhaps "wawa" for water or "Nana" for grandmother.

When Diane, for example, began to make the sound "baba" rather consistently in her babbling, her mother told her three-year-old that his little sister was trying to say "brother." Paul puffed up with pride and joy to discover that the baby's first word meant him. He responded eagerly and lovingly whenever Diane said "baba," and the baby quickly learned to associate the sound with him. The family used the syllables until Diane was able to say "Paul" properly.

Once your baby has grasped the idea that things and people have names and that he can form the names himself, it's better to shift to correct pronunciations for every word. Your child's speech will progress more rapidly and efficiently if you do.

You should begin reading to your baby from children's books by the time he's ten months old. Find a quiet place and time, when your baby isn't engrossed in crawling or trying to pull himself up on his feet, and cuddle him close as you read. Picture books that show familiar objects are good. So are simple stories. Encourage your baby to look at the pictures and to attempt to turn the pages. A few excellent books for very young children also involve the sense of touch by including sandpaper whiskers on a daddy's face to rub or a ring-shaped cutout in the page to slip a finger through or a cotton-soft bunny to feel.

Your baby won't understand every word that you read to him at this age, of course. But he will grasp more than most parents realize. And he will enjoy the cuddling and the sound of your voice and begin to associate books with pleasant feelings.

Your baby's experiments with banging, dropping, throwing, picking up and releasing, poking, pushing, and pulling will continue at this age. But if you observe closely, you'll see more purpose in what he is doing and more serious concentration on the results of his actions in contrast to the random behavior of a few months earlier. He now gets enormous delight from his increasing skill in coordinating thumb and forefinger to grasp and let go of small objects. He enjoys pursuing crumbs around the tray of his high chair and has great fun with small toys and objects of all kinds. (Do remember they'll still go into his mouth and must still be large enough to be safe.)

The amount of sensory stimuli and motor activity your baby has had during the first half of his first year of life will already be reflected in his learning behavior, as Dr. Piaget pointed out. For the more stimuli he has been able to store away in his brain and the more points of reference he now has for new objects in his environment, the more curious he will be and the more eagerly he will go about exploring his surroundings, instead of reacting with fear or indifference to new sights and new experiences.

cover-up: but that more subtle form of abuse, which parents
are often unaware of, is just as damaging. It deprives a
son or daughter of the assurance of knowledge of himself or
herself that is necessary to normalize his relationship to
the world. It prevents children from growing a protective
skin that can survive whatever comes...

5. The Insatiable Drive to Learn: Ages One to Three Years

The years between your child's first and third birthdays may
well be the most critical of his life. Never again will he
change so fast, learn so much, or accomplish such a formidable intellectual task as learning his native language.

During these two years, your youngster will change from a
baby into a child. He will gain enough control over his
growing body so that he can walk, climb, jump, run, and
manipulate without having to pay attention to making his
brain and muscles work together. He will learn to use
language to communicate, question, joke, demand, seek
help, and learn. His learning style will become more evident. His personality will be crystallizing, reflecting not only
his innate temperament and heredity, but his environment
and parenting. By three, it will be apparent, as it was not at
one, how competent he is likely to be later on. Critical
differences among three-year-olds that will foreshadow their
future will be obvious.

A child's home environment and his relationships with his
parents are particularly crucial during these two years, as
new studies make clear. Yet one researcher estimated that
perhaps only about ten percent of families give their toddlers
optimum rearing during this vital stage—in part because
they are busy with other demands in their own busy lives
and in part because knowledge about what young children
need during these years has not yet been widely reported.

Once your child has discovered how to pull himself up into

a standing position and to take a few staggering steps while hanging on to a low coffee table or chair and finally to walk independently, he'll begin to get a fresh perspective on old, familiar territory and his intense interest in exploration will increase. His curiosity now seems insatiable. He can push, pull, climb, grab, pick up the tiniest objects, and move about with surprising speed. His attention span is short. His energy seems triple that of adults caring for him. And his ability to get into everything will exhaust his parents long before he is ready to stop and nap.

How parents react to a toddler's insistent, persistent eagerness to learn and the kind of learning environment they provide for him will be a significant factor in the lifelong level of his intelligence and his attitude toward learning and new experiences.

The more research educators and child development experts do on children between the ages of one and three, the more convinced they become that these may be the two most critical years in a child's life. By age three, there are many measurable, important differences between children that predict with considerable accuracy how well they will do later on in school and how successful they will be interacting with their environment and with other people. The most crucial requirements for the development of competent, intelligent children, researchers have found, are freedom to explore in a safe environment and encouragement and help in learning language.

One of the first and most important of these studies was made by the long-term Harvard Preschool Project, which was intended to conduct ongoing research to gain basic, accurate knowledge about how young children develop ideally and why there are such great differences in the abilities of six-year-old children. These differences have become a major national problem because of the difficulties they create in schooling and because it seems to be almost impossible for the least competent youngsters to overcome their handicaps.

One of the first things the Harvard researchers, headed by Dr. White, did was to define precisely what the results of ideal rearing during the first six years of life should be. What is a competent, successful six-year-old?

The Harvard researchers began by studying hundreds of preschool children with a great variety of educational, ethnic, and socioeconomic backgrounds. They talked to teachers, parents, pediatricians. They gave tests. They observed youngsters carefully at home, at school, on playgrounds, in supermarkets. Then, they chose two groups of children. Half of these youngsters were rated high in overall competence, "able to cope in superior fashion with anything they met, day in and day out." The other half had no physical or mental abnormalities, but were "generally of very low competence."

Next, the researchers set out to analyze exactly what the differences between the competent and incompetent six-year-olds were. They observed the children carefully over an eight-month period, often recording their activities with minute-by-minute evaluations. The researchers didn't find much difference between the first graders in physical skills and abilities. But they did pinpoint several abilities that distinguished the competent six-year-olds from those who had poor ability to cope with their surroundings.

These are the characteristics that mark a competent six-year-old, according to the Harvard researchers:

—He is able to get and hold the attention of adults in socially acceptable ways, such as talking to them, showing them something, moving toward them, or touching them.

—He can use adults as resources when a task is clearly too difficult. He can get information or assistance in a variety of acceptable ways, without trying to get an adult to take over the task.

—He can lead and also follow other children his age in a variety of activities. He can give suggestions, direct play, act as a model for others to imitate, and follow the suggestions of others.

—He is able to compete with other children his age.

—He can take pride in his own achievements, in something he has created, possesses, or is doing.

—He can play-act an adult role or adult activity or talk about what he wants to do when he grows up.

—He can make good use of language and grammar and has a good vocabulary for his age.

—He is aware of discrepancies, inconsistencies, and other

kinds of irregularities in the environment and can talk about them and can occasionally act on these inconsistencies appropriately.

—He can anticipate consequences and act on them or talk about them.

—He can use abstract concepts and symbols, such as numbers, letters, and rules, in an organized way.

—He can put himself in someone else's place and can show an understanding of how things look to another person.

—He can make interesting associations, relating scenes, objects, or discussions to past experiences.

—He has the executive ability to plan and carry out activities that involve several steps.

—He can use resources effectively, choosing and organizing people and/or materials to solve problems.

—He can do two things at once, or concentrate on one activity and still keep track of what is going on around him.

Once the Harvard researchers had a working definition of a competent six-year-old, their next step was to trace how children acquire these abilities and what factors in their home life favor the development of these traits. As a beginning, they analyzed their massive records, which covered the development of more than one hundred preschool youngsters whom they had studied for more than two years, again sorting out the competent and the incompetent children. These studies turned up an unexpected finding: The competent three-year-olds had already developed most of the abilities that marked the competent six-year-olds. It was immediately obvious that the study needed to shift to an earlier age level.

Next, the Harvard researchers determined that there seemed to be very little difference at age one between those children who later turned out to be most competent and those who turned out to be least so. It was what had happened in the home when the youngsters were between the ages of one and three years that accounted for most of the crucial differences that were detectable by age three and almost impossible to change by age six, the Harvard researchers concluded.

In further studies, the Harvard group sought out families

that had already produced highly competent or markedly incompetent children and that also had another child who was a year old or younger. With parents' permission, the Harvard researchers observed these babies and toddlers carefully for up to two years, correlating the degree of competence they developed with the child care practices in their homes.

Harvard researchers then identified two areas of particular importance during the critical two years between ages one and three: freedom to move about in a stimulating environment and the use of language.

In the first months after he learns to walk, about the time of his first birthday, a toddler's newfound ability to move around—combined with his innate curiosity—produces a great amount of work and stress for his mother or whoever is taking care of him. How his mother responds to this insatiable into-everything activity of her toddler helps determine whether he will be highly competent or incompetent by the time he is three years old—and as a first grader.

Parents who raise the least competent children use playpens and gates to restrict their children's freedom to explore and move around much more frequently than do those whose youngsters are rated as highly competent, according to the Harvard findings. More effective parents arrange their homes so that their children are protected from dangers in the house—and the houses are safe from damage by the youngsters. Then, they give their toddlers free access to roam and explore. These parents in particular make the kitchen safe and useful and provide kitchen cabinet space and safe utensils for their children's play, according to Dr. White.

Regardless of how successfully they are developing, one- and two-year-olds spend much more of their time interacting with objects than they do with people, according to the Harvard findings. One-year-olds average 86 percent of their time with objects and 12 percent with people; two-year-olds, 81 and 19 percent. Most, but not all, of the objects that hold the attention of toddlers are small and can be easily carried about.

Toddlers between the ages of twelve and fifteen months spend much of their time looking intently at objects (an activity the Harvard group labeled "gain information—visual") or simply exploring the qualities of these objects. But gradually, children begin to devote more time to mastering simple skills. The toddlers who turn out to be most competent later on put in more time mastering easy tasks during this age period than do the less competent youngsters. Poorly developing toddlers tend to spend far more time in idleness than other children; these statistics Dr. White called "an index of emptiness."

The other major factor in how well a young child develops is the kind and amount of language his parents and the rest of his family give him, according to the Harvard studies. Talk between toddler and parent is often very brief, usually no more than a few words. Frequently the words come in direct response to what a youngster is doing or in answer to a short question from him, an interchange lasting no more than ten to thirty seconds. But because the language relates so directly to what the child is doing, because it comes when he is most open to learning, such talk is a powerful teaching device, the Harvard group reported.

"The mother's direct and indirect actions with regard to her one- to three-year-old children are, in my opinion, the most powerful formative factors in the development of the preschool children," said Dr. White. "I would expect that much of the basic quality of the entire life of an individual is determined by the mother's actions during these two years."

What makes an ideal parent for a one- to three-year-old? On the basis of the Harvard studies, Dr. White suggested, "Our most effective mothers do not devote the bulk of their day to rearing their children; most of them are far too busy to do so. Many of them, in fact, have part-time jobs.

"What they seem to do, often without knowing exactly why, is to perform excellently the functions of designer and consultant," noted Dr. White. "They design a physical world, mainly in the home, that is beautifully suited to nurturing the burgeoning curiosity of the one- to three-year-old." Such a home is full of "small, manipulable, visually detailed objects" and of opportunities to move about and climb, according to Dr. White.

The ideal parent he describes "is generally permissive and indulgent. The child is encouraged in the vast majority of his explorations. Although she is not usually involved directly in his activities, she is within earshot. When the child confronts an interesting or difficult situation, he goes to her and usually, but not always, is responded to by his mother with help or shared enthusiasm plus, occasionally, an interesting, naturally related idea.

"These effective mothers talk a great deal to their infants and very often at a level the child can handle," according to Dr. White. In talking to their offspring, these parents "consider the baby's purpose of the moment" and use language that is "at or slightly above his level of comprehension" and "do not prolong the exchange longer than the baby wants."

Dr. White also noted that "though loving and encouraging and free with praise, these mothers are firm. They set clear limits. They speak a disciplinary language the baby can understand. They don't overintellectualize or expect the baby to do more than he is capable of."

Said Dr. White: "Effective mothers seem to be people with high levels of energy. The work of a young mother, without household help, is, in spite of modern appliances, very time- and energy-consuming. Yet we have families subsisting at a welfare level of income, with as many as three closely spaced children, that are doing as good a job in child rearing during the early years as the most advantaged families."

If you've ever doubted that small children have an urgent, insatiable drive to learn, just watch a youngster in the running-climbing-questioning-chattering-getting-into-everything months between the ages of one and three. A two- or three-year-old can outexercise a professional athlete, outtalk a radio disc jockey, outrun most mothers in active training, and still have energy enough to fight going to bed. You're lucky if you can persuade your wiggler to sit still long enough to eat.

The years between one and three also include the four- to six-month stage called the "terrible twos." This is the frantic period—usually around two and one-half—when almost every toddler is in active rebellion against the restrictions placed on his free exploration by No-ing adults and when he's most frustrated by his inability to become more independent and to "do it all by myself."

102

If you give your youngster more opportunity to learn and to satisfy his curiosity and to become more competent, he'll be far easier to live with. If he has fascinating, challenging learning materials to play with and ample opportunities to exercise his exploding interest in language, he'll not be as likely to empty the wastebasket into the goldfish bowl or crayon the walls or flush socks down the toilet. And if you can help him learn to develop some degree of control over the everyday objects in his immediate environment, he won't experience nearly as much frustration.

During this twelve- to 36-month period, your child still needs great opportunity to learn through sensory-motor activity, just as he did in the earlier stages of his life. The more stimuli he can pour into his brain through looking, listening, tasting, smelling, and touching, the more intelligent he will become.

But now, as he changes from a baby into a preschooler, he needs more than just a variety of sensory activities. These experiences must be integrated into patterns that help him understand relationships and form concepts. He is better able now to think, to reason, to draw conclusions, to use objects as symbols for ideas and activities. The great surge of language that comes between the ages of one and one-half and four years not only helps him to express his thoughts, but also to formulate them.

During this period, too, your youngster's learning style begins to crystallize, and this will influence the way in which he goes about learning and his reactions to new experiences all the rest of his life. Your offspring's learning style is based partly on individual constitutional factors—whether he's quick or placid, impatient or relaxed, independent or clinging, happy-go-lucky or a born perfectionist. But it's determined to a greater degree by whether his attempts to learn at this age meet with enthusiasm and help from his parents, or whether the attempts are constantly frustrated, punished or minimized.

How can you arrange a rich, stimulating learning environment for a youngster between twelve and thirty-six months of age—in view of today's expanding knowledge about how the brain develops? It isn't as big a job as it sounds.

Basically, you'll discover that your youngster gives you

many useful clues to what his growing brain needs. You don't have to impose learning on him or try to teach him facts by rote, as a few misguided early-learning programs have prescribed. You don't have to try to force him to sit still to learn or even program ahead of time what he should be learning. Your job, generally, is to see that he has opportunity and encouragement to teach himself.

In the months after your toddler's first birthday, you can help increase his mental abilities by enlarging the environment in which he is permitted to play freely and safely. You can begin teaching him how to handle possible hazards—how to slide off an adult bed safely, feet first, and how to go up and down stairs sitting down, for example—so that he can be allowed more freedom.

When it's warm and dry outside, you can fence off a sizable portion of your yard, make sure it contains no hazards, and let your toddler explore freely. Or tote him to the nearest park to let him roam. You will need to watch him closely until he's outgrown the habit of putting everything new and interesting into his mouth.

To help make this greater freedom possible, you will need to teach your toddler the meaning of "No." But it is important that you do not say "No" too often or too harshly, or your toddler may get the idea that you love him better when he isn't trying to explore and learn.

You need not resort to slapping a toddler's hands or spanking him to teach him to respect the rights and property of other people. Slapping hands to discourage active exploration usually teaches a child to slap back or to hit other, smaller children. Spanking carries a feeling of humiliation that isn't necessary in helping youngsters learn to behave properly. Spanking should be used rarely, if at all, only with toddlers too young to understand your words and only when they are in immediate danger—reaching up to touch a hot stove burner, for example, or darting into the street.

For some adaptable, easygoing toddlers, it's enough to say "No," in a quiet, firm, disapproving voice, pointing out what is forbidden and offering a substitute object or activity. But most toddlers are more determined.

One good way to teach your toddler "No" without curtailing his exploratory drives or resorting to slapping or spanking is this: First, be quite clear in your own mind what objects you don't want your child to touch or what you don't want him to do. Keep this list as short as possible. Whenever your youngster reaches out to touch one of these objects or to do something you are forbidding, sit down in front of him and hold him securely by his forearms, so that his hands press against his cheeks and you can turn his head to face you squarely. Now he has to listen to you. Keep him facing you for about half a minute, saying firmly, "No" and "Don't touch."

When you let your toddler go, give him a hug. This method compels him to pay attention to you and lets him know that you mean what you are saying, but it avoids the idea of punishment. A toddler who is trying to fill his brain's urgent need for stimuli should not be punished; he merely needs to learn a lesson about the property rights of others and the dangers inherent in this fascinating world.

You'll probably have to repeat this strategem a few times. But after that, your child should understand the meaning of "No" and be convinced that you mean what you are saying. But you will have to be consistent. A little later, you can begin adding a short reason to the "Nos" you give your child: "No, that will burn you." "No, that is Daddy's." "No, that will break." This gives your child information he can apply in other situations (you are trying to raise a thinking, reasoning, independent adult—not obedience-train a puppy), and it will help convince him you aren't arbitrary and mean.

If you are giving your toddler plenty of opportunity to explore and fill his brain with sensory information, if you love him and he knows it, he'll accept your "Nos" in good grace—most of the time. If you begin this way, if you are warm and loving, if you understand your child's real needs, you'll find you almost never have any need to punish him and discipline is just not a problem in your house.

Once your toddler has his walking well under control and can get where he wants to go without paying attention to his feet, his interest shifts to talking.

In the six months after his first birthday, your youngster will probably add only about two dozen words to his speaking vocabulary. But his understanding of what you are saying will increase enormously. You should talk to him whenever you are with him—when you dress him, while he's eating, while you're doing housework and cooking, when you take him on an outing, when you rock him. Asking him to carry out very simple directions can turn into a happy learning game in which he takes great delight, especially if you praise him and hug him when he's successful. The more language your child hears now, the larger and richer will be his vocabulary when he begins talking explosively, about the time of his second birthday.

By the time your toddler is two, you probably won't be able to total up his vocabulary. By two and one-half, he'll hold up his end of a conversation quite effectively, even if he has to invent a string of nonwords to do so. And by age three, you'll be wishing that he'd stop talking for a few minutes so you can have some peace.

A great many parents do a superb job of helping their youngster acquire the mechanics of language—simply by filling the child's environment with good language models, by matter-of-factly correcting his mistakes, and by responding to and praising his efforts. The child delights in his increasing competence with words and in the power that words give him to function in his world. Parents usually enjoy his learning so much that they can't resist quoting him to any adult who will listen.

So receptive is a child of this age to the language he hears about him that he learns to speak it precisely as he hears it, whether it is French, Hebrew, Chinese, Bostonian English, Southern drawl, or slum patois. In homes where parents are too busy, too unschooled, too ignorant, or too uninterested to provide good models of language for their young children to absorb, the loss is almost impossible to make up later on without enormous effort. The lack of opportunity to learn correct language easily and naturally during the first few years of life is probably the major factor that depresses the learning abilities of disadvantaged children.

The sooner your child learns to talk well enough to communicate his needs and feelings, the happier he will be and the easier he will be to live with. Many of the frustrations and tantrums of the "terrible twos" are triggered by a toddler's inability to let his parents know what he wants.

The whole area of discipline becomes simpler, too, when your child can understand language well enough so you can explain rules and safety regulations to him, instead of enforcing them by physically removing him or preventing him from hurting himself.

You don't need to teach your child to talk by drilling him on syllables, of course. But you can help him absorb the words he needs most by talking to him casually whenever you are together. For example, you can name the part of his body he may not have learned yet as you bathe him—shoulders, heel, thigh, chest, chin. Then, when he knows them, let him tell you in what order he wants to be scrubbed. You can describe each article of clothing as you dress him—white undershirt, blue overalls, red sweater. Then, as he learns to say these words, you can give him some choice about which clothes he'll wear. In the supermarket, you can ask him to bring you products he knows and to put them in your cart—crackers, paper napkins, bread, cake mix, salt.

You should not put words into your toddler's mouth before he has a chance to say them. (Sometimes when a two- or three-year-old is unusually slow to talk, it's discovered that his mother—or perhaps an older sister—is anticipating his needs so completely that the child feels no compelling urge to speak up himself and doesn't.) But there are tactful ways in which you can supply him with the words he needs but doesn't know.

For example, Stephen's ball is stuck so far under the chair he can't reach it. He tries to explain the situation to his mother and asks her to get it out. But his vocabulary is so limited he can't make her understand and he's getting so angry and frustrated he's about to cry.

Tactfully, his mother can hold out her hand and suggest, "Show me what you want me to do." When she sees the ball, she can remark in a friendly fashion, "Oh, your ball is stuck under the chair. I'll pull it out for you." Or she can say, "Let's get the yardstick to push it out." This sort of conversation supplies a small child with words he needs and helps him discover for himself how he can use language effectively.

Just by carrying on friendly conversations with your toddler, you can supply him with words he needs to describe his activities, his feelings, his experiences. "Daddy's chin feels scratchy when he needs a shave," you can comment. "The dog is making tracks on the kitchen floor because his feet are wet." "I like the way this sprig of pine smells when you hold it in your hand."

Even at the age of eighteen months, when a youngster can say only a few words himself, it's not too soon to begin using language as a way of encouraging him to think, to see relationships, and to formulate concepts.

This doesn't mean that you should start lecturing him or going into long explanations for everything you do. But in simple ways you can help him see cause and effect. ("If you turn the faucet just a little way, the water won't splash on you.") You can suggest time relationships. ("We're going to the grocery store now so we'll have hamburger to cook for dinner.") And you can supply facts that help him draw his own conclusions. ("This knife I am using is sharp, so I must be careful; scissors are sharp, too.")

Most parents help toddlers learn language so naturally that they may not be aware of how much verbal stimulation they are providing. For example, Ernst L. Moerk, a psychologist at California State University, Fresno, tape-recorded talk between a mother and a toddler named Eve for hour-long periods of time when the little girl was between the ages of eighteen and twenty-eight months. Analyzing this casual talk, he discovered that Eve's mother was actually giving her daughter six hundred to seventeen hundred bits of "linguistically instructional input" per hour—an incredible 3.5 million bits of vocabulary and grammar a year. And Eve's mother was casually structuring her talk to reinforce what Eve was doing at the moment, to supply her new words and grammatical constructions, and to restate or rephrase ideas Eve appeared not to understand.[1]

As a parent, you should be teaching your child about the relationships between his actions and possible accidents by the time he is eighteen months old, according to the American Academy of Pediatrics. "During this period, the child is learning the relationship between cause and effect," the pediatricians' organization pointed out. "In particular, he is learning that what happens may be the result of something he has done." Furthermore:

> When minor accidents do occur—and they will—the child should be helped to understand the extent to which something he did caused the accident. In teaching the child the dangers of his environment and why he must avoid them, it is of little help to blame inanimate objects. If we say, 'Oh, did the bad stove burn your hand?' we fail to show the youngster the true relationship between cause and effect, namely that the stove is hot, he placed his hand on it, and the hand was burned.
>
> Compensating minor accidents with cookies, excitement, or gifts only convinces the child of his innocence. A careful, patient explanation, along with appropriate sympathy for the injury, will help teach the child about cause and effect and about his responsibility to be alert to dangers and obedient to parental rules.
>
> At this age the child is learning obedience, which in some cases must be absolute. He should know and respond to the command, 'No.' But it should not be overused or it rapidly loses its effectiveness, or worse yet, stops the child from any investigation or experimentation. Its uses should be limited to situations that cannot be converted into learning situations.[2]

As your two-year-old becomes able to use words, you can begin playing word games with him. An easy one to start with is: "I'm thinking of something in this room that is red; what is it?" You can play it with shapes and sizes and other variations—and while you're doing dishes, cleaning house, or even driving the car. As soon as your toddler can talk well enough, let him take his turn quizzing you.

By the time your child is two and one-half, you can change the game to "Can you think of something that starts with the same sound as 'Timmy'?" Or "Can you think of a word that has the same sound at the end as 'cat'?" Games of this type sharpen a child's ear for the sounds that make up our language and provide him with an excellent foundation for learning to read.

Variations of the "silence game" used in Montessori schools can delight two and one-half and three-year-olds and provide them excellent training in auditory perception. You play it, basically, by encouraging your child to remain just as quiet as he possibly can—for the purpose of hearing and identifying a sound. Perhaps it's a train or a plane or a siren in the distance, or water swishing through the dishwasher, or a key turning in a lock, or pudding just starting to bubble in a pot, or a bird outside the window.

Or ask your child to play the silence game with his eyes shut and to guess what sound you make for him. Possibilities: a spoon striking a glass of water; keys jangling on a key ring; your hands clapping twice. Or have him play the silence game and listen carefully until he hears you whisper a simple direction he is to follow or tell him about a small surprise.

When he becomes adept at these games, set a time limit of one or two minutes and see which one of you can hear and identify the most sounds during this interval.

These games make excellent antidotes for the mother who feels like she is screaming at her offspring half the time to attract his attention and for the youngster who has learned to tune his mother out so often he seldom hears her at all. They are also good ways to help a busy, active youngster make a tearless transition to bedtime, bathtime, or meals.

Between eighteen and thirty-six months, your child's pleasure in books and in reading will grow enormously with even the slightest encouragement from you. If you haven't already, begin the practice of reading to him regularly. If you make it just before bedtime, it helps him relax, gets him into bed happily in anticipation of the treat ahead, and establishes the habit of a quiet evening talking time that you'll find invaluable at less communicative ages—such as seven, eleven, and thirteen.

You should let your two-year-old buy books of his own whenever you can afford it, even if they are just inexpensive paperbacks from the supermarket. Some PTA and library groups put on used-book sales as fund-raising projects, and here you can usually find stacks of hardcover children's books donated by parents whose youngsters have outgrown them; most are priced at only a fraction of their original cost. By now, your youngster should be making some of his own choices in library books as well. Toddlers often enjoy looking through magazines with you as you point out the babies, the toys, the chairs, an apple, a horse, a dog, a cat. Most toddlers like to have a stack of old magazines of their own, which they can look at by themselves.

At this age, most youngsters prefer simple, factual stories about other small children, about animals, about what adults do, and about the world with which they are familiar. Their lives are already full of so much wonder and magic—at the world outdoors getting a shower when it rains, at the light switch that can chase away the night in a second, at water that gushes out of a faucet at a wrist's twist—that they don't appreciate fairy godmothers and magic lamps as much as six-, seven-, and eight-year-olds do. Two- and three-year-olds are still greatly intrigued with absorbing information about the world around them and forming concepts about it and their relationships to it. Some of the best-loved books of two- and three-year-olds tell what parents do at work each day, about what they were like as small babies, or about a child's pride in learning a new skill.

Because two- and three-year-olds are so sensitive to language, most of them are fascinated by poetry. Even traditional nursery rhymes—most of which are actually old English political satires which have no meaning for today's children—interest them because of their sound patterns.

But parents who make the effort to find meaningful poetry to read to their children find that they enjoy it far more than "Baa, Baa, Black Sheep" and "Little Miss Muffet."

Two- and three-year-olds find great delight in poems like Dorothy Aldis's "Naughty Soap Song."[3]

Just when I'm ready to
Start on my ears,
That is the time that my
Soap disappears.

It jumps from my fingers and
Slithers and slides

Down to the end of the
Tub, where it hides.

And acts in a most diso-
Bedient way
And that's why my soap's growing
Thinner each day.

Or her poem "About Candy":

I say to lick a candy stick
Until it's sharp enough to prick.
If you have a lemon drop, then tuck it
Way inside your cheek and suck it.
To bite it would be very wrong
Because it would not last you long.

Better for today's two- and three-year-olds than nonsense
like Jack and Jill or the old woman who lived in a shoe are
poems that not only have rhyme and meter, but meaning as
well. For example, there's Aileen Fisher's "A Bug":[4]

I saw a bug
with twenty feet

Go crawling up
and down the street,

And wondered if
he stubbed ONE toe

If he would ever
really know.

You can find collections of many such intriguing poems for
very young children in almost every library—and a poetry
anthology is a good Christmas or birthday gift for any child
of two or older. There's nothing wrong with teaching your
child nursery rhymes, of course, and most parents do simply
because it's easy. There's nothing wrong with nonsense,
either. But this is all that most preschool children are given
for poetry. Your child will absorb more and enjoy rhymes

more if they have meanings that fascinate him as much as the sounds do.

You will find your child wanting you to read the same poem or story seventeen times, even though both of you know it by heart. This is a characteristic need of children at this age level, and such repetition is important for them to gain mastery of the ideas and language patterns. It is not time wasted.

You can begin now to introduce your two-year-old to the idea that reading is just another form of language, that writing is just talk written down. You can show him what his name looks like in print. You can suggest that he dictate short notes to you to send to his grandparents or to his friends. You can point out the titles on books, the names on records, and the labels on grocery boxes. You can write memos to him, pin them on his bulletin board or tape them on his mirror, and read them to him the next day. You can answer any questions he asks about words. (If these steps make him eager to learn more, you may want to read ahead in Chapter 7 about teaching a preschooler to read, even before your child reaches his third birthday.)

Even though a toddler learns much verbally in an enriched home environment, he still does a great part of his learning via sensory-motor activities. He still needs great freedom and opportunity to touch, to manipulate, push, pull, put together, take apart, group, rearrange, throw, and explore. He still must learn by doing as well as by listening and looking.

This is not learning that you can impose upon him or lecture into him. It's learning he acquires on his own, by exploration and experimentation, by trying and sometimes failing. (Remember this if you find yourself tempted to push him a little or pressure him into learning.)

This need for constant, reliable perception from which a child can draw conclusions about the world around him is probably a major reason why youngsters at about twenty-four and thirty-six months of age are so insistent upon routine and repetition. How can Johnny be sure just how far down a step is until he tries it over and over again? How can Jennifer learn that the same words written in her book always say the same thing unless she hears you read them in exactly the same way two dozen times? How can Tommy feel assured that the night will safely pass unless his frayed pink blanket and his teddy bear and his night light are all precisely in place?

A scientist's efforts to control conditions in his laboratory and to repeat experiments so he can test a theory are respected by his colleagues. Small children need the same respect and patience and understanding from adults in their absorbing efforts to control conditions and test out conclusions—even though they can't explain what they are trying to do, as the scientist can.

Of course you can't let your pint-sized Galileo test the law of falling bodies by dropping eggs from the top of your kitchen counter. Nor can he experiment with the principles of aerodynamics by throwing rocks at the neighbors' windows. But understanding more about the needs of his growing brain may help you to be more patient when your youngster demands the same bedtime story thirteen nights in a row or if he cries when you let the water out of the bathtub instead of waiting until he decides to do it.

Instead of being annoyed at your toddler's insistence on routine and repetition, you can take advantage of it to help him acquire habits of neatness and order and independence in personal care, as Dr. Montessori suggested decades ago and is done, for reasons of learning, in Montessori schools today.

A parent who uses Montessori techniques at home keeps her child's toys on low, open shelves where he can reach them easily and choose freely what he wishes to use. Each toy and learning material has its own specific location and the youngster is encouraged to return it to this spot before he begins playing with something else. A small basket or box is used to keep parts of games together. A parent marks items which should be shelved together with bits of bright-colored tape. All the pieces of one wooden puzzle are identified with a smidgin of red tape on the back, for example; all the parts of another with green; all the equipment for a game is tagged with blue and kept in an open basket that is also marked with blue.

A low clothes rod and low pegs in his closet help make it possible for a small child to be orderly about his possessions. At this age, a youngster wants fiercely to become as independent as possible about his own dressing and undressing, as you know if you've ever seen a two-and-one-half-year-old on the verge of a tantrum because he can't button his shirt and won't give in and let his mother do it for him.

A small child who can manage his dressing and undressing—because of the tactful, behind-scenes planning of his parents—develops a great feeling of pride and competency. He has control of a particular part of his environment, which gives him pleasure. And he has become independent of adult assistance in at least one area of great importance to him, at a stage in his life when he values this freedom enormously. If parents let a child grow past this sensitive period without helping him develop habits of orderliness, they often find themselves nagging at him for years about the state of his room and his belongings—with little observable results.

More than just neatness about possessions is involved in this sensitive period, according to Dr. Montessori. She felt that this stage of childhood could also be used profitably by parents to teach a youngster that tasks have a beginning and an end, that jobs begun should be finished, and that mental processes should be controlled and orderly, as well as physical surroundings.

A child's desire to be competent, to master as much of himself and his environment as possible, is particularly urgent when he is between twenty-four and thirty-six months old. If you take the time and effort to show a child how to perform easy tasks, he will usually learn with great concentration, interest, and obvious satisfaction. In the long run, it will take less of your time and energy to help him learn than it will to cope with his negative behavior and to try to amuse him and keep him out of trouble.

But few parents bother to think through how and what they try to teach a small child—whether it's to wash hands, tie shoes, button a shirt, or set the table. Adults usually work too fast, too automatically, for a child to follow and imitate. Dr. Montessori urged that an adult seeking to help a child learn should break down the activity into its component parts—the same technique modern educators call "programmed learning."

What precise steps are involved in buttoning a button? Adults do it so often without conscious thought that most of them can't describe the process without deliberately slowing down and thinking it through. But if you do break up the task of buttoning into its small, component steps and show your child clearly what these steps are, he will learn with delight and pride.

By using these steps, a child can learn how to perform a necessary skill—washing his hands, for example—successfully by himself at an age when it gives him pleasure to do so. The alternatives are for the mother to continue to do it for him, which usually makes him impatient and rebellious. Or he can do it inefficiently and unsuccessfully, which means his mother will nag, criticize, or send him back to try it again. The child need not continue to wash his hands in precisely the same way all the time, of course. The procedure will become automatic, and he will vary it as circumstances suggest. But he will be able to do it—at an age when he most wants to. Furthermore, the youngster learns a major lesson in how to go about learning. He discovers that there is a logical way to go about controlling his environment and accomplishing what he wants.

To help children isolate and practice the skills involved in dressing themselves, Dr. Montessori devised simple "dressing frames," which have since been updated for contemporary clothing design. Each square frame holds two pieces of cloth which can be fastened together in the center—by a series of buttons, snaps, ties, buckles, laces, or a zipper. Three-year-olds in Montessori schools often spend thirty to forty-five concentrated minutes snapping and unsnapping, buckling and unbuckling—by their own free choice. These frames can now be purchased from several sources, or they can easily be made at home. (One point: In constructing a frame to teach tying, when your child is three or four years old, make the left-hand ties one color and the right-hand ties another. This makes it easier for a small child to follow the tying action.)

Using programmed learning techniques, you can help

your two- or three-year-old learn many household tasks that will give him immense satisfaction, such as polishing furniture, scrubbing a tabletop, washing plastic dishes, or setting a low table.

It's important to remember that you are making it possible for your child to learn these skills because he wants to become more independent and because it gives him satisfaction. When he scrubs or polishes, he will do it because the performance gives him pleasure. So discipline yourself to let him polish and repolish, scrub and rescrub, as long as he wishes. Do respect his work; if you must redo something, never do it over in his presence.

To avoid putting undesirable pressure on a child to learn what he is not yet ready to learn, all of these activities should be completely free choice. Ask your youngster, "Would you like to have me show you how to button the button?" If he says "No," don't pressure or push or urge or coax or show any disappointment. Just change the subject and offer the suggestion again in two or three weeks. If your youngster is the kind who routinely says "No" to everything, you may change the question to a more positive, "Here, I'll show you how." But stop if he resists or isn't interested. And do it in a friendly manner.

Whenever your toddler begins to lose interest in a learning demonstration or wiggles away or says he's tired of it, stop. Put the material away and offer it again days later. This technique will not only protect your child from pressures, but it will help to avoid his developing a resistance to your teaching attempts.

Teach the very young with real things, as Rousseau urged long ago, is still a cardinal rule in helping toddlers to learn. Your house is full of utensils and equipment your child can learn to use effectively with a little help. And most of it is easier for small hands to manipulate than the cheap, flimsy miniatures made as toys.

But toys can, of course, be a delightful way to help feed your youngster's great need for varied sensory stimulation and motor activity during these vital years.

Look for toys that will give your child practice with concepts like "in" and "out" and "inside" and "on top" and "larger" and "smaller." Nesting blocks or cups make good toys for year-old children. So do small boxes with lids. Stacking cones with wooden rings that fit around a central core intrigue toddlers. Other possibilities: wooden blocks he can line up to make a simple train or pile into a tower; simple form boards containing a solid-color wooden triangle, square, and circle; a mailbox with geometric shapes to deposit and pull out below.

By the time he's walking, your toddler is ready for push-and-pull toys of every variety. Bright balloons are inexpensive playthings that help him absorb basic information about air and gravity (but don't let him bite or suck on one). He'll have great fun with a large cardboard packing box that's big enough for him to crawl inside, or with a sheet draped over a card table for a tent or cave. You can save milk cartons, wash and dry them thoroughly, and cover them with foil or bright contact paper to make easy-to-handle blocks.

Stairs hold great interest for a toddler. If you live in an apartment or ranch-type house, where your youngster has no opportunity to practice, you'll find him fascinated with stairs you encounter on shopping trips or on visits to other homes. Some toy stores sell sturdy, three-step wooden stairs that intrigue one- and two-year-olds.

Water play (which must still be well supervised at this age) delights a toddler. Sponge toys to squeeze, sailboats, floating animals, and pouring utensils increase his pleasure in the bathtub—or outdoors in a clean, shallow, plastic pool.

Simple games of hide-and-seek played with familiar objects appeal to almost every young toddler and help him form concepts about the permanence of objects not immediately in his sight. When he is very young, you'll have to hide the objects while he's watching. But even then, he'll laugh with joy when he discovers them.

Toys serve many other purposes in a small child's life. There are toys to love (the soft, cuddly, feels-good-to-touch stuffed animals and dolls that are always there when a parent turns out the light and goes away, that always listen when things go wrong). There are toys to trigger the imagination (paints, paper, dolls, doll house, sand, puppets—the more simple and less structured, the more creatively they can be used). There are toys to help a child try out the idea of being a grown-up (realistic dolls and their miniature paraphernalia, housekeeping toys, garden tools, doctor kits, costumes, trucks, trains, farmyard sets). There are toys to help a child find the action (tricycle, scooter, wagon, anything with wheels; swing, glider, climbing bars, tire-on-a-rope-hung-from-a-tree, slide, sled, small trampoline, rocking horse, balls of every variety, any equipment which moves and encourages a child to run or chase or sway or swoop or bounce).

Even though some of these toys seem chiefly to foster the development of a child physically, socially, or emotionally, they also encourage his mental growth. For there is an intellectual component in all of these areas.

There are also toys which are primarily for intellectual learning, whether or not they are so labeled. These are often the toys with which you are most apt to get your money's worth in terms of hours-of-play-value-per-dollar.

In addition to the general categories of toys already listed, your youngster can learn much and have fun with playthings like these:

- kindergarten blocks, in as large an assortment as you can afford, made of smooth, accurately cut, natural wood in squares, oblongs, diagonals, triangles, curves, half-circles, and pillars
- flashlight
- inlaid puzzles of wood or hard rubber (some have pieces which can be removed and used as toys)
- indoor wooden slide, with ladder
- simple rhythm instruments—bells, triangle, tambourine, drum, wrist bells, finger cymbals, small xylophone
- take-apart trucks and toys
- collection of hats for playing different pretend roles
- inlaid form board containing simple geometric shapes
- giant magnet
- unstructured playhouse

- counting toys and number puzzles
- cassette player or phonograph simple enough for a small child to operate himself. There are many excellent tapes available for very young children—and many toddlers recognize and enjoy a few musical comedy songs and folk tunes
- bean bags and baskets for targets
- large wooden beads to string or fasten together
- simple lotto games

Art and craft materials and projects suitable for youngsters older than two are described in Chapter 8. Some of the Montessori techniques and equipment listed in Chapter 9 can be effective with children younger than age three.

Taking your toddler on a variety of very short trips is one of the happiest and most effective ways of increasing the amount of stimuli he receives. Even a walk around the block can be a good learning experience, if you take the time to let him watch the ants hurrying in and out of an anthill and poke his finger into a puddle and scuff in the leaves and go up and down every step that beckons.

When you are outdoors with your toddler, you can encourage him to feel the rough bark of a tree, the prickliness of fresh-cut grass, the softness of a flower petal, the fur of the neighbor's friendly cat, the brittleness of an autumn leaf, the tickle of snow, the gooiness of mud.

Even your trips to the supermarket can provide opportunities for sensory stimuli. You can buy a box of cookies and let your toddler sample one. Let him try to drink from the cold arc bubbling out of the water fountain. Give him an orange to put in and out of a small paper bag. Let him feel the cold frozen-food package, a heavy bag of sugar, the softness of a loaf of bread. None of this will take any longer than scolding him to sit still or trying to prevent him from wriggling out of the shopping-cart seat in boredom.

A zoo and a farm and a pet store are all full of delightful learning possibilities for a two-year-old. If you can arrange it, let him have a chance to pat a horse, sit on its back, listen to it, and watch it eat—to learn about it through three or four of his senses. Then talk about the experience afterward and encourage him to put his feelings into words. He'll learn more this way than if you plop him into a stroller and try to cover the whole zoo in one afternoon.

Other good expeditions for two-year-olds include: A short trip on a bus. A train ride between two or three commuter stations. A visit to a bakery, a fire station, a shoe-repair shop. A trip to the beach and to as many different neighborhood parks as possible. An expedition to a fast-food drive-in, a greenhouse, an apple orchard.

The transition from this stage into the preschool period of three to six isn't a definite line that children cross in a birthday month. By about thirty months, a few youngsters will be ready for some of the activities listed in the next chapter, particularly if their parents have been enriching their environment since the earliest months of life. So you will probably want to read ahead in the sections about language, science, math, and perception before your child is fully three years old.

6. How to Stimulate Intellectual Growth in Three- to Six-Year-Olds

Peter, just six, is entering first grade this fall, already able to read independently and with great delight, at about third grade level. He can count as far as he wants to, do simple addition, subtraction, and division, and he has a good grasp of what numerical symbols mean. His vocabulary is probably about twenty-five thousand words, and he has developed many sound concepts about the natural and social sciences. He is eager, curious, fascinated by the world around him, responsive to adults, and happy. And because he is also self-confident, outgoing, and energetic, he finds it easy to make friends with other children.

But for Ted, also six, first grade is a threat. He can't talk well enough to make the teacher understand him. He has had no experience in interpreting even the pictures in his pre-primer, let alone the more complicated symbolism of the obscure black marks underneath the illustrations. It seems easier to Ted to withdraw, to look out the window, to keep quiet, rather than to try. Ted already feels that he is a failure, and he shows it in the classroom and on the playground.

Yet Peter and Ted started life—just a few miles apart in the same large city—with far less difference in innate mental ability than these first grade contrasts show. If they had been given an infant I.Q. test, they would both have scored in the same general range. They never will again. The differences between them now will almost certainly be self-perpetuating and will probably increase.

Peter, obviously, will be classified as a "bright" or "gifted" child. He will go immediately into the top reading group in his class. His eagerness to learn and his quick successes will delight his teachers. He will bask in their approval, and this, plus the joy he has already experienced from learning, will motivate him to keep trying and prevent him from being too discouraged if he draws a poor teacher or dull assignments. If he's lucky enough to be in an ungraded primary, he may even save a year of elementary school— time he can use to great advantage later for graduate study or for an earlier start in a profession.

It won't be long before Ted's teachers will stop expecting him to succeed. Even a patient, understanding teacher will find it hard not to become discouraged with Ted's obvious lack of effort and interest. Because of his lack of readiness and his deficiencies in language, Ted will be slow in learning to read and thereby handicapped in all of his other school-work. A sad, familiar cycle will probably begin. Because he can't keep up, Ted will begin to fail. Because he fails, he'll tend to stop trying. The less he tries, the less he will learn. Ted may spend an extra year in an ungraded primary. Or he, like about 10 percent of first graders, may have to repeat the year. Despite automatic promotions after that, he may be only a high school freshman or a sophomore before he is legally able to drop out of school and does.

The contrast between Peter and Ted is not an exaggeration. There are hundreds of thousands of Peters in our first grades today, the product of stimulating homes, of Montessori schools, of laboratory schools in university settings, of preschools where teachers practice early-learning principles. Happily, children like Peter are increasing rapidly.

Boys and girls like Ted, however, can also be counted by the hundreds of thousands. Most come from poor homes, often with only a single parent. But some of the Teds also belong to affluent families where parents are too busy or too uninformed or too uninterested in seeing that their children get the mental nourishment they need.

In between the Peters and the Teds are millions of other

youngsters whose minds have not been stunted as much as Ted's nor stimulated as much as Peter's. What they bring to first grade they have learned chiefly by osmosis in homes where they are loved and cared for physically, but where their urgent need for mental stimulation has not been fully recognized.

What can you give your child between the ages of three and six to boost his mental abilities and start him off to first grade confident and destined for success?

No preset curriculum can be devised that will fit all preschoolers, all homes, and all parents with their varying talents, responsibilities, and available time. Even if such a curriculum could be devised by extensive research, it would not be desirable. Youngsters are so active physically and mentally that no preplanned pattern of experience can take advantage of the opportunities for learning that constantly occur.

A small child's mind works so fast and reaches out in so many unexpected directions that you'd miss great teaching opportunities if you tried to stick to a prescribed, formal lesson pattern. One of the great advantages of preschool learning at home is that you can adapt it to the needs and immediate interests of each individual child—an opportunity for personalized learning that rarely occurs throughout your youngster's years of formal schooling until graduate level.

Here are general guidelines for the major areas you'll want to cover during the years between three and six. Like any good teacher, you'll improvise and adapt the suggestions for your own child. How fast he will go in which areas will depend on how much time you spend with him, his own individual speed and way of learning, how much early stimulation he has had before age three, and whether he attends a nursery school or day-care center which actively fosters intellectual development. That's why these guidelines are not grouped more specifically by age levels.

Language

Between the ages of three and six, your child's vocabulary will grow explosively and excitingly—and in imitation of yours. If you speak English correctly, so will your child by the end of this period. He will also pick up your swear words and pet expressions. One of the most important aids you can give your preschool child—and one which a disadvantaged youngster is most apt to lack—is a good language model to copy.

This doesn't mean that you have to speak copybook English with complete sentences every time you talk. But it does mean that you should use a full range of tenses, subordinate clauses, pronouns, adjectives, and adverbs for your child to absorb. He'll discover—without apparent effort—how to form tenses, plurals, and clauses without overt assistance from you, if you provide the example. His ability to do so is greater when he's a preschooler than it will ever be again.

Don't be afraid to use words your child doesn't understand. He'll absorb them and gradually decipher their meaning. That's how he learned to talk originally. It's easy to underestimate a youngster's comprehension vocabulary because, like almost all adults, he understands a far larger number of words than he uses.

Sometimes, for the delight of it, you can deliberately teach your child big words. Four- and five-year-olds often enjoy learning the precise names of various types of dinosaurs, automobile parts, or flowers, for example. Tyrannosaurus, brontosaurus, carburetor, and philodendron are great fun for a child to roll off his tongue, especially when he knows what they really mean.

Almost all preschoolers go through a stage in speech development when they seem to stutter. This may occur simply because their thinking outraces their vocabulary. "I don't have enough words for my thoughts," one three-year-old told his mother in a worried voice.

It's also been suggested that this stuttering stage comes just before the establishment of dominance by one hemisphere of the brain, where the control of speech normally becomes fixed during the early years of life. According to this theory, stuttering should disappear naturally about the time a clear-cut and natural handedness—either right or left—is established. It is known that stuttering often persists in a child who does not have a consistent preference for his right or left hand, or whose dominant eye and/or foot is not on the same side of his body as his dominant hand. It's also been observed frequently that stuttering may start in a child when a parent or a teacher attempts to force a natural leftie to switch to his right hand for most tasks.

Regardless of the cause, the type of normal stuttering that occurs in most children between the ages of two and one-half and four should be ignored. These "disfluencies," as speech experts call them, almost always disappear as a child's skill in using words increases (or perhaps as the speech center in his brain becomes better established).

But a parent who calls a child's attention to his hesitancies and disfluencies may, with the best of intentions, turn his youngster into a persistent stutterer, some speech experts warn. There is risk, they caution, not only in telling your child not to stutter, but also in even suggesting that he pause and think, or take a deep breath, before he talks. This tends to make the youngster so conscious of the mechanisms of speech that the hesitancies and disfluencies increase and turn into habit.

One way you can help is this: Give your preschooler the courtesy of listening to him with as much respect and attention as you'd give an adult guest in your home. If your youngster feels that you are really listening to him, he won't try to rush through what he's saying, and there's less danger that he will stumble over sounds or skip syllables. This courtesy will also increase his feelings of self-confidence and personal worth and make him less inclined to whine for your attention.

Most youngsters continue to mispronounce one or two speech sounds even until kindergarten or first grade, speech therapists say. Unless your child's speech is almost impossible for others to understand after about his fourth birthday, you needn't be concerned about a few mispronunciations until school age.

As your child begins to acquire a beginning command of the mechanics of language, you'll want to help him learn how to use this marvelous tool. Language is so closely related to thought that some theorists even consider them almost synonymous.

During your child's irreplaceable years between three and six, you can help him learn to use language to foster thinking. When you talk to your child, you can encourage him to plan ahead ("When you have helped me put away the dishes, we can read a story together"). And to consider alternatives ("Should we make cookies or would you rather go to the playground?"). And to avoid mistakes ("If you move your glass of milk toward the center of the table, you won't knock it over with your elbow").

Helping your preschooler learn to put his feelings into words makes life easier for everyone in your family. If your youngster knows he can make you understand what he is feeling with words, he won't be so likely to whine or sulk or throw things or have a tantrum or pat the baby too hard.

You can also use words to help your preschooler understand the feelings of others and begin to act accordingly. "I know you are angry because the baby grabbed your toy car," you might say. "But you see, the baby admires you so and she is trying to do everything you are doing. She wants to grow up and be just like you. Will you help me teach her how to become as fine a person as you are?"

You can make it become a fascinating game if you sometimes ask your preschooler to choose precisely the right words to describe a cloud, a feeling, the taste of a new food, the touch of a fabric, the beauty of a flower. He'll delight in these verbal treasure hunts if you let him know you enjoy the aptness of his choices and join in the game, too.

A parent who listens with respect and interest and without being condescending or all-knowing can have delightful conversations with a preschooler. If you make it a happy habit to converse with your child (not talking down to him or issuing orders or preaching at him) when you're driving in the car, riding the bus, tucking him into bed, doing the dishes, or whenever you can find time, you'll not only stimulate his mental development, but you'll keep open lines of communication with him which are invaluable later on in his life.

It will help your child's vocabulary to grow and his skill in using language to flourish if you give him something interesting to talk about. A trip, a visit to a museum or zoo, a shopping expedition, or a kitchen-sink science experiment not only provides a child with new words to use, but spurs his desire to try them out. Another incentive is for each member of the family to take turns telling the others what he did that day.

Television can be turned into a stimulus for your child's vocabulary development, too, especially if you encourage him to discuss programs he's seen with you. This gives you a good opportunity to help him sort out fact from fiction—often very difficult for preschool TV viewers—and to clear up misunderstandings he may have about what he has seen. Television can also whet a thirst for more information about a subject—space travel, rockets, airplanes, a foreign country, the ocean, the presidency—which you can help him find in a library, newspaper, or encyclopedia. These conversations can aid your youngster in developing critical judgment about television, and he'll be less inclined to watch indiscriminately when he is older.

Good parent-child talk is often silly, funny, absurd talk, as any parent knows whose youngster has twisted Pooh Bear's "Help, help, a Heffalump, a Horrible Heffalump" around and around on his tongue with delight. A quick, happy sense of humor is one of the most common characteristics of gifted children, research shows. And the more your child enjoys the fun of jokes, riddles, verbal puzzles, puns, silly rhymes, and absurdities, the brighter he probably is. The more you join in his fun, the more he'll come to enjoy words and the more open he will be to learning through language.

You can build on this interest by suggesting games to heighten your child's awareness of sounds and sound patterns—a fundamental step in learning to read. You can help him recognize similarities and differences in beginning sounds by asking him to see how many words he can think of that begin with the same sound as "Maggie" or "book." Or you can take turns thinking of all the words you can that end the same way as "Sam" or "Dad" or "pop."

Skill with language involves listening and understanding, as well as talking, and there are many happy games you can play with your child to help him sharpen his listening ability. Simon Says is a good game for three-year-olds. May I? is fun for children old enough to count to ten. I Packed My Sister's Suitcase appeals to four- and five-year-olds.

Reading to your child should continue to be a shared

pleasure, even after he is old enough to read easy books for himself and well into the early elementary school years. A child's level of comprehension is much higher than his reading level for many years and he needs to have you read to him to sustain his interest in books and to provide him with mental nourishment until he can find enough for himself.

Regular trips to the children's room of the nearest library should be a routine part of your offspring's life, starting no later than the age of three. As a special treat, he should be permitted to choose books to own on gift occasions, or whenever you can afford it. Books, generally, cost less than many toys, especially when figured on a dollar-per-hour-of-pleasure basis. Providing your child with his own special bookshelf or bookcase or bookends—and with inexpensive bookplates that carry his name—will also increase his interest in books.

It is important to keep reading a pleasure, not a task or a lesson. For example, you can show your preschooler how much fun it is to spread out a blanket under a shady tree on a summer afternoon and read together. Or let him cuddle up in bed with you on a stormy night while you read to him. Or let him substitute a story session for a nap on a day it's too hot for sleep. You can suggest that he help you in the kitchen, then reward him with a story. You can encourage him to avoid boredom by reading a book when he must wait for the dentist or for the next motel with a "vacancy" sign on a vacation trip.

"When I was about four years old, I used to get these awful earaches," recalled a teenage boy. "I'd wake up in the night crying because it hurt so much. My mom would get up and give me the medicine the doctor sent, and then she'd sit beside my bed and read to me all sorts of good stuff, until the hurt let up. She told me that reading couldn't kill the pain, but that it would fill up such a big part of my brain I wouldn't pay so much attention to the hurting. Sometimes reading still makes me feel good, like it did then."

You should make certain your child realizes that reading is also an adult activity you enjoy independently of him. You should let him see you read often for pleasure and for information. You should make your trips to the library a time for you to select adult books, too. You can request books as gifts for yourself (a paperback is one of the least expensive material presents a child can choose). And you can comment often on what you do read. A youngster who grows up seeing his parents get most of their information and entertainment from television is quite likely to do likewise and may never become happily addicted to reading.

Your child's interests and responses will be your best guide to the type of books you choose to read to him. As they did at the age of two, many preschoolers still prefer factual books that explain the world around them and books about children much like themselves to fairy tales. A book about thunder and lightning can seem just as wondrous to a four-year-old as a story about fire-breathing dragons, yet it gives him information he craves about a familiar phenomenon. Given a choice, he'll usually take reality, at least until he's a little older.

Often a book for small children that is considered cute or charming by an adult will have almost no appeal for a four- or five-year-old. Some books for preschoolers are condescending in tone and far too limited in vocabulary and content.

In helping your child select books, a guiding principle should be that it's better to challenge his mind than to bore him. Your youngster's response to books will be a clear guide to his level of comprehension—far more accurate than any prepared book list (although you might consult one as a starter). If a book matches your child's mental development, he'll probably ask you to read it to him again and again, and he'll listen quietly and carefully. If it's too easy or too difficult, he'll probably wiggle away and begin to play with something else.

Good poetry stirs great interest in three- to six-year-olds and you should continue to read poems to him all during this preschool period. Encourage him to memorize those he especially enjoys—not so he can recite them for your friends, but so he will have them in his mind for his own pleasure.

Your reading to your child shouldn't be limited to books, of course. You can also stimulate his interest in printed symbols by reading to him traffic signs, labels, historic markers that you encounter on vacation, menus when you go out to dinner, directions that come with toys and games, words that flash on the TV screen, signs that help him tell the difference between the "men's room" and the "ladies' room," reminders that you chalk on your kitchen blackboard for yourself and for other family members—anything that helps him to understand that printed letters make words which have meanings.

Reading

If you've been following the suggestions in this book, your youngster will probably be showing clear signs of readiness to learn to read sometime between his third and fourth birthdays. He'll be fascinated by books, questioning you about the meanings of signs and labels, wanting to learn to print his own name, interested in pictures and adding to his speaking vocabulary faster than you can keep count of the words. Chapter 7 will tell you, in detail, about teaching him to read easily and happily yourself.

Second Language

The years between three and six, when your child's ability to absorb language with great facility is at its peak, are the ideal time to introduce him to a second language, if you are lucky enough to have the opportunity.

At this age, your youngster can learn a second language almost as readily as he learns English and without any sort of formal lessons, provided it is taught in the same way he learns English. He merely needs to hear it spoken frequently, naturally and well by someone who can speak it like a native. A grandparent, a parent, a day-care teacher, a neighbor, or a household helper can be an effective teacher simply by speaking to your child only in the second language (or by speaking to him only in the second language in a special part of the house or during certain hours at the day-care center). Your youngster figures out for himself that to get what he wants and make himself understood, he must talk in one way to you and a different way to the person in his life who is using the second language or in the special area where the other language is spoken. He won't confuse the two languages, and he will use them with the appropriate person.

Your goal should not be to help your preschooler build up a large vocabulary, but rather to establish the basic units of the second language in his growing brain, as described in Chapter 2. Then he can build on them later instead of having to learn the second language cold, using English sounds or speech units when he's a teenager or an adult.

It is important that whoever teaches your child the second language speaks it correctly. Bilingual children who come from disadvantaged homes where neither English nor their parents' native tongue is spoken well, usually do poorly in school, research shows. And experiments in teaching a foreign language in elementary schools, using teachers who do not have a mastery of the language and who do not use a "direct" or "mother's" method, usually seem to be a waste of time.

If you aren't fluent in a second language yourself and don't know anyone who could teach your child by the "mother's method," you will probably not be able to give your child this opportunity. It just doesn't seem to work when parents try to teach a child a second language that they do not know via phonograph records or coloring workbooks or other techniques. Parents who try to learn a second language along with their youngster find that he learns more quickly and easily than they, as immigrant families for generations have discovered.

Math

Even if you never were a whiz in math yourself, you can help your preschooler discover and absorb many basic mathematical concepts long before he's ready for first grade. Whether he is eventually taught in school by traditional or new-math methods, he'll profit greatly by these early-learning experiences.

In fact, your child will begin learning mathematical ideas in very simple form while he is still a toddler. Concepts such as "bigger" and "smaller," "light" and "heavy," "tall" and "short" are basically mathematical in nature. Grouping toys together, such as a pile of blocks and a handful of marbles, helps lay a foundation for set and subset theories. Simple matching games teach math concepts of "equal," "odd" and "even," and "more" and "less." Each concept helps lay a foundation in math on which your child can build later on.

The key to teaching a preschooler about math is to set the stage for him to make his own discoveries and to present ideas in the form of games which you both enjoy or practical uses for mathematical relationships he encounters normally in his life. You gain almost nothing by trying to stuff his head with number facts learned by rote.

Because your preschooler will learn best by perceptual methods, mathematical ideas should be taught with interesting materials he will enjoy handling. For example, don't just teach him to count to ten by rote, or by pointing to his fingers one at a time. Instead, encourage him to use anything he can move into groups—buttons, raisins, blocks, cookies, pennies—as he counts. Otherwise, he may get the idea that "four" means the fourth in a series, rather than all four in a set of objects.

Once your youngster has learned to count, you can invent dozens of delightful counting games to play with him. You can have him turn his back or cover his eyes and count how many times you rap on the table with your hand or bounce a ball or tap a glass with a spoon. You can ask him to count out the silverware and napkins to set the table for dinner or the number of small balls or peanuts or marbles he can drop into a clean, empty cardboard milk carton. You can go for "counting walks" together and look for items you've listed in advance: four white flowers, three rocks, two red cars, and one black dog. Or you can take a clipboard and help your youngster record his count of whatever objects interest him.

You can help your child learn about repeating patterns by giving him three or four kinds of macaroni and a sturdy string. Create a pattern by stringing one of each of the pasta shapes on the string, then challenge him to fill up the string and make a necklace by adding more macaroni in the same sequence you began.

You can teach your child the names of geometric shapes—

circle, square, rectangle, oval, triangle, sphere, cube—and help him look for them wherever he goes. A tabletop can be a circle or a rectangle, for example. A circle can be seen in a button, a jar lid, a drop of water, or a slice of carrot.

You should also introduce your preschooler to the idea that "zero" is a number, too. The correct number of giraffes in the bedroom is zero. So is the number of bears in the bathtub. It is not "none." The difference may not seem important when your child is counting giraffes and bears that are not there. But it is crucial when he begins constructing written numerals. In writing the number 40, for example (meaning 4 tens and no ones), the second number is not "nothing," but "zero." The concept is even more obvious with larger numbers. There is a "zero," not "nothing" between the 5 and the 7 in the number 507 (which means 5 hundreds, no tens, and 7 ones).

Once your child has learned to count from 0 to 9, the next step is to show him how to write the numerals he is counting. Most youngsters learn more quickly if you make large-size numerals for them to trace with their index and middle fingers. In Montessori schools, big sandpaper letters are used for this purpose. These can now be purchased for use by parents at home, or you can cut out a set of numerals from sandpaper yourself and mount them on squares of cardboard. Wooden jigsaw puzzles that match numerals with the proper number of dots or pegs or small animals are also available.

Several Montessori techniques can easily be adapted to teach mathematical concepts to your preschooler at home. For example, after your child has learned to count and to identify numerals, give him an egg carton with ten compartments numbered from 0 to 9 and two compartments taped shut and forty-five beads, beans, pennies, or buttons he is to distribute correctly into the compartments. The carton will give him some degree of self-correction and make it possible for him to practice and learn independently.

For another game, write a single digit on several slips of paper and put them into a bag. Let your child draw them out one at a time and then get for you the corresponding number of items—blocks, leaves, buttons, or books.

Dice make an excellent device for helping preschoolers to

learn about numbers in a games context and to reinforce learning already acquired. In one nursery school, for example, four- and five-year-olds play long, concentrated games in which one child shakes the dice and calls off the numbers to other children who chalk them on a blackboard and then add them up.

Any board game that involves dice or a spinner and counting can be useful in helping a child grasp number concepts. Four-year-olds can do quite well at Sorry and Parchesi if one opponent is an adult or an older child who can help out, if necessary. A preschooler may shake a 3 and a 4 on the dice, for example, and count as he moves his marker, "one, two, three, one, two, three, four" to find the seventh space. But it isn't long before he announces "seven" after his shake, without the preliminary steps.

A deck of playing cards can also be turned into a learning game. You can explain that the ace card means one, then encourage your child to count the spots on the cards from ace to nine and match them with similar number cards from all four suits.

Playing bingo is a delightful, no-pressure way in which to help a child learn to identify and pronounce numbers between 10 and 75, especially if you call out the numbers as "fifty-seven, that's five, seven." In a game situation, a child often wants to play and win so badly that he absorbs basic mathematical concepts without even realizing it.

Rummy-type games that give practice in number concepts are available in most toy stores, but are generally intended for elementary school–age youngsters. Four- and five-year-olds with some experience in math can usually play the games, but lack the ability to hold enough cards in one hand. This difficulty can easily be overcome by giving each youngster a large cardboard box, turned with its opening on the side facing the player, in which he can spread out his hand in secret.

Once your child has learned to read numerals, it's not difficult to teach him to tell time and to read a thermometer. Both of these skills are well worth the teaching effort. A preschooler finds it easier to accept the fact that it's bedtime or that it's too-soon-before-dinner-to-have-another-cookie when the clock makes the ruling and not an arbitrary parent with whom the child can argue. Many a parent has side-stepped arguments about whether a child needs a heavy jacket or just a sweater by posting a code that goes approximately like this: above 70, no wraps; 65–70, sweater; 45–65, light jacket; below 45, heavy jacket and cap or scarf.

To teach your child about money, begin by helping him learn the names of a penny, nickel, dime, quarter, half-dollar, and dollar. Then, you can explain to him that we use money to trade for things we want and that we have different kinds of money so we can pay different prices for these things. Then play matching games with him to show him that one nickel will buy as much as five pennies; that a quarter is equal to two dimes and one nickel or five nickels or twenty-five pennies or one dime and fifteen pennies, and all of the other combinations. After several short sessions of practice with these coin equivalents, your child should be quite knowledgeable about money and ready for a small allowance.

To teach your preschooler the concept of "odd" and "even," you can make a series of number cards, using index cards marked 0 to 9. Then let him place the corresponding number of buttons in pairs under each card so he can easily tell whether there is one left over or not.

Make a second set of cards and you can teach your child the concept of "same" or "equal" by putting out two identical numerals and corresponding numbers of buttons and by having him pair them off. Then, using two different numerals, with the correct number of buttons, help him discover the meaning of "more" and "fewer."

These cards and buttons are useful, too, in introducing your child to the idea of addition. First, lay out two numerals, with matching buttons, the sum of which is less than 10. Have him combine the buttons into one pile, count them, and find the matching numeral from your stockpile. Then you can show him how to write down what he has done, using the appropriate plus sign. Subtraction can be introduced in this same way.

In Montessori schools, the concept of "tens" and "hundreds" and "thousands" is taught by means of golden beads. These beads are available for the children to use as single units, in strings of 10, in squares in which 10 rows of 10 beads are securely fastened together, and in cubes which are painted to resemble 10 of the 100-bead squares.

The child learns to match the printed numeral 10 with a 10-bead string, the numeral 100 with the 100-bead square and the numeral 1000 with the cube. Then, for example, if he chooses a printed card that says 1000, another marked 600, a 50, and a single numeral card 3, he can stack them together to form for himself the numeral 1653.

Montessori-type golden beads can now be purchased by parents, although they are expensive for individual use. Mothers who have used Montessori methods at home have devised several ingenious substitutes. For example, instead of beads, you can fasten sticky-backed tape which has a small, unitary design—flower, Santa Claus, circle, or bell—onto a cardboard and cut it in the required sizes. You'll need single units, rows of 10, and squares which contain 10 rows of 10 figures. For the 1000-unit cubes, you can tie 10 100-figure squares together.

You'll also need some filing cards. On one set of cards, with a marking pen, write large-sized numerals: 1000, 2000, 3000, 4000, 5000, 6000, 7000, 8000, and 9000. Before marking the second set of cards, cut off about one-fourth from one end, so that they can cover only the last three digits on the thousands cards. Then number them in ink: 100, 200, 300, 400, 500, 600, 700, 800, and 900.

The third set of cards is cut in half and numbered: 10, 20, 30, 40, 50, 60, 70, 80, and 90. The fourth set is only one-fourth as wide as the full-sized cards and it is marked with single digits from 1 to 9. By stacking these cards in proper sequence, a child can construct any numeral from 1 to 9999.

One game you can play with your child is to put the cards in piles on a table. Then say to your youngster, "Please get me four thousands." When he has succeeded, instruct him to find a certain number of hundreds, tens, and units and have him stack the cards properly to make the correct numeral. Then challenge him to lay out the same number of whatever equivalent you are using for the golden beads.

When your child can handle this game easily and happily, you can progress to more complicated forms of addition. First, have him construct two different numerals—1433 and 6354, for example—and lay out the "beads" that illustrate both numbers. First, he counts the number of unit beads in both piles, combines them into one pile, and finds the numeral card that corresponds. In this case, of course, it is a 7. In a similar way, he counts the tens, the hundreds and the thousands, until he has 7 units, 8 tens, 7 hundreds, and 7 thousands. He forms the corresponding numeral and has the sum of the two original numbers.

At first, you'll want to use numbers that can be added without involving carrying. But when your youngster has become adept at adding, you can show him graphically how to carry. When he has 10 or more units, he can take 10 of them back to the original stockpile and exchange them for a strip of 10. Similarly, he can exchange 10 10-strips for one 100-square, or 10 hundreds for one 1000-cube. It's easier for him to understand if he performs the operation first with the beads and then sets up the numerals to match his answer.

If you wish, you can teach your child to subtract by much the same method. The easiest way is to have him set up a number with both beads and cards. The subtrahend should be formed only with the cards. Beginning with the units, have your child take away the number of beads called for in the subtrahend. When he has finished the operation, he can construct the correct answer with the cards. Your first numbers should not involve the concept of borrowing. But after the basic process has been mastered, you can introduce borrowing by having your child actually exchange a 10-strip for 10 units or one 1000-cube for 10 100-squares, so that he can perform his subtraction operation.

You can also show him how to check his results by adding the difference and the subtrahend to form the original number.

Short division can also be taught to a preschooler, using these Montessori-type materials. First, give your child a four-place number (with each digit an even number) to set up, using both beads and cards. To show him how to divide by 2, have your youngster take turns with you removing one 1000-cube at a time from the pile set up to illustrate the dividend. If the dividend is 8682, for example, each of you would have four 1000-cubes. Do the same with the remaining digits, until each of you has four 1000-cubes, three 100-squares, four 10-strips and one unit. Then you can set up the number cards to indicate your quotient. In Montessori schools, the directress may vary the divisor by asking additional children to participate. For fun, she may suggest that the youngsters march once around the table each time they take a unit or a square or a cube.

When this step has been mastered, you can vary the dividends so that the digits cannot be divided equally by the number of individuals used as divisors. Then you can show your child how to change the leftover thousands or hundreds or tens into hundreds or tens or units which can be divided equally.

Another excellent tool for helping preschoolers understand mathematical concepts is a set of number rods. Both Montessori-type rods and Cuisenaire rods are now available for home use. Both will help your preschooler to acquire basic mathematical ideas by perceptual methods and to make many of his own discoveries about mathematical relationships. But you will need to spend some time learning about the rods yourself before you set the stage for your child to make his own mathematical explorations.

Science

A preschooler comes equipped with a probing, poking, questioning, exploring, insatiable interest in science of all kinds. Or at least he does until a parent or a teacher has discouraged or ignored or scolded him out of it.

Even if you can't tell a pipette from a test tube, you can do much to encourage the scientist innate in your child. Your aim shouldn't be to pressure him to memorize scientific facts, but to absorb scientific attitudes—to question, to make sensitive observations, to look for cause and effect, to test conclusions, to wonder, and to marvel.

(Your encouragement of scientific interests and attitudes is important for your daughter as well as for your son. Research shows that most girls start out with the same type and degree of scientific interest as boys, but are discouraged by lack of support and encouraging feedback from adults and are shunted away into other areas of interest long before junior high school.)

With practice, you'll discover many ways in which to

encourage your preschooler's natural scientific bent. For example, find every way you can to help your child become more sensitive to his environment, to look beyond the obvious, to use all of his five senses to explore the world around him. In March, you can help him hunt for the first signs of spring in the tender shoots of green under snow-sodden leaves. You can encourage him to notice the differences in the shapes of leaves, the coloring of birds, the shapes of clouds, the sounds of a city or a suburb.

You don't have to live on a seacoast or on a farm or even in a wooded suburb to find natural phenomena to delight your child. You can make a special expedition to a park to watch a rising full moon on some crisp, clear October night. You can make the acquaintance of animal babies in a zoo or in a pet shop. You can collect leaves in a park. Find tiny fossils in crushed stone in a driveway. Watch a parade of ants scurry along a sidewalk. Grow small plants in jam jars on a windowsill. Marvel at floating castles and gray dust-rolls of clouds. Take walks in the fog and in a warm rain. Learn the feel of the wind as it whips and whispers down apartment house canyons.

One of the most fascinating ways in which to make nature intriguing to a city child—or any youngster—is to buy a good hand lens or magnifying glass. Even the tendrils of ivy clinging to a building, a spider on the wall, a stalk of geranium in a flower box, or a few grains of sand take on a magical aura when magnified.

One preschool science teacher suggests that simply giving a three-, four-, or five-year-old the cardboard center of a roll of toilet paper or paper towels to use as a viewer is useful when looking for interesting objects outdoors. Looking through the cardboard roll helps a child focus his eye and attention on a specific leaf or flower or other object and makes it easier for him to study it closely.

Another experiment you can conduct outdoors—either in a suburban backyard or a city sidewalk—is to encourage your child to stand perfectly still and try to identify all of the sounds that he can hear.

Your job isn't to try to teach your child precisely about what he observes. You don't have to know exact scientific names or explanations or make lessons out of what you do together. All you really need to do is to be interested yourself and invite your offspring to share your wonder.

Often, just following your child's lead is enough. Four-year-old Jeanne, taken by her mother on a routine shopping trip, became intrigued with smelling the flowers in the raised concrete boxes decorating the shopping center's walkways. She tugged on her mother's hand to share her discovery. Mother and daughter spent almost half an hour smelling the various types of flowers, comparing their scents, their shapes, and their coloring—happy and oblivious to other shoppers. This, too, can be called science.

"Now that Jeanne is ten and much too dignified to smell flowers in public, I remember that day with special delight," recalls her mother. "You need a small child for an excuse to take time to appreciate the small, daily wonders of living."

Do try to answer your child's questions—even when they come when you're frantically busy trying to feed the baby, finish making dinner, and get the laundry started. If you must postpone his queries, take the initiative in reopening the subject. If you're on a crowded bus when your youngster asks you why that lady sticks out in front, or what happened to the leg of the girl wearing a brace, or why that man has no hair, you'll have to whisper you'll tell him later. Then do. You want him to understand that it's all right to question, but that sometimes questions should be saved for a more appropriate time. After you've done this several times, you can probably avoid embarrassing questions in a childish treble by a look that says "Later" in recognition of an unspoken "Why?" in your offspring's eyes.

Sometimes, you'll discover that your youngster is satisfied with just a short, quick answer. "Why is that cloudy stuff coming out of the teakettle?" "Because it is hot."

But more often than most parents realize, a child is seriously questioning a physical phenomenon and would be fascinated by a more complex explanation of steam. And his interest could lead to a number of learning experiments with boiling and freezing water.

When asked a what-is-steam type of question, one mother replies to her child, "Do you want a long or a short answer?" Almost always the youngster answers, "Long!" and wiggles comfortably in anticipation of a fascinating learning session.

If you don't know an answer, tell your child, "I've wondered about that myself; let's find out together." Teaching your youngster how and where to find information to feed his boundless curiosity is one of the most valuable gifts you can give him during his early learning years. If you're stumped about finding adequate source material, ask the nearest librarian. Invest in an elementary science encyclopedia and look up answers with your child. Other possible sources of knowledge: a science museum (many exhibits are not too old for preschoolers), a natural history museum, a TV science program, or a science-discovery kit from a toy store.

Sometimes when your child asks a what-would-happen-if kind of question, you can answer, "Let's experiment and see." What happens if you bring a snowball into the house? If you keep it in the refrigerator? The freezer? Is it really pure, clear water, if you let it melt? Is snow always the same? Do snowballs pack better in some snowfalls than in others? Can you make snow again if you refreeze the water? Can you make ice again after it has melted?

There are many excellent books describing experiments in the physical sciences which are written, usually, for elementary school youngsters, but which are also suitable for preschoolers with the help of parents. The library nearest you should have several of these books. The experiments are not only stimulating learning activities, but also delightful rainy-day fun for you and your offspring.

In trying these experiments, you can begin to encourage your child to have a scientific attitude about them. Before you begin, talk over these questions: "What are we trying to find out?" "How can we set up an experiment to discover the answer?" "What do you think will happen?" "What materials will we need?" Whenever possible, let your youngster perform the experiment himself. He'll learn far more that way than he will watching you.

When the experiment has been completed, urge your child to review precisely what did occur. Then ask him, "Do you think it would happen again this same way if we did it again?" "What did this experiment teach us?"

Your child will do a better job with these experiments if you've given him opportunities previously to pour water, to wash plastic dishes, and to measure dry materials and liquids with measuring cups and spoons.

No more than a brief sampling of science experiments for preschoolers can be included here, but they will give you an idea of materials you can find in your library.

For example, to help your youngster sense the reality of air, suggest that he crumple some newspaper at the bottom of a glass or a glass jar, turn the glass upside down and submerge it, straight down, in a pan of water for several seconds. When he removes it, he will find that the newspaper is not wet because the glass was already filled with air, which kept the water away from the paper.

To see the air itself, have your child repeat the experiment, this time turning the glass on its side after it is submerged in the pan of water and watching the air bubble up.

For a third experiment, suggest to your child that he submerge an empty glass in the water and turn it on its side so it fills with water. Then, show him how to tuck the end of a piece of rubber tubing into the top of the glass, turn it upside down again in the water and force the water out of the glass by replacing it with air blown through the tubing.

Demonstrate to your child how he must empty the air out of a medicine dropper before he can fill it with water. Let him blow up a balloon and watch it jet around the room when he releases it. (On a visit to the nearest big airport, you can point out the jet planes that fly on this same principle.) Help him make a pinwheel on a pencil to demonstrate the force of moving air. Let him watch firsthand how you put air into a tire at the gas station and how beach balls and footballs are filled with air to make them more fun to play with.

Another experiment for a sunny day outdoors, or for a bathroom in wintery weather, is to give your child a chance to blow bubbles, using a straw and a small container of water mixed with liquid detergent. You can show him how to dip the end of the straw into the water, lift it out and blow gently to form a bubble. You can talk about how the air got inside the bubble and why the bubble soon pops, leaving a trace of water on the grass or on the bathroom floor.

You can even turn the pouring of fruit juice or a soft drink from a can into a science experiment. Punch one hole in one can and two holes in an identical can and encourage your small scientist to observe which empties faster. See if he can deduce why.

Experiments with water hold a special fascination for a small child, especially when he is permitted to perform them himself. For example, you can help him learn about evaporation by having him measure out a tablespoon of water in a shallow dish, set it in a warm place, and observe what happens to it. Add a drop of food coloring, if you wish, to make the experiment more interesting.

Next, suggest that he set out three shallow dishes, the first with one tablespoon of water, the second containing two tablespoons, and the third three, and watch to see whether the amount of liquid in the dishes affects the rate of evaporation.

Here's another experiment you can try when your preschooler comes indoors from play with a pair of wet mittens. Suggest that he put one in a warm place and another in a cold spot and observe which one dries more quickly. If it isn't mitten weather, try the experiment using dishcloths or washcloths dipped in water and wrung out. On a windy day, your youngster can experiment to see whether a wet dishcloth hung on a line in the breeze dries faster than one hung in a bathroom. On a hot, sunny day, you can give your child a squeeze bottle filled with water and let him make a design or a drawing on a sidewalk and keep track of how long it takes for the water to dry up.

To teach your child about another property of water, have him fill a small glass or a wide-mouth jar to the brim with water. Gently and slowly have him stir in about two tablespoons of sugar or salt, using a thin wire, such as a straightened paper clip. He should notice that the water does not run over, because the sugar and the salt will dissolve. Then have him repeat the experiment using sand and see what happens.

If your youngster has begun to understand about evaporation, ask him what he thinks will happen if he lets the salty or sugary water evaporate. Suggest that he experiment to check his conclusions by spooning out some of the salt or sugar solution into a shallow dish and check later to see what has happened.

When your youngster has grasped the idea that the air picks up water, ask him if he thinks the water can ever be taken out of the air again and suggest that you try to see if it is possible.

One of the easiest experiments is to take a glass of ice water and let it stand a few minutes on your kitchen counter on a hot, humid, summer day or at a time when your kitchen is warm and steamy. Your child can observe the drops of water collecting on the outside of the glass.

Other ways to demonstrate condensation: Let your child squiggle or letter on a steamy bathroom mirror after a warm shower. Show him how you can boil water in a pan on the stove and how the evaporated water will collect on the bottom of a second pan you have filled with ice and hold over the steam. Let him feel summer dew and autumn frost and make the connection between these phenomena and the idea of condensation. Let him run his finger over a car window that has fogged up in cold weather; talk about why it happens and how the car's defroster functions.

Your preschooler can have great fun experimenting—in the kitchen sink, bathtub, or plastic outdoor pool—to see what kind of objects will float and which will sink. Help him to keep a record of his experiments as he tests such every-day materials as blocks, bottle caps, paper clips, pennies, paper, pencils, crayons, cloth, capped empty bottles, capped bottles full of liquid, various types of soap, cork, empty milk cartons, and milk cartons full of water. Encourage him to form conclusions about why some objects float and others do not.

Some bright, sunshiny day, you can let your youngster—and his friends, if you wish—put on swimming suits and turn on the hose in the backyard so they can run in and out of the water. When they are ready to try something new, twist the nozzle of the hose so it produces a fine spray, angle it so the sunshine catches the water drops just right and makes a rainbow for them to wonder about. You can talk about the colors they can see and how the drops of water act like prisms to break up the colors in the sunlight.

Experiments with sound usually delight preschoolers. For example, one of the simplest ways in which to demonstrate that vibrations produce sounds is to make a cigar-box guitar or a cereal-box banjo by stretching rubber bands of various thicknesses around the box. Your child can be helped to observe that the thinnest rubber band produces the highest notes when plucked and the thickest band the lowest. Tuck a thin block of wood or a strip of plywood under the rubber bands to act like a violin bridge. Have your child listen to the change in sound as you move the block to stretch the strings.

To help your child understand that the more vibrations per second, the higher the sound, tape a playing card to your child's upended tricycle so that the edge of the card is flipped by the spokes of a wheel as it revolves. Let your child spin the wheel by rotating the pedals and observe that the faster he turns, the higher the sound the card produces.

To demonstrate to your youngster that sound can travel through other media than air, suggest that he take two wooden blocks or two flat stones or two small pot lids and bang them together, listening carefully to the sound. Then, in the bathtub or in a backyard pool, have him duck his head under water and repeat the banging. He'll discover that it's much louder, because of the sound-conducting property of the water.

One child discovered an interesting variation of this principle. Lisa found that if she put one side of her face tightly against her brother's, she could hear him scratch his opposite temple much more clearly than if his face were only an inch or two away from hers when he was scratching. Her father explained to her that bone is also a good conductor of sound.

For other sound-conduction experiments, put a watch on a bare, wooden table and have your child press his ear to the other end. He'll hear the ticking quite clearly. If you blow up a balloon and press it tightly between your child's ear and your ticking watch, he'll also be able to hear it distinctly.

You can use a stretch of garden hose as a telephone, with you on one end and your preschooler on the other. Or you can tap a signal to your child from one room to another or from one floor of your house to another using a water pipe to conduct the code.

You can make your child a can telephone this way: Find two empty metal cans with no sharp edges where the lids have been removed. In the center of the bottom of each one, punch a small hole with a nail. Through each hole, thread one end of a long, stout, cotton string and tie it into a large knot or around a little stick to anchor it securely. Stretch the string tight and use as a telephone, with you speaking into one can while your child holds the other against his ear and listens.

For a variation in sound-conduction experiments, you can cut a piece of cotton cord about one yard long. Loop the center of the cord around a teaspoon and have your pre-schooler hold one end of the string in each of his ears, as he bends over slightly, balancing the spoon. If you strike the spoon with another spoon or a nail, your child will hear a sound like a church bell.

The world of growing things abounds with opportunities to help your young sprout gain a firm grounding in science, and you don't have to have a green thumb yourself to plant seeds of interest. Even if it isn't green-up time in the suburbs, there are dozens of experiments you and your budding botanist can try.

To demonstrate how a plant grows from a seed, buy a handful of large, dried beans. Let your child try to break one of the beans open. When he finds it too hard to split, remind him that seeds usually need rain to start growing and suggest that he see what happens if he soaks several of the beans overnight in water.

The next day, your child will be able to peel off the coating of a bean seed and open it to discover the tiny shoot and root inside. Tell him that the surrounding sections of the bean, called seed leaves, are food for the baby plant.

To show your preschooler how the baby plants grow, try this: Line a glass with a wet paper towel. Keep water in the bottom during the experiment. Tuck one of the soaked beans between the towel and glass, where your child can watch it grow.

Cut off one of the seed leaves from a second soaked bean,

carefully leaving the embryo plant, and add it to the glass. Do the same with a third, removing one entire seed leaf and half of the second. The difference in the growth of these three tiny plants demonstrates how much they need the food contained in the seed.

Radish seeds can be used to point up other essential needs of growing things. Fold two paper towels in the bottom of each of three glasses. Have your child put ten radish seeds in each glass and cover each glass with a third folded paper towel.

In one glass, have your child sprinkle only a few drops of water. Soak the paper thoroughly in the second glass. Have your child fill the third glass almost full with water. Label each one and check the results in about five days. Help your youngster to understand that the seeds in the first glass did not get enough water; those in the third didn't get enough air.

Plants need proper temperature to grow, too, as you can help your child to learn. In the bottom of each of two cups have your preschooler put a pad of wet, absorbent cotton. Sprinkle with bird seed. Cover the cups with saucers; place one cup in the refrigerator and keep the other at room temperature. Compare the results every day for a week.

Seeds can sprout in the dark, if they are wet, airy, and warm enough. But they also need light to grow into leafy plants after they have used up the food within the seed. Demonstrate this to your child like this: In each of two bowls, have your youngster place a wet sponge and sprinkle it with bird seed. Keep half an inch of water in the bowls during the experiment. Place one bowl on a sunny, warm windowsill; cover the other with a large pot or keep it in a very dark spot. Have your child check them every day for two weeks, but be careful not to let the second bowl stay in the light longer than a minute.

You can show your child other ways in which to make new plants besides starting them from seed. For example, put young pussy willow stems in water in your home and watch new roots grow from the bottom. After they are well rooted, you and he can plant them outdoors.

Here's another way. Let your child cut a long leaf from a snake plant into two-inch pieces. Have him plant each piece about an inch deep in damp sand in a bowl. Keep the bowl covered with glass and in the light until new plants grow.

A favorite experiment to show how plants use water is this: Cut off the end of a white carnation stem under water, place the carnation in a glass of water colored with bright ink, preferably red, and let it stand in the sunlight. Within a few hours, the petals will turn the color of the ink. You can even split the bottom half of the stem carefully and put each section in ink of a different color to obtain a two-tone bloom.

If you can't get a carnation, the experiment works, too, with a leafy stalk of celery you have freshened in water for half an hour.

On sunny days, you can help your child look for shadows when you are outdoors together, noting that shadows aren't always the same size or in the same place. Then early one morning, you can suggest keeping track of your youngster's shadow for a day. Have him pick a spot to stand on the sidewalk and mark it with chalk. Then outline the shape of his shadow. Come back once or twice during the day—at noon and late in the afternoon—have him stand in the same place and observe what has happened to his shadow. Then you can give him a flashlight and help him experiment to see that shadows are produced when light cannot go through a solid object, but that light can go right through a drinking glass or empty plastic bag without making a shadow.

Encourage your preschooler to make collections—insects, leaves, rocks, shells, pressed flowers—for the beauty of the objects and the pleasure of having them. When he runs out of shelf room to keep his collections, suggest that he begin to compare and classify his treasures, to keep his prizes, and to discard his duplicates. Then help him follow where these interests lead.

For example, suggest that your child start a collection of seeds and keep a count of how many seeds and what kind he finds in apples, grapes, peaches, cherries, watermelons, peanuts. Let him study closely dandelion seeds, milkweed seeds, an acorn, a coconut, and a maple seed. Ask him to guess how seeds can travel from one place to another. Then give him an opportunity to plant some of his seeds and watch them grow. (You'll have to do some background research first to guide this experiment to a fruitful conclusion.)

If you can manage it where you live, give your preschooler a chance to learn about a pet firsthand. If you can't house a dog or a cat, try goldfish, tadpoles, a hamster, a gerbil, a parakeet, or an ant farm. In learning to care for another living thing, your child will gain much information about the needs of all creatures for food, rest, water, protection, and clean living quarters, and he will also learn about the inevitable cycle of birth and life and death.

Today, there is only a thin line between scientific learning materials and some types of toys; both help your child learn more about physical phenomena. For example, magnets make fascinating playthings, especially if they are extra large and your child has a collection of nails, paper clips, and metal buttons with which to experiment. Help your preschooler to make a list of the household objects that can be moved about by a magnet and the ones that cannot. And you can put paper clips on slips of paper that have the letters of the alphabet or the numerals he is learning and let him go fishing for them with a magnet that is on a string attached to a stick. He can "read" you the ones he hooks and throw back into the "pond" those he misses.

Other materials that can help children absorb scientific ideas in the guise of play include: a large-sized prism, field glasses, a see-through alarm clock that permits observation of gears in motion, and a stethoscope (a real one isn't expensive and permits a child to hear actual heartbeats and chest sounds).

Perception

Perception, as the word is usually used by educators, physicians, and psychologists, means the ability to transmit stimuli to the brain and interpret them accurately. It involves recognizing a voice as being mommy's, a doll as being small enough to fit into a wagon, ice cream as being cold, a picture as representing reality.

Perception includes all of the senses—hearing, seeing, smelling, tasting, feeling. But because seeing is the key ability in learning, perception usually refers to the ability to see and to comprehend accurately in the mind.

Even though a child's eyes may function perfectly, visual

stimuli may be modified or they may be misinterpreted or not recognized in the brain itself. These distortions can be so great in some children that they have great difficulty learning in school. They may not be able to separate background and foreground, for example, or recognize left from right, or focus on one part of a scene or on one word on a page.

Children who have perceptual difficulties may number from 5 to 15 percent of the average first grade class, according to some estimates. Sometimes these learning disabilities appear to be caused by minor injury to the child's brain before, during, or after birth. Sometimes they seem to be related to a general lag in neurological development. Often there is no evident cause. Many youngsters with perceptual problems also have what doctors call "soft neurological signs." They may be clumsy, overly active, impulsive, irritable, explosive, and may also have a tendency to stutter, an unusually short attention span, and/or poor powers of concentration.

Special training in perception does seem to help most of these youngsters, researchers have discovered, especially if it is begun before a child has tried and failed in first grade and before emotional problems are piled upon his neurological difficulties. In fact, every child can profit from training and practice in perception before he starts school, many educators and doctors now believe.

To help your child sharpen his perceptual abilities, try playing some of these games with him:

—Arrange two to four blocks in various patterns and let your youngster copy the layout with identical blocks.

—Conceal a small toy in a paper bag. Let your youngster put his hand in, without peeking, and identify the object by touch alone. Vary the game by hiding several toys in the bag and by calling out which one he is to find and remove.

—Invent matching games of all types with lotto cards, color swatches from the paint store, numbers, letters, and magazine pictures pasted on cardboard.

—Try the Montessori activity of giving your youngster a box containing a dozen of each of four kinds of unshelled nuts which he is to sort by type into four smaller dishes. When he's adept at this, challenge him to try it blindfolded.

—Have your preschooler lie flat on the floor and ask him

to identify different parts of his body as you point to them or call out their names. Vary the game by playing it while he is standing, sitting, and kneeling to help strengthen his perception of his body position in space.

—Set up an obstacle course for your child to follow through the house that will include crawling under a table, over the end of a sofa, around a chair and jumping, hopping, rolling, and climbing. For fun, cut out foot, hand, and knee outlines and make a trail for your child to follow.

—Make a walking beam for your youngster, using a two-by four-inch board at least eight feet long and mounted on three supports that hold it about two inches off the floor. A youngster can have all the walk-the-railroad-rail delight with it, while he is developing visual-motor coordination and perception of his own body position in space.

—Help your child learn about right and left. Identify his right sock and shoe and then his left sock and shoe as you dress him. Call out which arm he is to put into his sweater or coat first and which mitten he is to slip on first. Teach him that his knife and spoon go on the right, his fork on the left. When you are driving the car, point out when you are making a right or a left turn or ask him to tell you which direction you're going as you do it. And when you read to him, call his attention to the fact that words go from left to right along the lines of a page.

—With a small box and a block, have your youngster follow the directions you call out, putting the block into and out of the box, in front of and behind it, under it, to the left, and to the right of it.

—Invest in two small pegboards. Set up a simple pattern with colored pegs on one for him to copy on the other. Make the designs increasingly complicated as he progresses.

—Put several small objects on a table and let your youngster look closely at them for about one minute. Then ask him to close his eyes while you take one of the items away. Let him try to remember which object you've removed.

—Look at large pictures in a magazine with your child; encourage him to talk about what is going on in the foreground and what he can see in the background.

—Challenge your child to tell you, in order, all of the

things he can see on a trip to the grocery store or on a walk to the playground or on some other familiar short trip.

—Plan walks with your child—to the park, through a shopping center, down a busy street, early in the morning, at dusk, in the winter, and when the weather's fine—to look for specific things. These could be colors, objects smaller than a breadbox, everything round, anything that is making a sound, people at work, or objects moving in the wind.

—Play a game with adverbs. Ask your child if he can demonstrate how to walk sadly, slowly, loudly, softly, proudly, fearfully, bravely.

—See how many different types of roofs you and your child can find in your neighborhood or on a car trip—hip, gable, flat, single and double pitch. Or count how many different kinds of building materials you can see in the buildings you walk or ride past.

If your child is unable to succeed with at least some activities like these by the time he is five, if he seems particularly clumsy, if he is unusually prone to temper tantrums, is overly active and has more behavior problems than most children, he may have a perceptual handicap or learning disability. It's a good idea in that case to call these symptoms to the attention of your pediatrician. Good techniques are now available to help these youngsters considerably.

Concept Formation

Whether you help him or not, your preschooler will constantly be sorting out and combining and reorganizing and shifting the great mass of sensory impressions he is receiving and the perceptions he is acquiring, as he tries to understand the world around him. Often he makes mistakes. Often he draws incorrect conclusions. But usually the fault is not in his way of thinking or in his reasoning abilities. He just doesn't have enough of the right information to begin with.

Four-year-old Carolyn hears her mother tell her father that Mr. Simpson, next door, has gone to the hospital. "What will they name the baby?" she comments, for her only knowledge about hospitals concerns mothers who have returned from hospital stays with new infants.

Donna, also four, is listening when her mother remarks to her older brother that she only has a dollar in her billfold. "Why don't we go to the toy store and get some more money," Donna suggests helpfully. Her brother hoots and calls her a dummy. She cries and through her tears says to her mother, "Well, every time you buy something in the toy store, you give the woman at the counter money and she gives you back more money." Donna's observations have been correct; she simply has not had the opportunity to learn that money can come in different denominations.

The exposure of small children to television has compounded this problem of concept formation. Television gives youngsters great masses of information and impressions for which they don't have enough background knowledge. Why does the Indian lady who comes to see the President wear a long sort of dress, instead of moccasins and a feather? Why can't we use magic to make our kitchen floor shine like the man does on TV? Is that cowboy really dead like the robin we found in the backyard the other day?

Preschool children actually want to learn, can learn, do learn enormous amounts about history, geography, and economics without overt adult help, educators and psychologists are now acknowledging. They formulate surprisingly complicated explanations for facts they can't comprehend—not so much because they enjoy fantasy and magic, but because they crave understanding. And they are capable of dealing with important and significant ideas about the physical and social world.

Some educators who understand early-learning concepts are experimenting with ways to teach major concepts about social studies, economics, and the physical sciences to children in nursery schools and kindergartens. These programs generally take inspiration from the contention of Dr. Jerome Bruner, of the New School for Social Research, that "any subject can be taught effectively in some intellectually honest form to any child at any stage of development." They are backed by studies in which researchers and preschool teachers have recorded and studied the conversations of small children who strive to understand major concepts about life and death, God, outer space, the community in which they live, the world of work, cause and effect, and natural phenomena.

"It is important to see and accept the fact that young children are not 'unready' for the many challenges involved in intellectual experience," explained Dr. Wann. "Unreadiness is a concept as fruitless as it is difficult to determine. The notion of unreadiness arises from overgeneralization about a given period or age in the development of children. It is more helpful to think, rather, of individual children as being ready at all times for some kind of learning, ready perhaps for different kinds of experiences, a different approach, another level of concept development. This way of looking at the problem leads to action whereas dismissing children of a given age as 'not ready' leads to stagnating inactivity. The children, meanwhile, go on with their trial-and-error learning which involves much misinterpreting and misconceiving."[1]

Designing new curricula for preschools and kindergartens to meet this new awareness of the intellectual needs of small children is underway in many day-care centers, nursery schools, and kindergartens. And research is being done in many academic fields to try to determine more precisely what the "key concepts" are that small children should acquire as a basis for future learning. These key concepts are not to be taught by rote, researchers emphasize. But learning experiences should be designed to help small children discover and use these understandings for themselves.

It is rare to find a preschool where your youngster's needs to form significant concepts about the world are appreciated and directed. Even if you do, you as his parent still have the major role in guiding his development of accurate concepts.

What can you do to help your youngster? Several guidelines have emerged from the ongoing research: It's a help, first of all, just to appreciate your child's need to form concepts. Listen to what he says and try to understand the information or misinformation behind his remarks. Let this guide you into activities that provide him with facts he is apparently missing or has distorted in his thinking. Carolyn's mother and father just laughed indulgently at her, for example. But her mother might have made it a point to read her a beginning book about where babies come from. She could have taken Carolyn to see the neighbor's new kittens and to the zoo to visit baby animals and talked casually about how they grew inside of their mothers. Some museums have exhibits depicting the development of unborn infants and displays in which baby chicks can be observed pecking their way out of their shells. Her mother could also have read her books about hospitals and what happens to people there and about the role of doctors and nurses. None of this need be formal teaching. All of it can take place naturally and easily in the course of relaxed and normal interaction with a child.

For Donna, a complicated game of playing store might be useful. In some experiments with intellectual development in kindergartens, playing store has been successfully used to help youngsters understand not only the role of customers, food producers, manufacturers, and retailers, but also about profit and pricing.

Donna's mother might have helped her daughter set up a grocery store in one corner and used it as a way to teach her about money, about making change, about the problem of getting produce and products to sell and about how prices are determined.

In the course of such activities, a parent can guide a child into formulating questions he does not have answers for and can suggest that he take his queries to people who can supply him with missing information. A grocery store manager, for example, would probably be willing to explain to a small child the answer to a question he has thought through ahead of time with your help.

In addition to helping your child gain experiences that supply him with information to correct his misconceptions, you can also guide him into new ways of thinking about the information he has.

A bus trip, for example, can be much more meaningful to a preschooler if you help him fit it into an overall concept about transportation. Help him to think of all the kinds of transportation he can—boats, horses, cars, buses, trains, planes, trucks, roller skates, rockets, bicycles, feet, helicopters—and talk about when he would use each one. Which methods would he use for hauling big packages? Which if he were in a hurry to go a long way? Which would probably cost the most money? This gives more meaning to short excursions on which you take your child and provides a foundation for future learning.

Children younger than first grade can absorb a surprising amount of learning about time, given some help, researchers have discovered. One good way to begin is to make a short, simple time line for your child. In a piece of string or rope, tie a knot about every foot to represent each of your child's birthdays to date. Then explain to him that the section of string in between the knots represents a year of his life. Talk with him about what events occurred during each of these periods—the time when he got his first tooth, when he first learned to walk, the summer you took that vacation trip to California.

Then make him a time line for yourself and point out some of the major events—perhaps when you started school yourself, when you were married, when you moved into your present home, when he was born.

Then you can tell him that a time line back to when Abraham Lincoln was president would stretch around your living room and kitchen twice. And one back to the era of George Washington, when our country got started, would go to the end of Jeff's driveway. A time line reaching to the year Columbus came to America would extend to the corner of your block and one showing the period of the first Christmas, when Jesus was born, would go all the way to his school. To make a time line that would represent the era when dinosaurs lived on this earth, you could need a time line that would stretch from your house to his grandmother's in the next state and back again thirty times, you can explain, for example.

It also helps your child gain some understanding about the changes that come with passing time if you can take him to a museum of history. Seeing the tools used by Indians or in ancient civilizations or even by pioneers in the United States gives him more observations upon which to base his developing concepts.

A preschool child won't be able to grasp completely the immeasurable periods of time that have swept over this earth, or even to sort out all the events he has heard about according to chronology. But, Dr. Wann emphasized, "to assume that we should wait to encourage and help children to gain concepts of time and change until they can handle true chronology is to deprive children of one of the important learnings of early childhood. To defer help and encouragement in this area is to frustrate a basic intellectual need of today's young children."

Maps make a good tool to help you orient your preschooler in your community, in your country, and in the world. Researchers who have worked with four- and five-year-olds, especially kindergarteners, find that they can grasp many major ideas associated with maps.

You might begin, for example, by helping your child draw a map of his room—locating chairs, bed, lamps, windows, door. He can learn that north is always at the top of the map and something about the concept of scale. Next, the two of you might construct a map of your block or your neighborhood, laying it out on the floor on a large sheet of white plastic or wrapping paper. You can crayon in streets and driveways, construct houses and buildings out of blocks and use toy cars and trucks for traffic. From this point, it's relatively easy for your child to use and appreciate a map of your community and, eventually, a map of the United States. He'll be able to follow your route in a trip and to locate places talked about on television news programs with some assistance.

Because of frequent television programs about rocket launchings, most preschoolers have acquired many small pieces of knowledge about outer space. You can help your child form this smattering of facts into useful concepts by showing him a model of the solar system and explaining how it functions. (You can buy solar systems in the form of mobiles for his room or make one yourself with his help.) He's not too young to look for mountains on the moon with you or to grasp the basic principles governing eclipses, should one be visible in your area.

Adult occupations is another subject about which most preschool children have garbled knowledge and misconceptions. Where Daddy goes in the morning—and Mommy, if she holds a job—and why can be the basis for much learning, both by conversation and by actual experience. If possible, it's a valuable learning experience for a small child to go to work with his father or mother—perhaps on a Saturday or on a parent's day off—riding the train or bus, sitting at the parent's desk, and watching the kind of work that goes on for a few minutes. Both parents should make a point of talking to a child about what occurred in the course of their day and helping him understand not only what his parents do, but why.

You can also talk to your child about what other parents do—police officers, pilots, doctors, firefighters, salespersons, factory workers, construction workers, truck drivers, musicians, photographers, TV anchors, teachers—and the relationship of this work to the community's welfare. You can encourage him to make some beginning discoveries about the division of labor (perhaps by comparing the amount of time it takes you to check out of a supermarket when the checker does the sacking and when both a checker and a packer work on your purchases together). You can also note the tasks both mother and father do at home and help him discover why this kind of work is also important to the family.

You should also be helping your child learn that the old lines between male and female work are fading and that most jobs are now open to both men and women. A girl, in particular, needs to understand that police officers can be men or women, that girls can grow up to be doctors as well as nurses, that her sex should not be a limiting factor in what she will eventually choose to become. This may not be difficult in a family where the mother works outside the home or if there are career women among the adults your child knows. But if the only women your daughter comes in contact with are full-time homemakers or are working in such traditionally female jobs as supermarket checker or teacher, you may want to make a special effort to give her opportunities to see women in other occupational roles if you can.

A child's sense of sexual identity is established early in life and you don't want your daughter's ideas about being female to become limitations on the development of her ability. The changing role of women in society is something you should talk about with your child—boy or girl. You should discuss with your offspring how you and your spouse divide up family responsibilities and how you feel about what you both are doing. You can point out other families you know where parents have made different decisions about how to handle their responsibilities for home and job, and that some women combine jobs with homemaking while others do not. The point is to make your offspring—especially a daughter—aware that she does have choices about her life, that her sex need not be a limitation on the vocational or professional goals she may want to set for herself and that there are many possible ways to combine home and career into a satisfying lifestyle.

If you are fortunate enough to have a two-parent family, you should make sure your child understands the special contributions both father and mother make. If you are a single parent, you should also talk to your youngster about how your family works and how you sometimes play both parental roles for his benefit.

A study of occupations can make a good, basic frame of reference for many of the short field trips you take with your child. For example, if he is getting bored with helping you buy groceries, suggest that he try to count the number of different types of workers in the supermarket on your next trip. Help him to observe which jobs take the least training and which require experience. And encourage him to speculate on other kinds of jobs which might be done behind the scenes or by other workers in other places.

Often you can take advantage of events in your neighborhood to help your youngster learn important concepts. For example, if there's a new house or apartment building being constructed in your neighborhood, you can use it to stimulate your child's formulation of concepts. Why do you think a bulldozer is used to dig the foundation, instead of people with shovels, you can ask your child. (His reasoning should lead him to observe other situations in which machines are employed to spare people hard, physical labor.) Why does one group of workers only put in pipes while another crew does nothing but lay brick? Why is insulation placed between the inner and outer walls of the house? Why is a building inspector's permit tacked on that tree in front? What is the purpose of the blueprints the builder is reading?

You also should be aware that your child is constantly forming concepts in the area of social relationships. Often these concepts can be distorted, psychologists and doctors have discovered, by misinformation and incorrect assumptions garnered from television.

Melissa, age five, had been unusually weepy and upset, clinging to her father and unwilling to play with her friends, for the past two weeks. After much cuddling and questioning, she finally told her mother that she was afraid her parents were going to get a divorce. Melissa's mother could think of no reason why her daughter could have had such a mistaken idea, but finally the little girl whispered something about "that lady who had dinner with Daddy."

Then Jane Whitman remembered that she and her husband had invited a woman business associate of his to dinner about two weeks earlier. Melissa had connected the woman with a family-situation drama she'd seen on television in which a divorce had been precipitated by a dinner-table incident involving another woman.

Her mother assured Melissa that she and her husband intended to stay happily married and looked for experiences which would help the child understand more about family relationships. About this time, the entire family was invited to a wedding. Jane spent several days before the ceremony explaining to her daughter what would happen, what words would be said during the service, and how seriously she and her husband took the marriage vows they had made in the same way, long before Melissa's birth. Melissa listened spellbound to the marriage ceremony and for weeks afterward played "wedding" with her dolls.

One reason television has such a powerful effect on small children is that they usually can't separate reality from make-believe on the programs they watch. Often you can suggest play activities to your youngster that will aid him in making this distinction.

Lindsey's mother, for example, was concerned because her four-year-old seemed to believe everything she saw on television as being true and real. So she arranged for the child to visit an audience-participation show, see the cameras, and watch the program being produced. Then she encouraged Lindsey to play "television show" at home.

Together they made a television "camera" by mounting a cardboard box on an old doll carriage base. Then they talked about whether they would put on a real-life program or a pretend story. For factual programs, Lindsey gave weather reports, neighborhood news, and helped her mother stage a cooking demonstration. For "made-up story" shows, she had her dolls act out policewoman plots and talking-animal dramas. And now she asks her parents to label programs she watches as being made-up or true whenever she isn't sure.

If you observe carefully how your child plays with other children and relates to them, you can also help him form intellectual concepts that will guide his social behavior in the future. Why should you share your toys with your guest? you can ask your child. How would you feel if you were Billy visiting at our house? Why do you suppose good manners are important? Why does Jamie act like such a bully and how can we help him to play in a nicer way with other children?

As your child begins to grasp new concepts based on his observations, you'll often notice that he plays them out, in variations, with his toys and with other small fry. If you listen to his conversations and watch his play, you'll usually discover how much he has actually grasped of the concepts you want to help him learn, and you'll have a good guide to the type of experiences to offer him next.

It will be years before your child can fully grasp and use most of the concepts you introduce him to as a preschooler. But they form a basic framework upon which he can build his future learning and make sense out of the great masses of information and detail his brain is recording.

Your child is going to be gathering information and forming concepts whether you help him or not. But with your assistance, he will form more useful concepts and fewer misconceptions and his future learning will be more efficient.

Toys

The years between three and six are the peak years for toys, the ages when your child most needs and most enjoys playthings. Many of the toys listed in Chapter 5 for toddlers are still appropriate for three- to six-year-olds. Some of the best playthings for preschoolers have already been mentioned in this chapter. But here is a quick summary of basic learning toys for this age group. Your child won't need them all, of course, and many he can use in the park or at a nursery school. Common objects around your house may be good substitutes for some of the items. But generally, he should have access to some playthings in each category:

—Blocks—well made and in as large an assortment as possible; simple, fit-together construction materials of wood or plastic, block cities, giant cardboard or hollow wooden blocks, if you can afford the money and the space.

—Toys to imitate grown-up activities—dolls, doll house, doll clothes, doll carriage, doll equipment, telephone, cash register, trains, trucks, planes, play money, an unstructured playhouse that can serve a multitude of purposes, doctor and nurse kits, farm and zoo animals, housekeeping equipment, gardening tools, carpenter tools. (Whenever possible, give your child the real thing instead of a toy. It works better, lasts longer, and gives a great sense of pride and accomplishment.)

—Materials to encourage creative arts—crayons, finger paints, colored pencils, chalk, blackboard, clay or the equivalent, poster paints, paper of all kinds from little colored note pads to large sheets of wrapping paper for murals. Invest in a stand-up easel if you have the space for it.

—Musical equipment—record player, drum, tambourine, finger cymbals, triangle, bells, xylophone.

—Props for dramatic play—costumes, costume box full of discarded clothing and large pieces of cloth, masks, hand puppets, hats, wigs, materials for playing store and school.

—Games that teach numbers—dice, counting puzzles, dominoes, simple board games that involve counting, measuring tools, number rods, telling-time games.

—Toys for loving—cuddly baby dolls, stuffed animals (which small boys need as much as little girls).

—Equipment for active, physical play—swing, wheelbarrow, wagon, scooter, tricycle, balls, trampoline-type bouncing pad, climbing apparatus, tree house, crawling tunnel, roller skates, ice skates, merry-go-round, ride 'em trucks and trains, punching toy.

—Toys to encourage sensory learning—inlaid puzzles, peg boards, geometric insets, Montessori-type dressing frames, lotto games, color-matching games, teleiodescope, flannel board with number and letter cutouts.

—Science-discovery equipment—magnifying glass, magnets, prism, seeds, ant farm.

7. Should You Teach Your Preschooler to Read?

Teaching a preschool child to read is one of the happiest, most worthwhile, and most satisfying forms of early learning. It is also the subject of widespread research—with bright youngsters, disadvantaged children, three-year-olds, youngsters who are mentally retarded or emotionally disturbed or brain-injured, children of average I.Q., four-year-olds, two-year-olds, and bilingual preschoolers.

Reading is being taught to preschoolers by parents at home, by psychologists in child-development laboratories, by educators in day-care centers, and by six-year-olds who like to play school in the family room. It's being taught phonetically, by sight-word techniques, by combination methods and by no method at all. It's being taught with sandpaper alphabets, with newspaper comic strips, by first grade primers, by television, by programmed readers, by cassette tapes, and by computer programs.

Regardless of method or motivation, most of those who try to teach preschoolers to read in any consistent way are generally successful. Those who have written about their experiences—in professional journals or in letters to the editors of newspapers—usually comment on the great joy, eagerness, and enthusiasm with which the preschoolers have learned.

Several years ago, the *Chicago Tribune* and dozens of other newspapers in the United States and England ran a thirteen-week series of daily cartoon strips which showed parents how to teach small children to read by a simple, phonetic method. A year later, a mother in a small, northern Illinois town sent this letter to mark the anniversary of the *Tribune*'s series, an event which she said "is celebrated at our house by much reading."

Mrs. John M. Sullivan wrote:

I doubt if you are fully aware of the door to a world of knowledge which the *Tribune* opened to children in the Chicagoland area. I do not see how you can begin to imagine the hesitant and curious way in which two of my little girls and I opened that door. Our doubt and curiosity soon gave way to an overwhelming enthusiasm and eagerness.

The older little girl started first grade this fall, reading as well as her second and third grade brothers. Our four-year-old spends many happy hours each week educating and entertaining herself. In our home there are no longer moans of 'What can I do now, Mommy?'

My two little daughters and I have developed an understanding and a closeness that I never dreamed possible from our association in the field of education—an unexpected bonus from the reading strips. I am looking forward to the same delightful experience of opening the door to learning for my other two babies and only wish, dear *Tribune*, that you had been around when the eight older ones were small.

Contemporary interest and research about teaching preschoolers to read began in the late 1950s. It was touched off, generally, by the discoveries about the functioning of the human brain itself and by concerns not only about providing learning stimulation for gifted youngsters but also about equipping disadvantaged children to succeed in first grade.

Now, it is commonplace to find youngsters entering first grade already able to read well. Now, popular TV programs like "Sesame Street" help youngsters learn to identify sounds and words. Now, many day-care centers and nursery schools make it a policy to offer reading readiness programs and beginning instruction in reading.

But the idea that children as young as three and four can learn to read if given a little of the right kind of loving, relaxed help is still not universally accepted. Many parents assume that teaching a young child to read would take more time than they can spare; if they cannot find a day-care center that offers a reading program, they see no problem in waiting for traditional instruction in first grade. School systems which have access to considerable data showing the benefits of providing preschoolers with early help in reading—either via programs for parents or in school-sponsored child-parent centers—often can't find the money to pay for such innovations. Others have been concentrating so much on school integration programs and on special education classes that they have not been able to develop major new curriculum ideas.

Despite an enormous amount of accumulating evidence that preschoolers can learn to read easily and happily and with great immediate and long-term benefit, interested parents may still get some negative feedback from teachers they ask about the possibility. Some teachers still tell parents: Don't try to teach your child to read yourself. Reading is such an enormously complicated mental endeavor that even trained teachers sometimes fail to teach it successfully. So how can you possibly succeed? You'll use the wrong methods. You'll pressure your child. You are too emotionally involved to help your youngster. He'll ruin his eyes. Besides, he can't possibly learn until he has a mental age of six—maybe even seven or eight—so you're wasting your time and inviting emotional disaster.

Some well-known books on child care still echo these messages. Some learned educators still write scholarly papers for professional journals analyzing the reading process in ways that make it seem too impossibly difficult for anyone ever to learn, especially small children. Debates still persist about sight-word methods versus phonics versus combination techniques, about grouping and mainstreaming pupils, and about other obscure technicalities involved in the reading process.

It's no wonder that many parents, especially conscientious mothers and fathers eager to do what's best for their offspring, are still getting the message to keep hands off the reading process. As in the past, some parents are still reluctant even to answer their children's questions about letters, words, signs, and labels. Many unwittingly, but effectively, still blunt their children's spontaneous interest in words—an interest which first grade teachers are instructed to build again slowly and often with some difficulty.

After the *Tribune*'s preschool reading series began to appear in print, dozens of parents wrote the paper with comments like this: "We're so glad to know it's all right to help our child with reading. He's learned so much on his own, from watching television and asking us questions about words. But we were afraid the school wouldn't approve."

One of the most curious facts in the history of American education is how long the mistaken idea persisted that children need a mental age of six or six and one-half before they could learn to read. The notion was based on several studies that were made during the early 1920s and 1930s which showed that among first graders, those with a higher mental age learned to read better than their classmates.[1]

These findings were generally interpreted to mean that the older a child, the better he could be taught to read, and that youngsters with a mental age of less than six could not read. The occasional child who did come to first grade already reading was thought to be so highly intelligent that he learned to read almost spontaneously. Or his parents were suspected of pushing him to alleviate their own neurotic feelings of inadequacy.

Contemporary critics who have reviewed this evidence point out that all it really shows is that the higher a child's I.Q., the easier he will learn to read. Furthermore, they point out, it isn't valid to draw conclusions about preschool reading from research which deals only with a small number of six-year-olds taught by a sight-word method in a formal classroom situation. As a result of this poorly done research, almost no attempts were made for decades to teach reading before the age of six and almost no children learned to read before they reached first grade. It was easy to assume that they couldn't.

But challenges to this smug assumption eventually developed—prompted in part by concerns about the worrisome percentage of youngsters failing to learn to read well in school and by new neurological findings about how the brain acquires and uses information.

As long ago as 1954, for example, Dr. Arthur I. Gates, then professor at the Institute of Language Arts, Teachers College, Columbia University, said about early reading:[2]

> Certain factors suggest both the possibility and the advisability of helping a child to learn to read long before the sixth year, indeed, perhaps during the fourth year.
>
> Children learn to understand spoken English and to use it long before the sixth birthday . . . Children are getting an increasing amount of experience with picture books, comics, radio, television, and other visual-auditory media almost from infancy. The result of this is that children are well advanced in getting information and stories of all kinds, long before they learn to read. The difficulties of teaching reading to a large class are so great that the average child learns rather slowly. By the end of the first grade, the typical child cannot read material anywhere nearly as complex as he can secure through other media. This puts reading at a very great disadvantage . . .
>
> Readers of this article may feel that the writer's comments on the difficulties of learning to read in the first grade are hardly in harmony with the suggestion that children learn to read earlier. The reader is reminded that the difficulties and confusions attending the new and strange group life, the necessity of learning in a distracting group situation, the teacher's difficulty in giving each child much quiet individual guidance, and the meagerness of the content of what a child can read in the first grade in comparison with what he can get from spoken words and pictures may comprise greater hardship than those attending easy-going guidance and self-employment at a younger age.

Today, the teaching of reading to preschoolers is well underway in many different places in the United States.

Today, there is no doubt that preschoolers can be taught to read—in several happy, satisfying, successful ways. For example:

In a Montessori school in Oak Park, Illinois, Bobby, four, spreads out a small, individual mat on the floor, then takes a collection of simple picture cards from a nearby drawer. One by one, he lines up the pictures in a row, down the side of his mat. He studies the first one, a dog. Slowly, Bobby sounds out the word under his breath. Still repeating the initial "d" sound, he goes to an open rack full of colored letters cut out of sandpaper-covered cardboard. He locates a "d," takes it back to his mat, and places it beside the picture. Next, he finds an "o" and then a "g," sounding out each letter as he walks back and forth.

Bobby successfully spells out "man" and "cat" and "hat." Then he tries "bus." But he can't remember what letter makes the initial "b" sound. So, for the first time, he asks for adult help.

"What says 'b'?" Bobby asks the Montessori directress. She goes with him to a bin of large-size sandpaper letters that are glued on cardboard rectangles. Gently, she guides the fingers of Bobby's right hand so that his fingertips trace the sandpaper shape of "b," while she repeats the sound of the consonant. After learning the "b" sound through his eyes, his ears, and his fingers, Bobby is easily able to find it himself.

Without any more help or supervision, Bobby spells out the rest of the names on his picture cards. Then, he sits back on his heels, contemplates his work for a minute, and quietly returns all of the materials to their proper place.

No one has instructed Bobby to do the reading-spelling lesson. No one has supervised him or graded him or pressured him or even praised him for doing it. He could have chosen any of dozens of other activities. But he was sounding and making the words because he enjoys the learning and the sense of competence it gives him.

Dr. Montessori discovered that preschoolers could learn to read and write and enjoy the process enormously when she was developing her first slum-area school at the beginning of the century. Ever since, Montessori schools have taught preschoolers to read and to write. Dr. Montessori's textbooks—now published in several new editions in the United States—are full of descriptions of the eagerness and the enthusiasm with which her poverty-level youngsters learned to read. After studying their progress, degree of interest, and rate of learning, Dr. Montessori concluded that children learn to read most easily at ages four and five.

The widespread and enthusiastic revival of Montessori schools in the United States has been due in part to parents' interest in early reading. For the Montessori method of teaching reading and writing is one of the best and most complete available to preschoolers today. Much of the entire Montessori program aims at educating a youngster's five senses and is designed to culminate in the joyous and exciting discovery by preschoolers that they can communicate by reading and writing.

A child in a Montessori school learns to write before he learns to read. And he learns with such ease and pleasure that most elementary school teachers find it difficult to believe. He begins by learning how to control the muscles in his hand—by manipulating equipment designed for this purpose, by working with geometric form boards and inlaid puzzles and by tracing and filling in geometric shapes with a pencil. Then he practices tracing sandpaper letters with his fingers as he learns the sounds these letters make. In this way, he learns all of the physical motions necessary to write before he ever risks making a mistake by actually trying to write with pencil on paper. When he is ready to try, he usually succeeds immediately and joyfully.

Dr. Montessori's classic book, *The Montessori Method,* describes the tremendous excitement and delight with which her small preschoolers discovered that they could indeed write real words, as a result of previous training of the senses and having learned the sounds of the letters. "The first word spoken by a baby causes the mother ineffable joy," she wrote. "The first word written by my little ones aroused within themselves an indescribable emotion of joy."[3]

Only after a child has learned to write well does he learn to read, Dr. Montessori believed. He should be taught reading by sounding out the words phonetically, then repeating them rapidly until he understands them. Often reading, too, comes with the same burst of excited joy with which a child discovers that he can write.

Four-year-olds, on the average, take only a month or six weeks from the first preparatory exercise to achieve their first written words, said Dr. Montessori. Five-year-olds need only about one month. "Children of four years, after they have been in school for two months and a half, can write any word from dictation and can pass to writing with ink in a notebook," wrote Dr. Montessori. "Our little ones are generally experts after three months' time, and those who have written for six months can be compared to the children in the third elementary. Indeed, writing is one of the easiest and most delightful of all the conquests made by the child." Moving from writing to reading takes about two weeks, reported Dr. Montessori.

The same easy progression from writing to reading has also been noted by Dr. Durkin in her studies of youngsters who learned to read at home before they entered first grade. More than half of these children were intrigued with printing words before or at the same time they became interested in reading. Such a child would draw or scribble with an ordinary pencil, or write on a blackboard at home. Then he would start to copy letters of the alphabet. Soon, he would begin to ask questions about words ("Show me my name!") and about spelling. And from this interest, he would advance naturally into reading.[4]

The idea that a preschooler will almost teach himself to read, if given the opportunity to explore freely in an environment that contains the proper stimuli, was also basic to an elaborate "talking typewriter" teaching device developed by Dr. Omar K. Moore, professor of sociology at the University of Pittsburgh. Dr. Montessori called her schools, with their carefully designed learning equipment, a "prepared environment." Dr. Moore called his computer-operated learning device a "responsive environment."

Each talking typewriter was installed in a small wood-paneled booth in a private area of a nursery school. Children were invited to take turns using the machine, which was programmed to call out the letters and words that the children typed on it, to guide the youngsters through the learning of new words and to dictate material for the youngsters to type. The program was designed to demonstrate Dr. Moore's theory that reading and writing are "autotelic," that is, they have intrinsic interest for small children who want to learn solely for the pleasure of learning and not because they are motivated by fear, reward, approval, or competition. Dr. Moore's research showed, too, that not only did the children learn to read and to type on the machine, but they also began to act like gifted children, even though they had been carefully chosen because they had an I.Q. in the average range.

Dr. Moore insisted that his talking typewriter be used only by preschoolers when and if they wished to do so. No one praised them or urged them to try it or made any comments about what they accomplished or reported to parents about their progress. Their only motivation was the pleasure of learning in itself.

Yet when given the choice of working on the talking typewriter or remaining with their play group, almost all of the youngsters eagerly took their turns at the typewriter.

Both Dr. Moore and Dr. Montessori took great precautions against pressuring a child into reading. The youngsters' only reward, in their programs, is the joy of discovery, the feeling of accomplishment and mastery, the fun of knowing. Yet even skeptics who aren't convinced of the value of preschool reading acknowledge with surprise the intensive interest, concentration, and delight with which children use the reading materials. The same kind of fascination and enthusiastic concentration marks much newer computer programs that are designed to help young children learn to read. In preschools, kindergartens, and first grades where they are available, children are generally so eager to use them that careful schedules of taking turns must be worked out.

The warmth, praise, and enthusiasm of human teachers play a greater role in some of the other ways in which preschoolers are being taught to read today. It is almost impossible for parents to play the detached, neutral role of a Montessori directress or to refrain from reacting with excitement and enthusiasm to a child's happy successes in decoding written words.

A few of the reading materials available to parents who

want to teach a child to read at home are built around what is essentially a sight-word or look-say method of reading in which the youngster is encouraged to identify words by their shape as a whole instead of decoding them phonetically. Some preschoolers can—and do—learn to read in this way.

However, phonetic reading methods, which teach a child from the very beginning that printed words are just written-down sounds which he can easily learn to decode, do a better job of teaching reading than sight-word techniques. (Debate does still persist on the sight-word versus phonics issue. But almost all of the best-conducted and most complete research studies on the subject show a clear-cut and continued advantage for youngsters who learn by techniques that introduce phonics at the very beginning of instruction.)

Almost all Japanese preschool children begin to read at home at age four without any formal teaching. In part, this is because most Japanese mothers are intensely interested in their offspring's education, recognize the importance of early learning, and regularly buy books for them and read to them. Another reason is that books for young Japanese children are written in a highly regular phonetic writing system called Hiragana. These phonetic symbols are easy for young Japanese children to learn, and tests show that only about one percent of them cannot read at least some Hiragana by the time they start elementary school.

When the *Chicago Tribune* decided to develop a comic-strip feature to help teach preschoolers to read at home, a phonetic plan was chosen. This one was developed by a nursery school teacher, Mrs. Dorothy Taft Watson, and included several games and learning activities.[5]

"This is a game to teach you what the letters say," a parent begins by telling a preschooler. Showing the child the large letter "h" in the comic-strip panel, the parent points out, "This looks a little like a chair."

The next panel shows a little boy running. The parent reads, "Harry ran home so fast, he was out of breath." With the next panel, "He fell into the chair and all he could say was 'h - h - h - h - h.' "

Then the parent encourages the youngster to run across the room, pretend he's out of breath, and collapse into a straight-backed chair as he makes the out-of-breath "h" sound.

Finally, the parent suggests that the child listen for the "h" sound in words like hat, helicopter, heart, and hammer. If the child is still interested, the parent asks him to think of words he knows that begin with an out-of-breath sound and writes them down for him, calling his attention to the initial "h."

"A very young child usually does better if he doesn't even know the names of the letters at first, except for the vowels, which sometimes make the sound of their own name," explained Mrs. Watson. "Later on, you can easily teach your youngster the alphabet by means of the familiar alphabet song," she suggested. The sounds that the letters make are what's important in decoding printed words—not the names of the letters.

The second comic strip teaches "m," linking the sound with Mary, moon, mouse, milk, and monkey and the shape with a pair of child's mittens held together, thumbs outside. Next comes "p," associated with the noise a papa makes puffing on a pipe. This time the parent writes down a series of words starting with "p" and asks the child to draw a circle around each "p" as she sounds out the words. (Lower-case letters are used throughout the initial parts of this program and most others for preschoolers; capitals are taught later on.)

Parents should play the game of letter sounds with a child for only a few minutes at a time, according to Mrs. Watson. She suggested that each session be no longer in minutes than the youngster's age in years—three minutes for a three-year-old, five minutes for a kindergartener. But the game can be played several times a day, provided the child is interested and enjoys it.

As a child learns the sound of a letter, he is encouraged to look for it in places other than the comic strip—on cereal packages, highway signs, labels, headlines. Many mothers wrote the *Tribune* that they had invented games to be played in the car or while doing housework which involved the child's listening for initial consonant sounds in strings of words or sentences concocted by the parent.

"Remember that for preschoolers, phonics is still very

much a game—just as learning to walk and to talk were games," advised Mrs. Watson. "Keep it light, happy, and relaxed. Your child has no deadlines to meet, no tests to pass, no possibility of failure."

"Your child will often forget the sound of the letters, particularly at first," explained Mrs. Watson. "Just tell him the right answer at once. Don't make him guess or wallow. Do praise him delightedly for each sound he learns and each word he sounds out. Your child will learn far faster when he's motivated by praise. And most important, do share his excitement at his own cleverness and the new world that is opening to him."

Next, "s" is taught, linked with snake. Then comes "w" with its windy sound, emphasized by having the child hold his hand in front of his mouth as he says witch, wild, wagon, wolf.

The letter "t" is learned in association with the *t-t-t-t-t-t*-tick of a clock and "r" becomes the *r-r-r-r-r-r-r-r* sound of a big, cross dog, which a child can have ferocious fun imitating.

When a preschooler has learned the sounds and shapes of these six consonants, all of which make a consistent sound, he's ready for his first vowel. Parents can tell preschoolers that vowels are "fairy letters" because they can do magic tricks with other letters and because every word must have one, Mrs. Watson suggested. The first one to teach is the short sound of "a" as in apple.

Then comes the exciting minute when a preschooler is ready to roll consonants and a vowel together to make his first word, "hat." To emphasize the smoothness of this procedure, the *Tribune*'s comic strip shows a snow-suited child rolling the "h" and "a" and "t" into a snowball.

Starting with the eighth comic-strip lesson, a preschooler is able to read a very simple comic written for him, using only the sounds he has learned to identify and blend together. For the rest of the thirteen-week newspaper series, he gets a new comic every day to read by himself, as well as instructions in a new sound or reading technique.

"When your child begins putting consonants and vowels together to make words, it's important that he learn to do it smoothly and quickly, so he will recognize the word he is sounding out," Mrs. Watson stressed. "You may have to work with him several days before this comes easily and naturally. Tell him he need not sound a word he already knows. He should just read it right off."

As the lessons proceed, a preschooler learns the sound of "j," "l," "z," "b," and "d," reading easy comics and playing simple games based on letter shapes or sounds. For example, a child can act out "d" by marching about, making the d-d-d-d-d sound on a pretend drum.

The fairy letter "e," as in egg, comes next. The letters "ck" together are taught as a "k" sound. With "g," a preschooler learns the hard sound, as in "gag." But he is also told that sometimes "g" sounds like a "j," and if he can't make sense out of the word using the hard "g," he should simply try the alternative.

Parents are encouraged to make up simple games to play with their children, using these basic sounds. For example, a sixteen- or twenty-square bingo-type card can be drawn, using letters instead of numbers and raisins or small gumdrops as markers. A mother can be cooking or washing dishes as she calls out the sounds for the youngster, who shouts out his own name when he has succeeded in marking a row up or across. Then he gets to eat the markers.

After a youngster has learned the consonants and short vowel sounds, the *Tribune*'s reading program begins to teach him shortcuts. First, he learns a few common digraphs—two letters which join together to make a special sound of their own, such as "ch," "sh," "qu," "ph," and "th."

Linguists point out that "th" actually makes two different sounds, as in "then" and "thin." But this is a subtlety that doesn't trouble preschoolers. Almost always, without being told, they will choose the correct pronunciation without realizing the difference.

After the common digraphs come phonograms, groups of letters which almost always sound the same, such as "ook," "ank," "ink," "all," "ight," "atch," "or," "er," "aw," and "oy." These word patterns make it easy for small children to learn some of the most irregular vowel sounds and consonant combinations. And by blending these parts of words with initial consonant sounds, a preschooler can increase his reading vocabulary rapidly and easily.

At this point, a parent should teach a child the names of the five vowels, according to Mrs. Watson. A youngster is taught one simple rule about when a vowel says its own name: When two vowels come together in a word or have only one other letter in between in a short word, the first one usually says its own name and the second one keeps quiet. For example, if a youngster already knows how to pro- nounce "at," this rule makes it easy for him to learn "ate" and "eat." And it gives most children a wonderful sense of mastery and competence to be able to apply this rule to read "rob" and "robe," "kit" and "kite," "hat" and "hate," and "bat" and "boat" and "bait."

Critics of phonetic reading methods always point out the inconsistencies in the English language, such as the different sounds of "ough" in "cough," "rough," "bough," "dough," and "through" (the worst single example of sound-spelling inconsistency in English) and subtle shades of differences in the pronunciation of vowels. But advocates emphasize that 85 percent of all English words are completely phonetic and almost all of the rest are at least partially so. And it's far easier to learn the spelling of the forty-four basic English sounds and a few rules about when to use which than it is to memorize every word by its total shape, as some reading methods teach.

When a child does discover such an inconsistency, a parent should merely tell him that it is a "naughty letter" that doesn't follow the rules, Mrs. Watson suggested. Most preschoolers are delighted at this idea and have no further difficulty.

As he begins to read easy books (many of which are still being written from word lists used with look-say methods, rather than according to phonetic principles), a child will encounter a few common words which don't follow the phonetic rules he's learned so far. It's easiest just to tell him what each word says when he comes across it and have him learn it as a sight word, according to Mrs. Watson. Such words include: could, father, friend, once, one, pretty, said, says, shoes, sure, there, to, too, very, where, would, and you.

Once a preschool child has learned the sounds of the consonants, the sounds of the long and short vowels and rules about when to use which, and a dozen common sight words, he can proceed independently in reading. Eventually, he should be taught the names of the consonants. And he should learn the alphabet. (It's easiest with the familiar song that follows the "Twinkle, Twinkle, Little Star" tune.) But from this point on, he'll absorb almost everything else he needs to know from practice.

"Julie was four when your first lessons started," one mother wrote to the *Tribune*. "She whizzed through about sixty of the lessons, but then lost some interest. She just wants to read books instead. Now she has very little trouble reading her sister's third grade reader. And she's trying to teach her little three-year-old brother to read. Thank you for making reading such a wonderful experience for our little girl."

"Parents should not be afraid of helping their children with reading," emphasized Mrs. Watson. "The subject has too frequently been surrounded by a maze of technical terms and suggestions. Too many people think of reading as being far more complex and difficult than it really is and tend to find deep and complicated reasons for any simple mistake a child may make.

"Teaching a child to read is actually quite easy," she said. "You can hardly go wrong. Anyone can easily learn the simple, basic letter sounds suitable for a preschool child. And it is surprising to see how easily and enthusiastically an extremely young child will often learn them. Phonics can be started—as a game, of course—when the child is just learning to talk.

"My own children began as babies, running in and out of my kindergarten and picking up their letter sounds along with nursery rhymes. If they saw a picture of a cow, they knew the cow said 'moo,' and if they saw a printed 'm' they knew it said 'm-m-m.'

"It is easy to teach a child the rudiments of reading," commented Mrs. Watson. "It is also a privilege and such an enjoyable experience that it would be a pity to miss it. Moreover, these early years are usually periods of high intellectual curiosity in the child. His interest is keen. He wants to learn. And he will do so more easily than he may later on. A four- or five-year-old who discovers the magic of letters will often spend endless hours experimenting with every bit of printed matter he can lay his hands on. Presently, he will discover that he can read—and then the world is his."

Giving parents a preschool reading program for their children via a newspaper comic strip was such a revolutionary concept in education that it might stir up a controversy, *Tribune* editors thought. First grade teachers, especially, would disapprove of the suggestion that part of their primary job could be done at home by a parent.

So the great burst of enthusiasm that greeted the preschool reading series caught the paper by surprise. What was intended as a public-service feature suddenly became one of the hottest circulation ideas in years. More than sixty thousand parents asked the *Tribune* for reprints of parts of the series they had missed or mislaid. Almost twice that many have bought paper-covered reprints of the reading strips since the series ended. The entire thirteen-week reading program has been published in many other newspapers and repeated twice since in the *Tribune*. Thousands of delighted parents have written the *Tribune* about their experiences using the material with their youngsters. The *Tribune* now even gets an occasional letter from a college student thanking the reading program for setting him on a successful academic career that has led to admission to a prestigious university.

"My three-, four- and five-year-old children are learning so much about reading from your comic strips," wrote one mother. "Our two-year-old listens and our nine-month-old baby eats whatever she can reach—the reason why we are missing two of the lessons. Can you replace them, please?"

"We need the last four comic strips," wrote another parent. "We were out of town for the weekend. The neighbors were saving the papers for us, but decided to keep the reading strips for themselves."

The mother of a four-year-old boy and a thirty-month-old girl described her experiences with the reading lessons this way:

Jimmy, my oldest son, will be five in December. He was very enthusiastic about learning to read. Last summer, he was more interested in going over his comic strips than playing outside with his friends. 'Reading' his new sound was the high point of each day.

The time spent daily in learning each new sound and going over the old ones varied from two or three minutes to fifteen. I found it very important for the child, as well as myself, to find a time when there were few distractions, such as a favorite TV program for him or demands of caring for the two youngest children for me. When either of us was tired, rushed, or had our mind on something else, nothing was accomplished.

I had some difficulty in convincing him that the sounds could be put together to form words. Jimmy has now reached the point where he can recognize on sight most of the common short words and is not afraid to tackle the long words.

After the first eight weeks, I purchased a beginner's dictionary, which I found was very helpful in building up Jimmy's self-confidence. Now he is reading books in the easy-read series. He reads to anyone who will listen to him—his father, sister, friends, even delivery men cannot escape without listening to a sentence or two. Another side effect of learning to read is that his speech has improved; each word is said clearly, and mistakes in pronunciations can be corrected easily.

Linda was only two and one-half when the reading strips started and, like most younger children, she tries to imitate every word and action of her older brother. I intended to use the series with her next year when Jimmy starts kindergarten, but I have already shown her several of the comic strips to teach her sounds that she was unable to say. I now believe that she will complete the entire series and be able to read long before next September.

I have recommended the series to three mothers whose children are having difficulties with reading in the first grade. One of them even offered to buy the scrapbook I made of the comic strips. But I wouldn't part with it for the world. It will always have an honored place in my home. My son is a walking, reading testimonial to its effectiveness.

Kindergarten and first grade teachers did, indeed, make up the largest group of individuals writing the *Tribune* about the preschool reading program. But contrary to expectations, almost all of them had high praise for the idea. This was particularly true of former teachers who retired temporarily to care for small children of their own.

"I am a first grade teacher in an Indiana school," wrote one. "I think you'll be interested in knowing that my best student is also one of yours. Would you kindly send me the entire series so I can use it with all my pupils?"

"Would you please send me the first weeks of your how-to-read series?" asked another parent. "I resisted the idea for some time for fear my daughter would be bored in school and her teacher would object. Now my daughter's teacher has convinced me of my folly in not helping Lisa to read before school. By now, of course, my back issues of the *Tribune* have been hauled away by the junk man. (His children, no doubt, are all reading well!)"

In some schools, kindergarten and first grade teachers sent notes home to parents, suggesting the use of the reading strips. Explained one, "This kind of idea certainly helps the teacher of the first grade. The children entering the class then have some idea of phonics and reading and they aren't so lost."

"We have a kindergartener in our house and I am also a first grade teacher," wrote an Iowa mother. "I was overjoyed to find your excellent series. Now my five-year-old girl is delighted that she can read as well as her third grade sister. I only wish my own pupils had this same opportunity. This is certainly not pushing a child—but helping him develop his own potential. These children in my first grade class have good minds, but no one has encouraged them to use their minds. It is like having an arm in a sling; if it's never exercised, it will eventually become unusable."

Enough Montessori reading materials and instructions can be found by determined parents to teach a child to read at home by this excellent phonetic method.

The highly successful and well-researched Distar program, published by Science Research Associates, Inc., is also available in simple, modified, manual form for parents to use with young children at home. Those who work with the program say it is appropriate for bright three-and-one-half-year-olds and for average four- and five-year-olds who can complete the program and learn to read well in one hundred days of half-hour lessons.[6]

Distar is essentially a phonetic decoding program for learning to read. It aims to teach youngsters how to decode—read—words that they already have the ability to understand. It begins by teaching children the sounds that each letter makes—not the names of the letters, which play no direct role in reading—then how to say the sounds together fast to make identifiable words.

This program reshapes a few letters to help youngsters recognize and appreciate the different sounds some letters make. And it urges parents to use lavish praise and surprise when their children succeed in the lessons. "That's amazing. You are really smart," the parent is told to say. Or "I thought you'd have a lot more trouble than that. You're terrific. It also includes dozens of short stories that youngsters are able to read for themselves as the lessons progress.

An increasing number of computer programs designed to teach preschool children to read are also available now. Some are designed to be used in preschools, some at home with a little help from parents. Early reports show that four- and five-year-olds can learn to read—and to write their own original sentences and stories—with enormous excitement, concentration, and satisfaction.

What accounts for the remarkable success of these different reading programs, carried out in different ways, under different circumstances, by people with such varied interests and training?

One explanation may be this: All language, whether written or spoken, is a function of the brain, not of the ears or the eyes which receive it, or of the tongue and hand which produce it. Neither ear nor eye can comprehend the meaning of abstract symbols; it merely passes them along as electrochemical impulses to the brain, where they are interpreted.

Recognition and understanding are in the brain, regardless of where the sensory stimulus originated.

We have long taken it for granted that every child, except the most severely retarded, will learn to speak the language used in his immediate environment and to speak it quite well before the age of five. He will also acquire the accent, vocabulary, and grammar—good or bad—that he hears most frequently. And he will accomplish this learning with little apparent effort, without formal training, without pressure, and usually with considerable enthusiasm and satisfaction. He will also learn this language more easily than he will ever again acquire any other language because of the physical state of his developing brain.

Because understanding and use of language are activities of the brain, it should be just as easy for a child to learn printed symbols through the eyes as it is for him to learn spoken symbols through the ears, say many researchers. In fact, small children of deaf parents do learn sign language, with its intricate finger movements, more readily than verbal language.

In explaining why first graders sometimes fail to learn to read, some educators blame the fact that young minds are not able to deal with the abstract nature of printed words. These educators fail to realize that the spoken sound, "cat," for example, is just as abstract as the printed letters, "c-a-t." Both are merely symbols for a small, furry feline. If a child's brain has developed to the point where it can understand that an arbitrary symbol represents a cat, it should make no difference whether the symbol is first perceived by the ear or the eye for transmission to the brain.

In fact, it's likely that the printed word—which remains visible and constant for as long as a child wishes to study it—may be even easier for him to grasp than a spoken word, which vanishes in a fraction of a second and varies in tone and in volume depending on the speaker.

Suggesting that most children could learn to read in their fourth year, Dr. Gates noted, "they learn to understand spoken language quite well by their second year and psychologically, there is little difference learning as it were, 'to read' spoken words and learning to read printed words. Spoken words come to the child through sound waves and printed words through light waves. The main reason they learn to understand spoken words first is merely that it is more convenient for parents and others to use them than to present printed material . . . There is no evidence that printed words are more difficult to perceive or distinguish than spoken words."[7]

From the very first weeks of his life, a baby is surrounded with spoken words. He hears again and again, one at a time, simple words which are related intimately to him. His efforts to duplicate these words bring obvious pleasure and praise from those around him.

But printed words are kept hidden away from him for the most part. Those he sees in books, magazines, and newspapers are so small and jumbled together that he hasn't a chance of separating them and deciphering them.

Often the first words that a child learns to read are those which he sees large, clear, and one at a time—labels on cans, gasoline-station signs, brand names in the supermarket, key words on television commercials, names on billboards. These are all he's had a fighting chance to learn.

Because learning to read and learning to speak are similar as a brain activity and all normal children master speech as a matter of course, the reason why some children fail to learn to read, or have great difficulty in doing so, must lie with the way in which adults present reading to children, suggested psychologists Dr. Arthur W. Staats and Dr. Carolyn K. Staats.[8]

They pointed out three differences. First, speech is acquired very slowly. Learning sessions are short, frequent, and distributed throughout the day. No one expects the child to succeed immediately or to keep working at the learning task.

Second, when a small child does learn to speak a new word, his learning is quickly and strongly reinforced. If he says "water," he is usually handed a drink. If he calls "bye-bye," someone usually bye-byes back at him. If he asks for a "cookie," he usually gets one—at least until his mother is sure that he knows the word.

Third, these reinforcements of learning are immediate.

Yet none of these learning principles applies to the teaching of reading in typical first grades, noted these psychologists. Compared to the teaching of speech, spread out over all the early years of life, reading comes with great suddenness, despite readiness programs in kindergarten. And when a teacher must deal with twenty-five or thirty or thirty-five first graders, all learning to read, reinforcement of successes can rarely be strong, immediate, or individual.

The learning theories presented by the Staatses in professional journals and in textbooks are complex. But generally they made the point that small children can learn to read with no more effort than they learn to talk, provided they are given ample opportunity and encouragement.

The debate about whether children younger than six *can* learn to read has generally been resolved. It's obvious that preschoolers can read and read fluently and with great enjoyment. But some influential critics still contend that even though it's possible, it's not a good idea to help a youngster learn to read before he starts first grade.

The opposition to preschool reading uses several arguments. First, the critics charge, too much pressure is bad for preschoolers, and it must take pressure to get children younger than six to accomplish first grade level work. For example, commenting on the program developed by the Denver public schools to give parents television instruction on how to introduce reading to four-year-olds at home, one professor of education wrote in a professional journal, "We shudder at what can happen when thousands of eager parents launch an attack on their young children."

Pressure *is* bad for small children. Furthermore, it's usually ineffective. Even greenhorn parents who might be inclined to pressure a youngster discover long before their firstborn is two years old that pressure doesn't work—in getting a child to nap or to use the toilet or eat peas or to wave bye-bye or to say thank you to the nice lady for the cookie.

The Denver program reported no evidence of pressuring from parents. This sixteen-week experiment which gave parents instruction on how to teach their small fry about beginning consonant sounds, letter forms and names, and letter-sound associations for some consonants brought much enthusiastic response. Of parents participating, more than

80 percent said that the instruction was helpful to them and important for their children. About 75 percent said they would appreciate having more help with early reading and that they intended to continue beginning-reading activities with their offspring.[9]

Observers who have studied other early-reading programs have not discovered any evidence of pressures or negative emotional reactions. Even in the cases of four preschoolers, now reported in professional literature, who failed to learn to read in research programs—all twins with low I.Q., emotional difficulties to start with, and a family background of poverty—researchers found that the youngsters enjoyed the program and scored better on psychological tests afterward than they had previously.

Actually, an earlier start in reading reduces the pressures of learning by introducing a youngster to reading at the age when his brain is most able to acquire language and his fascination with words is at its peak. When reading is taught individually and informally by a parent at home, a child isn't pressured by first grade competition. He doesn't have to try to make the top reading group or feel humiliated in the lowest section. He doesn't need to be concerned about grades or tests or keeping up with anyone else. He is free of the fear of making mistakes in public.

Every first grade reading method requires much repetition of words and sounds. The writers of primers often boast about how many times they can use the same word on a page or in a story. The total vocabulary introduced in a first-grade sight-word reading program ranges from about 110 to 300 words. It's no wonder it takes rules and discipline to keep a six-year-old's eager, active, space-age, television-conditioned mind on "Oh, look. See the girl. See the boy."

But two-, three-, and four-year-olds enjoy repetition. What is boring at six can well be fascinating at three. What a first grader does only at a teacher's insistence, a three-year-old may easily do by his own choice and initiative.

The critics who still think no one but a trained teacher can help a child learn to read ignore not only the new research on the subject, but also a youngster's ability to learn spoken languages. They also ignore the skill with which a majority of parents learn to adjust their child-rearing methods and teaching techniques to the individual personality and progress of their child.

In studying the backgrounds of forty-nine youngsters who read before entering first grade to find out how they learned, Dr. Durkin found a surprising factor. Sixteen of the youngsters said in interviews that they had been taught to read by an older brother or sister. Checking out these statements with parents, Dr. Durkin learned that the older child had been solely responsible for the teaching of reading in only four cases. For twenty-four other youngsters, however, an older brother or sister did contribute to the reading instruction. Having a sister about two years older who likes to play school has a great deal to do with early-reading ability in a preschooler, suggested Dr. Durkin.

So easy can it be for some preschool children to learn to read that they almost seem to teach themselves. For example, William H. Teale, of La Trobe University, Bundoora, Victoria, Australia, compiled considerable research on children who learned to read before starting first grade. He found there were usually four factors present in their home environment: (1) A wide range of easy reading material was readily accessible, including not only books but signs, names, TV captions, and other material. TV program guides were favorite early reading matter for these youngsters, who also picked out words in newspapers, cookbooks, and labels on food products.[10]

(2) Someone in the home helped the child learn what the printed material says, both by volunteering information ("That sign says 'Stop' ") and by answering a child's questions about words, and made it clear to the youngsters that printed words convey important and interesting information. Parents in these homes did considerable reading to their preschoolers and one or both of them were avid readers themselves.

"The environment of early readers was filled with varieties of print, print that was being interpreted for them by parents or older siblings," said Dr. Teale. "In many ways reading became an integral part of daily living. The early readers saw people reading and responding to print. They themselves were read to and came to understand that reading is yet another mode of communicating. In short, the environment facilitated their discovering that reading is a pleasurable, unique, communicative experience."

(3) Children who learned to read early in these studies almost always had access to pencil and paper and enjoyed drawing and scribbling. And (4) people in the home environment who were important to the child—not only parents but brothers, sisters, aunts, or grandparents, for example— responded to what the youngsters were trying to do. "In short," said Dr. Teale, "the children got feedback about reading in response to their felt needs and in a manner which preserved the general language arts concept of reading."

A study of how thirty-seven youngsters in a class for gifted children in Palm Beach, Florida, learned to read, either before they entered first grade or almost immediately after, showed that generally the same factors were involved, with some individual differences. Several parents said they helped their youngsters learn to read, some by means of phonics, a few with a combination of phonics and sight words. Six children learned to read incidentally, largely by asking questions persistently about letters and words and names on TV. Two preschoolers started reading in Montessori schools, three in nursery school. The parents of almost all of these youngsters had read to them throughout the earliest years of their lives, beginning by the time they were first able to sit up.

Parents who are teaching reading at home are routinely cautioned to stop the instruction the second the youngster seems bored or frustrated or inattentive or uninterested. Most parents do this quite naturally and successfully, as letters to the *Tribune* indicate. One mother wrote:

> You should have seen how interested and excited my three-year-old boy was to learn the sounds of the letters. I believe now that if a child can tell a knife from a fork, he can tell an 'a' from a 'b.' It's that simple.
>
> I never pushed my children. Rather, they kept after me to teach them another sound. I only gave them one at a time and added another only when they could identify the last one on cereal boxes, newspaper head-

lines, and the like. I think we mothers don't always realize that we are really the child's first and most important teacher.

The wife of a missionary temporarily stationed in Portugal taught her four-year-old to read, using the reading strips from the *Tribune* mailed to her by the boy's grandmother. She wrote:

Jon just turned four in October. We began in September. Every day, five days a week, he wants a new letter. And we review from the beginning each time. His enthusiasm overwhelms me. My mother has been sending me a week's comic strips at a time, and if Jon happens to see them, he is quite insulted that he cannot learn the new ones right away. Tonight, as he went to bed, he asked, 'Tomorrow, will I learn a new letter?' Outside, he calls our attention to signs, and many times a day he can be heard muttering letters and words, 'h-a-m—ham!' and 'f-a-s-t—fast!'

I am thoroughly enjoying teaching him, despite the fact that I have never had any training. In fact, I've never had any college work.

A Wisconsin mother said, "Our kindergarten son has just turned five. I have not pushed him into learning these comic strips. In fact, I have to hold him back and now he has only two more letters to go. He has really enjoyed learning, and he has read at school for his kindergarten teacher and principal, who were delighted. Do you realize that you are not only helping children learn to read, but bringing parents and the child closer together?"

"Many thanks to you and the *Tribune* for the reading lessons from a two-year-old and a forty-one-year-old," a Nebraska mother wrote. "I don't know what other mothers have done, but I made the series into a scrapbook for Lynn. We have had much fun. For the minute it becomes no fun, we put it away for another day. Two years of age is young and the attention wanders. Ten minutes was all that we have ever spent in a single day. But I do want you to know how much Lynn and her mother enjoy the whole project."

"I am having very wonderful results with my little boy," a Georgia mother wrote. "Not only is it improving his speech, but it has sparked his interest in books, and he is very enthused over being able to read words. We are both having a marvelous time. Our littlest boy, age thirteen months, leans over his crib when we make the 'magic sounds' and imitates us. Also, when we are not studying, we talk about sounds and words as we see them on signs and on food boxes or in the grocery stores."

Another mother said:

Thank you for the joy of teaching my little five-year-old girl to read. We have been working for about four months, whenever we had time and felt like it. She thinks in sounds and now is reading little books, although she may ask me about one or two words.

She does attack big words as well as little ones, simply because things like 'spray starch' and 'frosted flakes' are as easy to read as baby words when you see sounds instead of alphabet letters.

My four-year-old knows all her consonant sounds well and a few vowel sounds, but so far hasn't made much progress putting the sounds together. I have not had too much time to spend with her. Even our two-year-old daughter goes around making the sounds and I'm sure, someday, will enunciate more clearly because of it.

Sometimes we play 'M and M' bingo. I give my five-year-old a card with words and my four-year-old a card with letters. The girls eat the 'M and Ms' when they are through.

A former teacher had this comment:

Our five-year-old is reading second grade readers with very little assistance and when he doesn't know a word, he can at least make an intelligent guess.

We spent very little actual time on each day's lesson. We usually did them at the breakfast table, and he eagerly looked forward to each day's lesson. Other than encouraging him to read various labels and signs that he was interested in, I used no additional aids or techniques. We merely went through each strip and read the words a few times. His eagerness to learn to read and his subsequent desire to read as much as possible have been my greatest satisfaction.

A Nebraska mother put her feelings this way:

Our five-year-old boy is an average sort—flashes of brilliance liberally mixed with die-hard ignorance. His excitement over lessons has been considerably less than fever pitch. Nevertheless, he is pleased over his many little victories and to be solving the reading mystery. When he shows signs of bogging down, we just put the lessons aside.

I work with my boy daily, except weekends, and I also take a week off now and then for assimilation, as he seems to need such breaks. We have completed forty lessons, and he can use all of these ideas with confidence. It is a true pleasure to be able to be his partner in this new adventure. It definitely enhances the parent-child relationship.

Many parents are troubled about what happens when a youngster enters first grade able to read competently and independently. They fear that such a child will be a problem for the teacher and out of lockstep with the educational processes.

But most kindergarten and first grade teachers are elated to find a pupil who is already able to read. Primary teachers are continually urged to try to meet the individual needs of their pupils—and it is easier to help the first grader who can read than the one who cannot.

Almost all first grades are divided into first, second, and third reading groups, with two groups working independently, while the teacher gives reading instruction to the third. Or they are organized about individual learning programs so that each youngster works at his own speed. As enthusiasm for preschool reading continues to grow, chances are that most first grades now contain more than one child who could read fairly well before the beginning of the school year. These youngsters can form their own reading group. Or, if one child is far advanced beyond the top reading group, it is quite easy for the teacher to keep him occupied and interested—if only by giving him a library book to read. Ungraded primaries and those with individual learning programs also make it easier for early readers to continue working at their own pace.

But what if an early reader draws a poor teacher, one who resents his accomplishments and lets him know it? It's difficult to conceive of an adult worthy of the name of "teacher" who would penalize a six-year-old for already knowing how to do something he is supposed to be learning. But it has happened and it can happen again.

If a first grade teacher is so insensitive to the feelings of a child and so unenthusiastic about achievement in learning, the whole class is probably in for a difficult and unhappy year. A first grader who draws such a poor teacher—and there are a few among the hundreds of thousands of elementary teachers in this country—will probably have unusual difficulty in learning to read in that class. Parents can count it a blessing that their youngster already knows how to read, if he's trapped in such an unfortunate situation.

Since a majority of youngsters do learn to read in first and second grade, why encourage a child to read at age three, four, or five? It isn't worth the effort, even assuming it succeeds, critics also contend.

On the contrary, a preschool reader gets a head start in first grade and maintains his advantage all through elementary school, according to increasing and well-documented evidence. His I.Q. is likely to be increased permanently.

An earlier start in reading is an advantage for children throughout elementary school, according to studies made in California and New York public schools by Dr. Durkin.[11]

In her first study, in California, forty-nine youngsters entered first grade able to read at grade levels ranging from 1.5 (fifth month of first grade) to 4.5 (fourth grade, fifth month). The median grade level was 1.9. Their I.Q.s ranged from 91 to 161. Five years later, fifteen of the children had been double-promoted. Of these, twelve were still attending school in the same community and were available for further testing. Their mental age ranged from 10.9 to 17.2, with a median of 14.0.

The earlier the youngsters started reading, the greater the advantage they gained, Dr. Durkin's research shows. For example, twelve of the youngsters began to read at age three; their reading level at the time of the last follow-up averaged 9.2. Fourteen children were five years old when they started to read. Although the average I.Q. of this group differed from that of the three-year-old readers by just one point, they were only reading at 7.6 grade level.

The lower the child's I.Q., the greater he profits from having a head start in reading, Dr. Durkin's research also suggested.

Preschool help with reading does not lead to problems of learning in school, Dr. Durkin stressed, in summing up the findings of her five-year study. None of the children involved in her research had an academic problem. And a majority of the bright, preschool readers did better in reading after only five years of school instruction than nonearly readers of the same I.Q. level did after six years of schooling.

No learning problems resulting from an earlier start in reading were detected, either, in a major, long-term study of the teaching of reading in kindergarten conducted in the Denver public schools between 1960 and 1966. The study involved about four thousand youngsters, who were followed closely from kindergarten through fifth grade.[12]

Organized reading instruction in kindergarten for youngsters in all ability ranges and from all types of background did not produce any harmful social or psychological results, the extensive Denver research showed. It did not trigger problems of school adjustment or create dislike for reading. No more of the early readers developed visual defects or reading disabilities than did the control-group youngsters who followed a traditional timetable for learning to read in school.

The kindergarten readers who got an accelerated reading program later on had significantly higher reading rates at the end of fifth grade than did the youngsters who followed the traditional program or who got a stepped-up reading program without the kindergarten head start. The kindergarten readers had a larger vocabulary. They did better on reading comprehension tests. And they also scored higher in word-study skills, in arithmetic concepts, language, social studies, and, to some extent, in science.

Reading can be "quite effectively" taught to large numbers of typical kindergarten pupils in a big-city public school system, the Denver study concluded. Pupils in all ability groups benefit proportionately. And the earlier start in reading has a measurable, lasting effect at least through fifth grade, provided the school program is adjusted to take advantage of the early start.

However, the benefits of the early start tend to be lost after first or second grade, if the traditional school program doesn't give the early readers a chance to build on their skills at a faster-than-usual rate, the Denver researchers found.

A preschooler can't see letters well enough to read, and he will ruin his eyes if he's pressured to try, some critics have also charged. This has been a common and persistent assumption, but researchers who have studied early readers have not been able to find any evidence of eyestrain or damage. Parents who know how fast very young children can discover tiny objects—pins, beads, buttons—on the floor usually discredit the theory that preschoolers can't see well enough to read. New studies about visual abilities of newborns have led doctors to revise their old concepts about vision in young children. Early reading, particularly if the letters are large and clear, may actually be good training in visual perception, some advocates of early reading explain.

The eyes of most children are physiologically ready for reading at the age of twelve months or before, according to ophthalmologists. Normal children can focus and accommodate at least by the time they are a year old. (Actually, by three and a half months, a baby's vision is almost as accurate as an adult's and probably better than that of most people over age forty.) So learning to read at an early age is not an eye problem.

Teaching a child to read will rob him of his childhood and prevent him from achieving the social and emotional growth which is the chief developmental task of the preschool years is another argument critics hurl at advocates of early reading.

But how many children have a life so full of fascinating toys and happy play that they can't spare even ten minutes for reading? (The Denver reading program found that youngsters made significant gains in reading ability if parents spent as little as thirty minutes per week working with them.) A four-year-old whining, "Mommy, what can I do now?" is a more typical picture of early childhood.

There are other arguments that are often used against early reading: Preschoolers won't read for meaning; they'll only call words or recite them like a robot. Young children don't hear well enough yet to discriminate between words and sounds. And they may not know the precise meaning or range of meanings of words.

All of these sound just like arguments against permitting a child to learn to talk. Yet no one worries about "talking for meaning." No one claims that a child is too young to handle the abstractions of spoken language, or that he may use a few words he doesn't completely comprehend. No one even frets very much when a baby who has just learned to say "Daddy" applies his precious new word one bright morning to the man who lives next door. Even the critics who contend that a preschooler can't understand a book if he reads it himself still urge parents to read to their children, yet they express no concern that the youngsters may not understand precise word meanings.

Some questions about preschool reading do, however, remain to be answered by extensive research in the future. For example, if six and one-half is not the minimum mental age at which a child can learn to read, is there in fact a minimum age at all? When Dr. Fowler was director of the University of Chicago Laboratory Nursery School, reading was taught to three- and four-year-olds using a method he developed which stresses sound-letter relationships, word patterns, play orientation, and careful programming. He found that bright three-year-olds often do as well and in some ways better than bright four-year-olds.

The Denver public school research suggests that the average child should be about four and one-half to profit from instruction in reading, although youngsters with special aptitude and interest could begin earlier. Some advocates of sight-word programs urge that a start be made at age two.

Montessori schools begin prereading sensory stimulation at about three.

Dr. Durkin suggested a simple way in which to tell when a child is ready to read: Give him interesting opportunities to learn and see what happens.

Can the advantages of preschool reading instruction be made available to all children, even those whose parents are not willing or able to help them at home? The experiences of the Montessori schools and those in a few other nursery schools and day-care centers do show that reading can be taught in a carefully prepared environment, without the one-adult-to-one-child relationship that is ideal for informal teaching at home. Television programs like "Sesame Street" also help give millions of children some exposure to reading fundamentals.

An increasing number of public school kindergartens now provide five-year-olds with some reading instructions, but it is rarely as much as an interested parent can give an eager child at home. More day-care centers and nursery schools are offering some very preliminary reading experiences. But most are laboratory schools in university settings to which most parents do not have easy access. A few educators have proposed moving the starting age for public schooling up to four, the better to capitalize on children's early learning abilities and to offer a start in reading. But such a school system reorganization is enormously difficult and most administrators are too hampered by budget shortfalls and other problems to tackle it.

If you have a preschooler now, you can't wait for reading instruction to become available at the nearest nursery school. What should you do?

You should teach your preschooler to read—because research to date shows he has much to gain and nothing to lose. Everything you teach him will help him, even if you begin teaching him and don't follow through to the point where he can read independently. Even if he learns only a few words or a few sounds, it will profit him. No matter which method you choose, he will not become confused later on in first grade if the teacher uses a different technique.

But don't try to teach your preschooler to read unless you

really want to, unless both of you will enjoy the process. Don't pressure him to learn so much every day. Don't drag him away from any other fascinating occupation to read. And don't attach any penalties to his not learning if he isn't in the mood. Stop the minute he acts the least bit bored or restless—or before, if you can manage it. Most people who have taught small children emphasize that you're more likely to bore a child by going too slowly than by proceeding too fast.

If you were not taught to read by a phonetic method when you were in first grade, you'll probably be surprised at how logical and simple a modern phonetic or linguistic reading program is. Investigate a program of this kind before you begin helping your child. You should use reading materials with large-size type, preschool educators say.

Your child may be one who enjoys making reading a formal game of "school," especially if he's itching to go to school with an older brother or sister. Unless this is so, don't attempt to make reading instruction anything formal. Just cuddle your youngster up close, as you do when you read to him. Show him a new sound or a new word. Review a few of the ones he already knows. Be enthusiastic about what he remembers. Tell him matter-of-factly what he has forgotten. Then give him a happy, loving hug before he goes back to other activities. You probably won't spend more than ten minutes a session. After your child has learned a few sounds or words, you'll find reading games are a delightful way in which to keep him happy.

The more you expose your child to printed words, the quicker and easier he will learn to read. Some parents have used the technique of hanging labels on a table, a toy box, a bed, a doll. Buy your child all the books you can afford. Make your local library a regular stop, and let him choose his own reading materials.

Do read to your child, happily, lovingly, frequently. The children who did best in the Denver preschool reading program were those whose parents read to them at least sixty minutes every week. A love of reading is one of the best legacies you can give your child—and one of the best assurances that he will be able to keep up with the future.

8. How You Can Encourage Your Child to Be Creative

Kim, four, spends a busy November morning digging up black dirt in the backyard and filling little cardboard boxes with it. When her mother asks her why, Kim explains that these are to be her Christmas gifts for her brother and the other boys she knows.

"What boys like best is to get dirty and play in the mud," Kim tells her mother. "When the snow covers all the ground, they can't find any mud. So I am going to give them some for Christmas."

Gregg, five, is a tinkerer. In the last month alone, he has tried to take apart the toaster, pull out and rewind a cassette tape that belongs to his brother, find out what makes the hands on the clock move, and discover how fast he has to slide back and forth in the bathtub before the water swooshes out.

Randy, three, asks questions almost nonstop every minute he's awake. "Where does the night go in the morning?" "Why is the sky always up?" "Where was I before you had me?" "Why amn't I Johnny?" "Why doesn't it rain up sometimes?"

All of these preschoolers give evidence of possessing creative intelligence to a high degree—as do most young children. Yet, according to recent research, it's likely that this gift will be blunted or ignored or misdirected or discouraged or punished out of the youngsters long before they reach high school, and their promise will be only partially realized.

"Creativity" is a name now given to a particular component—probably several components—of intelligence. (Researchers have identified dozens of separate intellectual talents comprising overall mental ability and estimate there may be almost as many more factors not yet recognized. The usual type of I.Q. test measures only six to eight of these elements.) Educators and psychologists have become especially concerned with creativity in children in recent years because it seems to be the essence of genius—and an essential characteristic of those individuals who make original contributions to the world.

Creativity means far more than talent in art or music. It includes the whole range of creative and adventurous thinking in every field: scientific discovery, imagination, curiosity, experimentation, exploration, invention. It is the ability to originate ideas, to see new and unexpected relationships, to formulate concepts rather than to learn by rote, to find new answers to problems and new questions for which to seek answers.

A creative child has intelligence of the highest order. (In fact, many researchers and educators now group children as "gifted/talented" or as "gifted/creative/talented.") But he may or may not score well on an I.Q. test, which measures chiefly academic areas of mental ability. Research on creativity in children is far from complete, and most of what is known has been learned in studies of school-age children. Valid tests of creativity are difficult to develop because by definition they are concerned with producing many fresh ideas and unorthodox solutions, rather than one "right" answer. So the tests are hard to score and evaluate.

But most researchers agree on these points: (1) Almost all small children possess a considerable amount of creativity. (2) Creativity can be increased by deliberate encouragement, opportunity, and training. (3) It can also be dulled almost out of existence by some child-rearing and educational practices.

It is important that parents understand how to identify and

cultivate creativity in very young children. For the tender sprout of creativity needs to be encouraged and guided almost from birth, according to Dr. E. Paul Torrance, chairman emeritus of the department of educational psychology at the University of Georgia and an expert on creativity in children. (In some cultures—and to a lesser extent in some cultural groups in the United States—certain kinds of stifling, early environments produce individuals who are not open to new ideas and whose production of good innovations is very limited.)

"If we observe how infants handle and shake things and twist and manipulate them in many ways, we find some of the earliest manifestations of creative thinking," said Dr. Torrance. "Since the infant does not have a vocabulary, he can learn little by authority. Thus, by necessity, much of his learning must be creative; that is, it must evolve from his own activity of sensing problems, making guesses, testing and modifying them, and communicating them in his limited way."[1]

Beginning about age three, a child's creativity usually begins to increase, according to Dr. Torrance and other researchers. It seems to reach a peak between four and four and a half. Then it drops suddenly about age five, when the youngster enters kindergarten (probably because of pressures from teacher and classmates to be more conforming). Creativity then rises slowly in the first, second, and third grades, said Dr. Torrance, until there is a sharp drop in the fourth grade.

What are the signs of creativity that you can watch for in your small child? Several researchers have compiled descriptions of creative children you'll find useful. For example, an enormous bump of curiosity is typical of a creative youngster. He loves to experiment, to test the limits of situations. He questions constantly and usually in a penetrating way or on an offbeat tack that can annoy a busy parent or a preoccupied kindergarten teacher who doesn't understand this special type of intelligence.

A creative child isn't often put off by an overly simple answer, or at least not until his basic creative instincts have been blunted. He is particularly sensitive to answers that don't make sense in relation to other facts he knows. Often he invents long, complicated explanations for phenomena he doesn't understand.

A creative youngster is particularly sensitive to what he sees, hears, touches, and experiences. You'll notice this sensitivity not only in the pictures he draws or finger-paints, but also in his surprising understanding of other people and other people's problems. He delights in learning precisely the right word for an object or a feeling or a color. And he enjoys sharing these special observations with an adult who is also aware of them. Because sensitivity is considered somewhat feminine, a highly creative boy may seem a bit less masculine than his friends, only because he doesn't quite match conventional stereotypes.

A creative child generates new ideas like sparks; many of them are offbeat or silly, but a few are surprisingly original and good in relation to his age. He often gives uncommon answers to questions, suggests unusual solutions to problems. He finds unexpected uses for common objects, like the five-year-old who constructed a "nutcracker" for her father's birthday present out of an empty paper tube, a heavy bolt, and a string.

In one test of creativeness designed for school-age children, youngsters are told to list all the uses they can for a brick, other than building. An extremely creative boy or girl may think of thirty-five or forty.

The imagination of a creative youngster is unusually active, delightful, and full of humor. Many preschoolers can turn this vivid imagination on deliberately and do so with great delight. Researchers who study creative children often comment about their "playfulness" and note that many highly achieving, creative adults talk about "playing" with ideas or inventions.

It is characteristic of a creative youngster to attempt tasks far too difficult for him. But instead of considering his failures frustrating, he accepts them as challenges—at least some of the time. His attention span is longer than usual for his age. And he may become so preoccupied with his own thoughts or projects that he may not pay attention to what his parents are saying to him.

Unusual flexibility is another mark of a creative youngster. He is open to suggestions, new ideas, to almost any activity an adult describes as "a new experience." Research shows that in comparison with others, a creative youngster tends to be more self-sufficient, resourceful, stubborn, industrious, introverted, complex, and stable.

Because creativity implies independent thinking, a creative child often seems to be in conflict with his teachers in preschool or kindergarten or with his parents. He may ignore or be ignored by many of his classmates. Teachers may consider him disruptive and impertinent. Deciding to what degree he will give in to social pressures toward conformity may cause him emotional upset, even before he reaches first grade. It helps if a parent is able to talk with him tactfully about these differences, encouraging him to develop his own ideas while still enjoying common activities with playmates.

This uncommon degree of independence may make a creative girl seem somewhat more masculine than her classmates. Social and family pressures to act more feminine may be one reason why many girls do not continue in scientific and engineering fields in which they often show creative abilities when they are very young.

Dr. Torrance, a pioneer in developing tests for creativity in children, often handed a youngster a toy and asked, "How could you change this toy to make it more fun to play with?" He reported that girls were often reluctant to deal with science toys and with a fire truck, objecting that girls don't know anything about toys like that. Boys, in turn, frequently refused to make suggestions about a nurse's kit, on the grounds that boys don't use girls' playthings. Some boys changed the name of the kit to "doctor," and then they felt quite free to produce ideas about improving it, noted Dr. Torrance.

Even parents who feel quite liberated and nonsexist about appropriate male and female activities may be surprised at how many sexist attitudes their offspring seem to absorb from television, playmates, and other sources. You may have to make a point of telling your youngster that toys and games and future plans aren't limited to one sex or the other.

Because he enjoys being independent, a creative child often objects strenuously to what he considers unnecessary rules and controls. He usually prefers to work by himself on his own projects, rather than to participate all of the time in the group-work that dominates so many day-care centers, nursery schools, and kindergartens.

How can you encourage and increase your child's creative abilities? Although research in this field is still incomplete, many positive recommendations can now be garnered from numerous studies. Many of the suggestions for increasing creativity in small children are virtually identical with recommendations already made in previous chapters in regard to overall intelligence. By stimulating a small child to see, to hear, to touch, to manipulate, to explore, and to try for himself, you can foster creativity. A parent who talks happily with a small child—and listens seriously in return—is helping creativity to grow. So is the parent who is enthusiastic about his child's achievements and projects and who encourages his innate curiosity.

In addition, experts on creativity make these recommendations:

• Help your youngster to feel and value his uniqueness, to find satisfaction in expressing his feelings, to experience the joy of creation. Too often, a child feels that he could not possibly think up a worthwhile idea, and so he doesn't follow through on the ideas he does have.

A child needs what Dr. Carl R. Rogers, of the Center for Studies of the Person in La Jolla, California, called "psychological safety" to express his ideas in new and spontaneous ways. A parent who laughs at a youngster's ideas, even in an indulgent way, or who pushes off suggestions with a what-could-you-know-you're-only-a-kid attitude usually convinces his child quite easily that his thoughts couldn't possibly be valuable or worth developing. Of all the image-makers in our society, none is more powerful or more damaging than the adult who casually derogates his own child.

• When you can, let your youngster plan some of his own and your family's activities and use his ideas when it's possible. Even a two-year-old can sometimes decide whether he'd rather have a picnic in the backyard or eat indoors as usual. A four-year-old should be permitted to select which of two or three play outfits to buy (after you have restricted the choice to those suitable in price, size, fabric, and style). Preschoolers should have occasional opportunity to plan family menus ("Which meat shall we have? What vegetables? What for salad?"), weekend fun, and treats.

Permitting a child to make such decisions not only makes him feel that his ideas are worth consideration, but it also helps him realize that decisions have consequences. If you recognize and respect your child as an individual, you'll find that his urgent drive for independence will not be so likely to erupt in undesirable ways.

• Encourage your child to become more sensitive to his environment, to ask questions, to experiment. Many of the suggestions already listed in the section on science in Chapter 6 are useful in this context, too.

• Science activities provide good opportunities to help your child understand that not all experiments succeed and that an experiment that doesn't succeed isn't necessarily a failure.

"Most parents find it extremely difficult to permit their children to learn on their own—even to do their schoolwork on their own," commented Dr. Torrance. "Parents want to protect their children from the hurt of failing."

It is important to teach children how to avoid failure when possible, of course. It is urgently necessary when their physical safety is involved. "But overemphasis may deter children from coping imaginatively and realistically with frustration and failure, which cannot be prevented," said Dr. Torrance. "It may rob the child of his initiative and resourcefulness. All children learn by trial and error. They must try, fail, try another method and, if necessary, even try again. Of course, they need guidance, but they also need to find success by their own efforts."[2]

If this sounds like too rigorous a concept to impose on your child, remember the process by which he learned to walk. How many times did he fail and fall? How long did he try without giving up? How much of the process did he do by himself, without active help or motivation from an adult?

As you study your own child and his reactions to experiences, you'll come to know about how much adult help he needs to function creatively and when he is apt to get discouraged and quit.

• Don't be deterred by traditional concepts of "readiness." New research shows that they are often inaccurate. If you constantly wait to introduce your child to new experiences and new materials until you detect signs of "readiness," you will keep him from being creatively challenged and stimulated.

"Readiness" too often becomes what Dr. Torrance called a "holding-back operation." He said that this reluctance to let children try for fear of failure is one of the most powerful inhibitors of creativity operating in the early childhood years.

"The usual defense of holding-back operations is the fear that the child will become frustrated by failure," said Dr. Torrance. "The ability to cope with frustration and failure, however, is a characteristic shared by almost all outstanding individuals. Certainly, almost all highly creative scientists, inventors, artists, and writers attempt tasks that are too difficult for them. If they did not attempt these overly difficult tasks, their great ideas might never be born."[3]

• Invite your child to try what one educator calls "creative calisthenics" with you. These aren't formal lessons, but games you can play while riding in the car or doing dishes or waiting in the dentist's office.

For example, you can play "How many ways could you use a pencil?" with your youngster. Take turns thinking up as many different, nonwriting uses as you can; for example, a mast for a toy boat or a perch for a birdhouse. Then substitute other common objects for the pencil, such as an empty milk carton, a paper cup, a spool, or an old tire. Be encouraging and happy about his responses—not critical.

• Apply the old necessity-is-the-mother-of-invention gambit. Give your child the need to think creatively by handing him an occasional mind-stretching problem or tough question to ponder: "What would you do if you were lost in the shopping center?" "How could you make a birthday party more fun?" "What can we make with the leftover lumber in the garage?" "How can we find out which is the shortest way to the park?" "What could we use to make trees around the doll house?" "What would help George stop being such a bully?" "What would you do if you had to be the teacher in kindergarten tomorrow?" "Can you invent a good game to play in the car?" "If you had a television station, what kind of programs would you put on?"

You can invite your child to hypothesize by asking him "What if. . ." questions and, if possible, letting him test out his answers: "What if you put a block into a glass that's full of water?" "What if we let a glass of milk sit outside of the refrigerator for a day or two?" "What if you mix red and yellow finger paint?" "And what if you then add blue and green?"

It's also fun to push a what-if game into the realm of fantasy. "What if it never got dark?" "What if everything you touched turned into gold?" "What if adults kept on growing as fast as children?"

• Encourage your youngster to appreciate new experiences—from watching a carrot top sprout in a dish on a windowsill to solving new problems; from observing the subtle shadings in a sunset to learning a new scientific concept (ice cream melts at room temperature, chocolate melts if left in the sun).

• See that your child has a quiet place and time to work on his own, without having to participate in a group, even a family group, all of the time. Most day-care centers and kindergartens, as well as elementary schools in general, place heavy emphasis on sharing and on group activities. Without your active efforts, your youngster may have almost no private time for individual, creative activity. Yet all good ideas begin in a single, individual, human brain.

Richie, a four-year-old attending a university lab school, was working with great concentration on discovering the relationships between number rods. He placed a four-unit rod next to a six-unit one, thought for a minute, and was reaching for a two-unit rod when Mike snatched the materials away. Richie shouted in protest and tried to wrestle the rods back. At this point the teacher intervened. She divided the rods between Richie and Mike and lectured Richie on sharing. But Richie's moment of discovery was lost.

"Don't interrupt a child who is working even to praise him" is a principle emphasized in Montessori schools to protect this irreplaceable instant of creative discovery.

One thing that makes it particularly difficult to provide young children with time to be creative on their own is television. If the TV set is turned on, it becomes such an easy magnet that youngsters simply relax and watch whatever is on without feeling a need to start a project of their own. The most effective way to prevent television from preempting too much of your child's irreplaceable early years is to turn it on only for a limited number of specific, carefully chosen programs and not permit indiscriminate viewing.

• Motivate your child to follow through on his ideas. Too often, brilliant innovations are lost because their inventor did not have the self-confidence or self-control to complete their development. During the preschool years, you can often encourage follow-up by questions like, "How are you going to finish your picture?" or "When you're done with your drawing, let's make a frame for it." Sometimes you can offer additional raw materials. Or you can suggest some positive actions: "I like your idea about rearranging your room. If you'll help, we can fix it your way right now."

• Don't worry if your preschooler enjoys making up stories or weaving fantasies or playing highly imaginative or imitative games. It's a normal part of preschool development. You'll probably be more comfortable about your youngster's use of his creative imagination in these ways if you help him label his stories "made-up" or "pretend" when they are. Set an example yourself by telling him whether the books you read to him are fact or fiction and the TV programs you watch are real events or play-acting.

• Often you can spur creative activity in a youngster by giving him a good reason for trying to be creative. Plan a backyard art fair, for example, with children's masterpieces clothespinned to a clothesline for relatives and neighbors to view, and you may stimulate a minor Renaissance on your block. Start a young marching band, and interest in rhythm instruments among preschoolers will double. Introduce word games on long car trips, and your offspring's awareness of words and their usage will sharpen. Write down some of your youngster's imaginative stories to paste in a scrap-book, and the quantity and quality of the stories will increase.

• Don't teach your child how to do everything step by step, but leave room for his imagination to flourish and for his brain to function. This doesn't mean, of course, that you let your youngster flounder with no preliminary guidance or instruction at all, or that you let him try to work out his own method for such basic physical maneuvers as tying shoelaces. Your youngster does need to learn, for example, the rudiments of using paint and brush, how to hold a pencil, how to manipulate scissors. But his creative feelings will be stifled if you insist on holding his hand to show him how to draw a horse or if you correct his drawing yourself when he has finished.

• You can make positive suggestions when your youngster seems to need them. Often these can be in the form of questions that stimulate his own thinking. If he crayons a horse, you might ask, "Where is the horse going?" "Is someone coming along to ride him?" "Is he standing in a field or beside a barn?" If your young artist is unhappy about the looks of his horse and asks for help, you can suggest that the two of you find some pictures of horses to give him more ideas, rather than tell him specifically what to do.

If your child is making up a story, you can say, "I'd like to know more about that doctor; what did he look like?" Or "Where do you suppose that spaceship came from?" Or "How did that boy feel inside when the giant grabbed him?" Sometimes you can suggest, "What other kind of an ending could you think of for your story?"

One good way in which to encourage creative storytelling is to play "Round Robin Story" with your offspring. He begins a story, starts to develop a plot, and then stops, often in mid-sentence, for you to pick it up. You carry the story line a little further, then toss it back to him.

You can set a pail of water in the corner of the sandbox to make sand-castling more successful. You can locate a big, empty cardboard packing box for your backyard cowboys and Indians to turn into a fort or a jail or for your miniature Martians to use as a spaceship. You can suggest costumes and props when your youngsters need new ideas for imaginative play—paper bags, empty cartons, and canned goods for playing store; stamp pad and index cards for playing library.

• Recognize that creative efforts are often messy. Paints spill. Bug collections add clutter. Experiments with seedlings take space and time. Cherished leaf collections gather dust and crumble. A preschooler who is constantly pricked by fear of being scolded or spanked for making a mess isn't going to feel much of the adventurous excitement of being creative. It's much safer and easier just to watch television.

You will need rules about cleaning up afterward and limits about where in your house finger paints may be used and rock collections displayed. But it may help to remind yourself that no one wins prizes or scholarships or fame for being neat. One mother commented, "I used to fret about how messy my children's rooms are most of the time. Now I just call them 'creative' instead of 'messy,' and I shut the doors when we have guests. I feel much better and my children are happier."

• Do reward your youngster for his creative efforts—by praise, encouragement and interest; by sharing with him the inner joys of creation; by valuing his creative results, even if they don't come close to adult standards. Your surprise and pleasure at what your youngster has discovered or thought or made or said will encourage him to keep trying; your indifference will dampen his innate creative sparks.

• Enjoy being creative yourself and share your feelings with your child. Talk about the color scheme you are trying to create for the living room; the effect you want to achieve in your garden; the solution to a problem you've just worked out; the new recipe you're experimenting with. Let him know when your efforts to be creative aren't spectacularly successful. If the new dessert sinks out of shape or the new casserole seems too dry, you can be casual about it and comment that at least you've learned something and the next one will probably be better. This will help your child to feel that he need not be assured of success before he undertakes a project, and it makes it easier for him to experiment.

Provide your child with plenty of good, simple art materials. Encourage him to use these experimentally and without constant supervision, discouraging criticism or fear that he will make a mess for which you will scold him.

All forms of creativity, even in scientific and engineering fields, are related, many researchers believe. Stimulating your child to be creative with art materials helps him develop sensitivity, originality, flexibility, and imagination—talents necessary for creative thinking in other areas.

Knowing just how much to supervise and suggest is a creative art itself. But if you study your child's individual reactions to your suggestions and comments, you'll soon discover just how best to encourage his efforts and his originality. This is one major reason for being aware of your offspring's need for creative stimulation: You are in a position to know him better than any teacher can and to work with him individually.

You should, of course, show your child the basic ways to use these art materials. But you shouldn't insist that he make his sky blue just because it is or form his clay dog into better shape yourself. It helps to spur your child on if you comment favorably on what he has produced. But your remarks should be sincere, specific, and enthusiastic, in proportion to the effort your youngster has expended.

"You always say what I have drawn is 'interesting,' and half the time you don't even look at it," complained one perceptive five-year-old. "I hate that word 'interesting.' "

Raw materials for preschool art range far beyond crayons and paper, although these will probably be the first craft materials your child uses. Creative art can also be inspired by:

—A package of white paper plates, to decorate with crayons, to turn into picture frames, to make into clocks by adding numbers and hands, or to edge with bells for a tambourine.

—Peanut shells, to paint or ink with faces and to use as fingertip puppets.

—Paper lace doilies, to color for place mats or to trim with ribbon for hats or to use as clothes for clothespin dolls.

—Large sheets of white, dull-finish oilcloth, to map out the streets of your neighborhood. Encourage your youngster to crayon in the houses he knows or to build them with blocks. Add toy trucks, cars, and tiny dolls for a working community.

—Assortment of small, multicolored pads of paper, to mark for parking tickets, plane tickets, paper money, or just to stimulate drawing.

—Old sheeting, to cut up and crayon for place mats or doll-house bedspreads or costumes. Colors will last longer if you place the sheeting color-side down on newspaper, cover with a damp cloth, and press with a hot iron.

—Finger paint in the three primary colors, to stimulate freewheeling art and experiments with color. You can buy it ready-made or mix your own, using liquid laundry starch and food coloring or powdered poster paints. Apply to white shelf paper dampened with a sponge or use it directly on a laminated plastic tabletop, which you and your pint-size Picasso can sponge clean quickly afterward.

For new varieties of paint, combine food coloring with a squeeze of toothpaste or a daub of hand lotion. Both make a delightful finger paint.

As an alternative to fingers in finger painting, try a comb, a small rag, a notched piece of cardboard, or an old hair-roller. To add a new dimension to a finger painting, let it dry, then add more color with a paint brush, or make a second finger painting on top, using a different color. Or try adding a few small dabs of finger paint to a piece of paper, smear slightly, fold in two and open to discover an unpredictable double design. Or finger-paint over squiggles of crayon.

One mother plopped her rambunctious Rembrandt into the bathtub, made "finger paint" by adding two or three drops of food coloring to several squirts of father's foamy shaving cream, and afterward cleaned up both art and artist easily with a soapy bath.

—Long lengths of brown wrapping paper, to make magnificent murals or life-size paper dolls by tracing around real children and crayoning in their features and clothes.

—Chalk, to use on bright or black construction paper, as well as on sidewalks and slate. Or soak sticks of colored chalk in cold water and rub on a sheet of paper that has also been soaked or sponged wet. You can draw with the sides or ends of the chalk, or even rub the chalk about with your fingers. Lay the finished design on a fold of newspaper to dry—and preserve it by spraying it with a fixative. (Hair spray does nicely.) On a sunny day, you can let your child chalk a design on the sidewalk, then decide how he wants to erase it: by letting the rain wash it away, by spraying it away with water in a squirt-type bottle, or scrubbing it away with a brush and a pail of water.

—Collage collection, for young pop art. In a box, assemble a big assortment of bright paper, bits of ribbon, interesting fabric swatches, trimmings, headlines, old Christmas cards, string, seals, stickers, buttons, old postcards, magazine pictures. Your young Michelangelo glues or rubber-cements his choices to construction paper or cardboard or posterboard to make original designs or unique birthday cards.

—Potatoes, to slice in half and use with paint or ink to stamp out patterns and designs. To make other unusual prints, walk fingers across the paper in paint patterns. Or try fork tines, bottle caps, half an orange, a celery stick, corks, carrot halves, clothespin heads, a spoon, checkers, or small blocks dipped into paint.

—Poster paints, for paintings. For unusual variations, instead of a brush, try a feather, a small sponge, a toothbrush, or a wad of paper towel. Or put poster paint and a little liquid laundry starch into an empty plastic squeeze-bottle and use it to apply paint to paper, varying the amount of squeezing, the distance from the paper, and the speed of hand movements. Combine with other colors, in other old bottles.

—Clay or its equivalent, for sculpturing. A five-pound bag of ceramic clay from an art store is most fun. But children also enjoy the homemade kind (equal parts of salt and flour, with water added gradually to the right consistency and powdered paint or food coloring mixed in, too, if you wish). Using cookie cutters, tongue depressors, pipe cleaners, and a rolling pin with clay may stimulate fresh ideas.

—Crayons, basically for drawings. Or your youngster can make crayon rubbings by laying an object with an interesting texture—penny, wood, leaf, corrugated paper, string design, sandpaper, or checker—flat on a firm surface. Cover with paper and rub over it, using the flat side of the crayon.

Or he can shave (with a dull knife or grater) flakes of old crayons into a sheet of shelf paper. You can cover this with another paper and press with a warm iron to melt the crayon. Then, your child can add more to the picture, if he wishes, with black crayon or he can scratch lines into the colors.

—Waxed paper, to make translucent pictures. Spread out a sheet of waxed paper, and on it arrange colored shapes and bits of bright tissue paper in overlapping designs. Add crayon shavings and wiggles of colored thread. Top with a second sheet of waxed paper, cover the whole creation with a piece of plain paper and press it into semi-permanence for your child with a warm iron.

• Enrich your preschooler's life with music in every way you can. Your preschooler will enjoy and profit from having an opportunity to use simple musical instruments, such as an octave of bells, xylophone, rhythm sticks, finger cymbals, a triangle, drums, a tambourine. Or he may also enjoy simple experiments with an autoharp, a piano, or an electric organ if you have one.

A phonograph or cassette player he can operate himself, plus his own records or tapes, gives a preschooler great delight and a good introduction to music. He will also enjoy and appreciate some classical music that has a definite melody, especially if you tell him something about the composition. Records or tapes which introduce the instruments of the orchestra are also helpful.

You've probably been singing lullabies to your baby since you brought him home from the hospital. Gradually, you can add other songs, folk tunes, ballads, musical comedy tunes. He'll enjoy learning a song in a foreign language and singing games and songs with accompanying finger plays.

You can help your preschooler discover more about music by talking about how music makes you feel or want to move about. Good examples: *Peter and the Wolf;* almost any Sousa march; *Swan Lake;* "The William Tell Overture," with its storm and quiet aftermath; "The Skater's Waltz"; "The Flight of the Bumblebee"; Dvorak's "Largo."

Just how much musical talent can be developed during the preschool years has been demonstrated in thousands of children by an extraordinary Japanese teacher of violin, Shinichi Suzuki. The Suzuki program begins at birth, with a mother playing tapes of fine music by her baby's crib and participating actively in music lessons with the youngster during the early years of his life, beginning almost as soon as he is able to hold a small-sized violin.

• Encourage your child to let stimuli from one artistic field suggest creative activities in another, related area. For example, suggest that he make up a dance to go with ballet music; or paint an illustration for a favorite poem; or make a dust-jacket design for a book you've just read to him; or dictate a story for you to write down about a painting he's just made; or finger paint to music.

• You can also suggest to your child that he try to express some of his strong feelings—sadness, fear, worry, joy—in creative activities such as artwork, poetry, or acting.

Nurturing your child's creativity is one of the most delightful privileges of parenthood. Many of your happiest hours with your child will be the times when you share his adventurous thinking and work together on creative projects.

It is urgently important that your child's creative abilities be firmly established before he starts first grade and encounters the stifling, stunting effects of groupism or a teacher who makes it clear to him that he'll get along better if he just obeys orders and doesn't ask questions. Perhaps your youngster will be fortunate enough to have a teacher who knows how to stimulate and value creativity; but even so she must deal with twenty-five or thirty other pupils and cannot give your child what you can. The conforming pressures of classmates will also begin to inhibit and blunt your child's creativity. Unless he has already been sold on the delights of thinking and creating for himself, he will find it easy to fall prey to demands for conformity and mediocrity and the desire not to be different in any way.

9. Montessori Ideas You Can Use at Home

What do little children like to do most of all?

To learn.

What should schools for preschool children teach?

To read, write, understand mathematical concepts, be self-disciplined, self-reliant, courteous, orderly, and to love learning.

Why?

Because the years between two and six are the time when such learning can be absorbed most easily and happily by a child's developing mind.

These tenets, basic to much of the recent research about early learning, were also held by Dr. Maria Montessori, an Italian physician, who put them into practice in the early 1900s with great success. In eclipse for decades in the United States, although not in Europe and India, Dr. Montessori's ideas, techniques, and equipment were rediscovered in the l960s by American educators and parents who see in them a practical and successful way in which to put into operation what the early-learning theorists are talking about. For Dr. Montessori not only formulated many of these theories herself almost a century ago, but she also worked out the best and most complete educational methods to date for implementing these concepts.

"Today, many educators go to great lengths not to admit

they are plagiarizing and mining Montessori for ideas in the field of preschool education," commented a school superintendent. (Dr. Montessori, for example, developed child-size furniture, educational toys, inlaid wooden puzzles, programmed instruction, and much of the other equipment now used in modern preschools.)

Since the rediscovery of Montessori ideas by American parents and educators, enthusiasm for Montessori education has grown enormously. There are now about six thousand Montessori schools in the United States. Many of them were started and are supported by groups of well-educated parents who realize that their three- and four-year-olds are ready for something more mentally stimulating than bead-stringing and finger painting and who appreciate the respectful care with which a Montessori program treats a youngster and protects him from pushing as well as from boredom.

Although most Montessori schools concentrate on three- to six-year-olds, some are now expanding to offer infant and toddler programs in response to the needs of single parents and employed couples. Parents who were enthusiastic about their children's progress in Montessori preschools have also pushed the development of elementary and junior high schools with a curriculum based on Montessori principles. An increasing number of public school districts in many states have set up Montessori elementary schools as magnet programs to give parents a choice in the kind of education their children receive.

Even today, Dr. Montessori remains one of the best sources for practical ways in which to stimulate the mental development of preschool children. There is much in her books and concepts and in the Montessori schools that you can adapt for use at home with your child, whether or not you wish to consider sending him to a Montessori school.

After Maria Montessori was graduated from a medical school in Italy, her first job was working with children in Rome who were classified as mentally retarded. So successful were the methods she developed to stimulate their learning abilities that many of these youngsters equaled or surpassed the records of normal children in school examinations.

So Dr. Montessori asked herself the logical question: What are we doing wrong with normal children that they can be outperformed by the mentally retarded?

Eagerly, she accepted the offer of a job to start a nursery school in one of the early Italian housing projects in an extremely poor area. The sponsors of the school had only one goal—to provide supervision for preschool youngsters while their parents worked and to keep them from damaging the buildings. But Dr. Montessori saw in the school an opportunity to test out her theories about how the minds of very young children learn.

So poor were the youngsters that Dr. Montessori told their mothers that if they had only bread and water to eat, they should make hot bread-and-water soup, so it would seem more filling. The curriculum also had to include such basic instructions as how to take a bath.

In this "Casa dei Bambini," teaching children from the most appalling slums, Dr. Montessori developed the educational philosophy and techniques which were to prove so successful with youngsters from every kind of socioeconomic background. Among the principles she worked out are these:

1. A child, unlike an adult, is in a constant state of growth and change, and the ways in which he changes can be modified greatly by his environment.

2. A young child wants to learn. The task of the adult who loves him is to encourage, to provide opportunities for learning, to permit him to learn by himself.

"Who doesn't know that to teach a child to feed himself, to wash and dress himself is a much more tedious and difficult work, calling for infinitely greater patience than feeding, washing, and dressing the child one's self," Dr. Montessori wrote. "But the former is the work of an educator, the latter is the easy and inferior work of a servant. Not only is it easier for the mother, but it is very dangerous for the child, since it closes the way and puts obstacles in the path of the life which is developing."[1]

3. The mind of even a very young child has great capacity for absorbing a tremendous variety of experience, even though he can't express it verbally. "The most important period of life isn't the age of university studies, but the first

one, the period from birth to the age of six," said Dr. Montessori. "For that is the time when man's intelligence itself, his greatest implement, is being formed."

4. A young child absorbs almost all of his early learning from his environment. To foster learning, his environment should be "prepared" so that he can choose freely from it the learning activities for which he has developed a readiness.

5. The very young child learns much through movement, and his movements should not be restricted any more than is necessary for his physical safety and to avoid interference with the rights of others. He needs great opportunity to move about, to explore, to learn through every sense organ of his body.

6. A youngster goes through specific stages in development when it is easier to acquire certain types of learning than it ever will be again. This is obvious in the development of speech, for example.

"Children pass through definite periods in which they reveal psychic aptitudes and possibilities which afterward dissappear," said Dr. Montessori. "That is why, at particular epochs in their lives, they reveal an intense and extraordinary interest in certain aspects of their environment to the exclusion of others."

7. Sensory-motor activities play a great role in a child's learning. The more opportunities a youngster has to feed sensory stimuli into his growing brain, the more his intelligence will develop.

8. Children learn best in an atmosphere of freedom combined with self-discipline and in an environment prepared to help them learn. The child, said Dr. Montessori, must be free within the classroom to follow his own interests, to move about, to work freely at activities of his choice. But freedom cannot exist without self-discipline and without the development of skills which make a child relatively independent of help from an adult. Limits also must be imposed to protect the rights of others.

9. The teacher must not impose learning upon a young child and must not intrude upon what the child is learning by himself. She should not substitute her will for the child's or rob him of the satisfaction of working on his own tasks.

10. A youngster should be able to learn at his own rate, at his own level of readiness, without being forced to keep up with or wait for a group.

11. A child develops a sense of his own worth by doing any simple task well—whether it is scrubbing a table, pouring water from a pitcher without spilling it, or multiplying 15 times 8. He needs great opportunity for such successes.

12. When a child is given a chance to learn when he is ready to learn, he not only increases his intelligence, but he also gains contentment, satisfaction, feelings of self-confidence, and a desire for further learning.

The great success Dr. Montessori had with her slum-area children drew distinguished educators and visitors from many parts of the world to the "Casa dei Bambini" during the early 1910s. Montessori schools were started and flourished in many parts of Europe and later in India. A few were opened in the United States. But teacher training in this country was generally inadequate. The movement ran headlong into the educational concepts of John Dewey; it was often misinterpreted and misunderstood and it quickly withered.

Dr. Montessori continued to teach, lecture, and write in Italy, throughout Europe, and in India until her death in 1952. It was not until the early 1960s that interest in the Montessori method began to revive in the United States, sparked by new research into the importance of early childhood learning and by the urgent need to find better ways of educating youngsters from poor and disadvantaged families.

The swift spread and obvious success of Montessori schools in recent years have been major factors forcing hard new looks at this country's traditional concepts of preschool education. Some early childhood educators, however, are critical of what they see as a lack of emphasis on social and emotional development in the Montessori curriculum and consider it too rigid and ritualistic for middle-class American youngsters. Others argue that all of the valid Montessori ideas were long ago incorporated into nursery school programs here.

It is true that some of the Montessori equipment, such as inlaid puzzles and child-size furniture, have become part of standard early childhood education. But many critics have taken the tools of Montessori while missing the blueprint for what the tools are expected to accomplish. They have not grasped the Montessori concepts about the absorbent mind, sensitive periods, freedom to work individually at learning tasks of a child's own choice, and the importance of intellectual work at an age when youngsters are so eager to learn.

Except for the size of the children and the furniture, almost everything in a Montessori school differs from what is found in the usual day-care center or nursery school. And everything in a Montessori school—from the colors of the learning materials to the tone of the directress's voice—is precisely planned to stimulate a young child to learn.

For example, when Eric, four, bounces into his Montessori classroom, he begins the morning by hanging up his own coat. First, he spreads it out on a low table. Then he inserts a hanger into the shoulders, fastens the buttons, and hooks the hanger over a low rod. He learned this technique through the programmed instruction which breaks down activities into small steps that he can master. The purpose is to capitalize on a preschooler's fierce desire to "do it all by myself" and to help him gain as much independence as possible from adults in his personal care.

Then Eric changes his shoes for bedroom slippers to help him feel comfortable and to keep down the level of noise which might distract the youngsters from their learning projects.

After a quick "Good morning" to the directress, Eric is free to choose any of the learning activities he wishes. He can use the material as long as he desires. And he is never urged to share it with any other child who happens to want it at the same time. His activity is respected seriously as "work" and no other youngster is permitted to interfere, in contrast to other types of day-care centers where sharing is emphasized regardless of what a child is attempting to accomplish by himself.

In a Montessori school, learning is an independent—not a group—activity. Each child works at his own speed, in his own way, with materials he chooses because of his own ability level and interests. He doesn't compete with any other child. He is neither held back nor pushed for the sake of keeping pace with the group.

The adult in charge of a Montessori classroom is called "directress" instead of "teacher" to emphasize the different kind of relationship she has with the children. Her function is to prepare the environment in which a child can learn, to guide his self-teaching, to answer his questions. She is a "catalytic agent," explained Dr. Urban Fleege, director of the Midwest Montessori Teacher Training Center in Chicago. She does not impose learning upon a youngster, but stimulates him to learn for himself. She seldom praises his accomplishments, so that he learns to look for satisfaction in his work and to learn to please himself, not someone else.

Eric walks quietly around his classroom for a few minutes. Then he pulls out a small piece of rug from a cubbyhole, spreads it on the floor, and picks up a set of number rods, marked off in alternating red and white units. With them he begins to set up a problem in subtraction. When he has arranged the rods to his satisfaction, he gets sandpaper numerals and a minus sign to illustrate his mathematical operation.

Jane, three and one-half, has chosen one of the "practical life" activities. Using a plastic pitcher, she dips water from a big plastic container marked "nice, clean water" and with a sponge and cloth cleans the tabletops. When she's finished, she pours the water into a second container labeled "dirty, old water" and puts her equipment away.

Over by the long row of windows, Jack, four, is arranging a "1000-bead chain," hooking together strips that each contain ten beads until they number 1,000. At each 100-bead interval, he lays out identifying numerals. Jack's project takes him almost an hour, but he doesn't tire of it. When he encounters large numbers later on in elementary school, he'll have a concrete idea of what these symbols mean.

Toby is taking apart and reassembling an inlaid wooden puzzle that is a map of the world, saying the names of the continents under his breath as he handles them. Julie is matching an assortment of bells with eight other bells arranged to make an octave, learning to appreciate subtle differences in sounds and in the patterns they make. Two five-year-olds are reading quietly to themselves. Another is writing words in his notebook.

Three-year-old Marcia is carrying a pile of pink blocks in precisely graduated sizes over to her small rug to build a tower. Like most of the Montessori equipment, the blocks are self-teaching and self-correcting. The youngster using them can tell for herself when she is right and when she needs to correct an error. Like almost all Montessori equipment, the pink blocks are beautifully designed and free of gimmicks that would distract from their purpose and their subtle sense of good design.

When each child has finished a project, he usually smiles in satisfaction, pauses for a minute or two, then puts his equipment carefully away in its special location. After that, he chooses another activity. Occasionally, the directress stops by his rug to see what he's accomplishing. But usually, the inner feeling of achievement is the child's only motivation and reward.

After the youngsters have been working with great concentration and interest for about ninety minutes, the directress quietly begins to walk along an oval stripe painted on the floor of the classroom. Soon, most of the children are following her, except a few who are still too intent on their own projects. Gently, the directress leads the youngsters in activity games designed to strengthen their muscles and give them more mastery over their bodies. They sing two songs in French and play a counting game in French.

Then comes the silence game. Seated around the oval, the children squeeze their eyes shut and sit as motionless as they can. The silence game has two purposes: to show a youngster his progress in self-mastery and to increase his auditory sensitivity.

When all is still, the directress calls each youngster softly by name. One by one, each tiptoes silently to his own little table, painstakingly pulls out his chair, and sits down.

"We teach the children to be silent, not because an adult says so, but in order that they can hear better," explains the directress. "We teach them how to pull out a chair quietly because it gives a child great pleasure to be able to control the chair and himself well."

Juice-break comes next at a Montessori school—but it differs from juice time in other nursery schools. Here, the children take turns pouring the juice themselves, carefully, with great control and no spilling. With great concentration and a tiny smile of pride on her face, a three-year-old carries a tray of little glasses to the other children and distributes them. The pitcher and glasses aren't plastic or paper, but glass; Montessori children take pride in knowing they can handle real things correctly, even if they are breakable.

The Montessori emphasis on self-discipline has raised doubts and opposition from some critics who may be confusing self-control and inner discipline with the rigid control imposed by adults. But Montessorians explain that only through inner discipline can an individual become truly free to learn. Only when he has mastered learning techniques and materials is he free to be creative. Only when he understands reality can he be truly imaginative.

The Montessori program for toddlers offers even younger boys and girls the same kind of orderly, calm environment full of a rich variety of attractive learning materials. Busy toddlers practice pouring dry materials such as rice and small nuts until they are adept at pouring water and fruit juice without spilling. They concentrate with obvious satisfaction on scrubbing tabletops, bathing and dressing dolls, putting together puzzles and stacking blocks, mastering self-help skills, walking along low balance boards, and testing their powers of observation with matching games.

The directresses in the toddler program use the same quiet tone of voice and respectful manner toward their charges as those in the preschool classes. And the youngsters learn to respond in the same courteous manner.

When a two-year-old boy suddenly begins to push a little girl off a rocking horse, yelling "You go away—now," the directress doesn't scold him or insist that the girl share the toy. Instead, she quietly reminds the girl to tell the boy firmly that she is using the horse now and that he can use it only when she is finished. It's a Montessori principle that a child's learning activities should be protected from interruptions, even for sharing.

Preparation for learning to read begins even in the toddler classes, as teachers play games that help the children listen and identify initial sounds of words and names. Even these lessons are designed to have a sense of ritual, to teach mastery of materials. For example, for a language game, a toddler gets an attractive woven mat from a low shelf and spreads it out carefully on the floor. Then he brings a small basket full of fruit and sets it precisely on the mat. As he takes each piece of fruit from the basket and puts it carefully on the mat, he calls out its name, emphasizing the initial sounds as the directress repeats the words as well: "orange, apple, pear, banana, grape." She then calls out the children's names in turn, again stressing the initial sound: "Alyce, Bobby, Michael, Peter, Betsy." When the game is done, the first child carefully puts the fruit back in the basket and returns it to its place on the shelf, then rolls up the mat and stows it properly. Again, he is learning not only self-control but that activities have a beginning and an end and that orderliness makes learning easier.

Not all Montessori schools are alike. Many, especially those affiliated with the American Montessori Society, have added more creative activities, more music and art, and new kinds of learning materials to the traditional Montessori program. But some schools still try to stick faithfully to the original Montessori methods. And others are simply day-care centers and preschools that have incorporated a few Montessori ideas and a little Montessori equipment and use the name "Montessori" without offering a genuine Montessori experience. As in choosing any day-care center or preschool, you should check into the qualifications and philosophy of the staff, observe the activities, and make sure it is what you want for your youngster and what he needs.

Whether or not you want to consider enrolling your child in a Montessori school, you may be interested in reading some of the books by or about Dr. Montessori which are listed in the bibliography. Parts of most of these books are obviously out of date and do not apply to contemporary children. But they still contain a wealth of ideas and insights into the gentle ways that can foster the learning development of small children.

Not all Montessori activities are applicable to homes and parents. Some depend upon the establishment of a large "prepared environment" in which a child is free to choose his own learning tasks. And a parent can't maintain the same type of low-key, rather impersonal relationship that a Montessori directress has with a child. Some of the equipment is expensive and difficult to obtain, although some can be ordered from the American Montessori Society, 150 Fifth Avenue, New York, N.Y. 10011. Montessorians warn that the equipment itself is no guarantee of success; it's essential that a parent know how to use it and when to introduce it to his child.

But many Montessori ideas and techniques do work splendidly at home. Accurate, well-made copies of some Montessori equipment can be found in good toy stores and in school supply catalogs. Other materials have been adapted into games and equipment quite similar to the Montessori originals. Parents who understand Montessori purposes can often make or find inexpensive substitutes that accomplish the same learning purposes.

In adapting Montessori ideas for your child, it helps to keep in mind these guidelines, which have been worked out for parents by Montessori directresses:

—Teach your child with real things. If you take time to show him how to handle materials and equipment carefully, he will be capable of far more than you realize.

—When you want to teach your youngster a new activity or skill, plan it out first as a programmed teaching exercise. Break it down into small, precise steps. What points of interest does the activity hold for your child? How can possible error be controlled by the activity itself, not by your verbal instructions? (In helping a child learn how to polish shoes, for example, a Montessori directress slips a piece of white paper under the shoe. The youngster can tell immediately when the polish is not going on the shoe because of the marks on the paper.) Can you isolate a single learning element you want your youngster to absorb?

—When teaching a small child, slow down your movements. Use as few words as possible. Let your movements guide your youngster's eyes to what he is to learn. (For example, in teaching a child how to use scissors, show him how to pick them up safely, to hand them to someone else, and to cut a straight line. Then let him practice, progressively, on thick straight lines, thinner lines, curves and angles, and finally on pictures.)

The purpose of this type of teaching is not to direct every move your child makes or to force your methods on him. It is simply to give him a successful way of doing something he wants to do urgently at this stage in his life. He can do it other ways if he wishes. But at least he will know one sure way that he can count on.

—Cultivate the art of not helping your child whenever he can do a task for himself. "Any unnecessary aid is a hindrance to learning," commented Dr. Montessori decades ago.

—Whenever you can, arrange your home and equipment so that your child can manage for himself. Make his table and chair low enough, his toy-storage shelves accessible, his clothing equipped with fasteners he can work, his closet rod the right height. Then don't do anything for him that he can do for himself.

—Give your child enough time to do a task without hurrying. He usually works at a slower, more deliberate speed than an adult and needs to repeat activities often, even after he appears to have mastered them.

—See that your preschooler has as much choice as possible over his own activities and learning. He can't live up to his potential unless he has the opportunity for independent work.

—Don't insist that your youngster try a new activity if he isn't interested. Don't make him stick at a learning task when he doesn't want to.

One reason for the great success of the Montessori method is this freedom of choice offered to the child. For a youngster's responses and interests are the best guide adults have to his level of readiness for learning. And this technique is a parent's best protection against undesirable pressuring and pushing.

—Make discipline in an activity interesting whenever you can. Say, "See how quietly you can close the door." Or "See if you can spread the peanut butter all the way to the edge of the bread."

—Don't ever rob a child of the feeling of satisfaction of having done a job all by himself. Don't do over any activity that he has done while he is watching. If he is not succeeding and is becoming frustrated instead of continuing his efforts, suggest a more simple, but related game or project that will help him acquire the necessary skills. For example, if he is having trouble controlling a pitcher when he wants to pour a glass of water, encourage him to try pouring easier substances, such as sugar or rice, from one container to another, until his muscular control has improved.

—Whenever you can, protect your child from interruptions while he is concentrating on any activity, even if it seems pointless and repetitious to you. His learning is work of the highest importance, and if you have respect for him and what he is trying to do, it will be much easier for you to teach him respect for others and their work.

—A useful Montessori way of helping a child learn the exact name of an object is called the three steps of Seguin (based on a teaching technique of Dr. Edouard Seguin, a nineteenth-century philosopher and educator who had great influence on Dr. Montessori). First, put three objects—for example, a paint chip of red, one of blue, and one of yellow—in a row in front of the child. First, point to the red and say, "This is red." Then, pointing, say, "This is blue" and "This is yellow." Then tell the child, "Point to blue. Point to red. Point to yellow." In the third step, the teacher or parent changes the order of the objects and pointing to each one asks the child, "What is this?"

Some learning activities based on Montessori techniques and ideas have already been described in this book. But here are others which you and your child will enjoy and which will help educate his senses and aid in his mental development:

—For a happy game that develops motor skills, draw a wide circle or an oval on the floor with chalk. First, let your child walk it, placing one foot directly in front of the other and precisely on the mark, until he can balance well. Then, encourage him to try it carrying a glass of water without spilling it as he walks, or a bell without letting it ring, or a bean bag on his head without letting it slip.

—To stimulate your child's tactile sensitivity, cut out matching pieces of cloth of several different textures—velvet, silk, seersucker, corduroy, chiffon. When your child can match them easily by sight and touch, blindfold him and let him try it by touch alone.

—Put a dozen simple objects in a paper bag, with the top tied just tightly enough to let your youngster slip his hand in. He is to identify each object by touch before taking it out.

—For a game to foster visual perception, you can get two sets of paint chips from a hardware store and mount each one on cardboard to make a color-matching activity. (Some mothers use two sets of spools of thread in a range of hues.)

A two-year-old can begin by matching just the three primary colors. Later, various shades of each color can be added to make the game more challenging. As he becomes more skilled, a child can learn to arrange the shades in order from lightest to darkest. (Children in Montessori schools learn to match and arrange sixty-four different shades.) Finally, in a color-memory game, you can show your youngster one shade, then send him into another room to choose the matching hue from a pile of all the colors.

—Obtain four small medicine-type bottles of opaque glass with droppers. Into one, put lemon juice and into another, vinegar. Into the third, put sugar and water, and into the fourth, a diluted syrup. Drop a little from one bottle at a time onto your child's tongue and ask him to identify whether it is sweet or sour. Most preschoolers delight in making appropriate faces for the sour substances.

—To sharpen your child's auditory abilities, take small, empty salt shakers or little cardboard boxes and fill pairs of them with different substances—sand, gravel, rice, pebbles, for example—that make a noise when your child shakes them. First, he should learn to match the pairs of sounds. Later, he can arrange them in order of loudness.

—You can play the same kind of game by obtaining half a dozen small glass or plastic bottles that you can cover with paper, three with one color and three with another. Then fill one of each color with a fragrant spice from your kitchen and repeat, using two more spices. Uncap the bottles and let your child smell them, then match them by their scent. You can add more pairs of spices as he becomes adept at recognizing them.

—This basic technique can be adapted to help your child

learn many different types of things. For example, you can buy or collect two identical, inexpensive sets of mineral specimens. First, have your child learn to match the minerals. Then teach him their names. Later, he can learn to arrange them according to hardness or group them into other classifications.

—Lotto cards of different kinds can be used to help your child learn about animals—first by matching them, then by learning their names, and finally by classifying them according to families or habitats. Other subjects you can use in this way include leaves, trees, dinosaurs, flowers, insects, birds, and geometric shapes.

—To help your child learn more about himself, have him lie down on a large sheet of wrapping paper and trace around him with a thick pencil. He can then crayon in his features and his clothing and cut out his outline.

—To stimulate his ability to observe accurately and record his observations skillfully, let your youngster use a window-pane instead of paper for drawing. He can trace the shapes that he sees through the glass on the window with crayon and learn easy lessons in perspective, shapes, comparative sizes, and structures by himself. He'll even enjoy polishing the window clean again with a commercial cleaning solution.

—For a game that combines finger dexterity with size discrimination, you can put screws and matching nuts of several different sizes in a small bowl. Your child can unscrew the nuts and put them on one side of the table and the screws on the other. Then he can rematch and reassemble them.

—Young children in Montessori schools voluntarily choose and enjoy a variety of "practical life" activities. You can arrange most of these experiences easily for your youngster at home. For example, you can provide him with two plastic bowls or basins, a small pitcher, a sponge, a small towel, and an apron. Then you can show him step by small step how to put on the apron, fill the pitcher with water in the sink, carry it over to a low table, and fill one of the basins carefully with water. Then, after your demonstration, he can dampen the sponge with water, squeeze it, and use it to wash tabletops or the floor, squeezing out the dirty water into the second bowl and freshening the sponge again in the first bowl. When he is done, he should empty the bowls in the sink, dry them with the towel, and put them and his apron away. For variations, your child can use similar equipment and procedures to bathe a doll or, with an added scrub brush, wash and dry dishes or clean other washable objects. Most young children in Montessori schools enjoy such activities and repeat them often.

HOW TO ...

10. Computers and Preschoolers

How much can a preschooler do with a home computer? Push a few buttons to call up some flashy graphics that hold his attention about as long as most new toys? Practice programmed drills with number facts? Begin to write before he learns to read? Discover some basic elements of computer programming that will ease his way into the technology of the twenty-first century? Nudge his brain into logical, orderly thinking? Stretch his mind with an open-ended opportunity for thinking in new ways?

Three-, four-, and five-year-olds are doing all of the above—with a concentrated enthusiasm that surprises traditional educators, but not computer buffs or adults keyed into early-learning concepts.

It's not yet clear what role computers will eventually have in day-care centers, preschools, kindergartens, and elementary schools. But there's no doubt parents by the millions—out of their own excitement about computers or their eagerness to help their youngsters learn—are introducing young children to computers at home. There is a major market for new software programs created for preschoolers and a substantial share of home computers are bought by families with at least one child younger than age seven.

Few extensive studies about the effects of computer use by preschoolers are yet available. But rich, detailed reports of experiments with computers in university-connected laboratory nursery schools and of individual experiences in homes with computers bubble with enthusiasm. Computers, say their boosters, not only help children with traditional kinds of learning, but offer the possibility of entirely new dimensions in thought and logic.

The early childhood educators who raise doubts about the benefits of giving a preschooler computer access do so because they consider a computer rather like another television screen—a mesmerizing medium that tends to deprive a youngster of time to socialize and interact with the real world. Or they see it turning a home or school into a video arcade hypnotizing children with moving stick figures and flashing lights. Teaching, they protest, should be left to human teachers.

But educators and computer experts who have actually been involved with children using computers almost all are convinced that young children not only can use a variety of software programs, but can learn some simple computer language and create simple programs of their own.

"Everybody I know who is working with computers and children is finding that our old models of what children can do are changing," said Dr. Ann McCormick Piestrup, who heads the Learning Company, which designs computer programs for children. "They can understand coordinates at ages three and four, and do plotting of computer graphics. They can visualize things in three-dimensional space with positive and negative numbers at the age of seven—which is the youngest I've tried it; perhaps younger children could do it—and then perform transformations on these objects similar to what is taught in college and graduate school.[1]

"Why? There was never before a medium that makes these abstract things concrete the way a computer does. Computers can build a success orientation that's as good as the best that teachers can do. Children can be on the learning edge, where they are challenged but feel competent.

"It is possible to make the computer smart enough that a very young child can approach it and use it as a world to experiment in—rather than have a simple sequence that concludes with 'You're right' or 'You're wrong.' It is possible to make the computer like a sandbox, where you fill up a little cup with sand and pat it down and turn it over. And if it doesn't make a nice little sandpile, you can think, 'Well, maybe if I wet the sand . . . ' "

"Good computer programs give young children the opportunity to enhance their pretending, learning, and experimenting," said Fred D'Ignazio, associate editor of a computer magazine. "Good software should meet the acid test of letting children do something they can do only on a computer. Otherwise you might have just bought an expensive pencil."[2]

Children as young as three can begin using a computer advantageously, agree most of the educators and computer enthusiasts who have tried it. Although they need some close supervision and adult help at first, preschoolers can become quite independent. Three- and four-year-olds can learn to operate a computer properly and to take good care of it and the diskettes they use. They can use a keyboard and even create simple programs themselves.

In fact, the sense of control and competence young children seem to feel about using a computer suggest that it may be a good way to help them develop feelings of autonomy, one educator said.

Some educators have worried that computers would push youngsters into isolated interaction with a machine. But just the opposite seems to happen when a computer is put into a preschool, a kindergarten, or a day-care center. The children rarely work at the computer alone. Usually at least one other child and sometimes a group gathers around to watch and make suggestions.

Typically, children help each other figure out what to do, especially if their teachers have had little computer experience. In fact, teachers usually report that cooperation and interaction among youngsters may increase when a computer is added to a classroom. For example, sometimes it's the children themselves, rather than a teacher, who figure out a way to make sure everyone gets a fair share of computer time.

To counter these concerns, some computer programs are deliberately designed to be what is called "pro-social"—to encourage group play and person-to-person interaction. Two youngsters may discover, for example, that winning a computer game may depend on how well two players can work together; one person alone can't win.

"Another social effect of using computers appears to be that a child's sense of self or self-esteem is fostered by the confidence and satisfaction generated by having control of the computer, making choices during a program, learning to program, and so on," suggested Mina Spencer and Linda Baskin, in a report on the use of computers by young children for the National Institute of Education. "Self-concept development has been noted by several teachers working with young children."[3]

Computers can provide several types of learning for young children—with some start-up help from adults. Software programs are being introduced so rapidly by such a variety of computer companies and educational publishers that it is impossible to critique individual examples here. But for youngsters, admirers of computers see them as playing these roles:

Electronic flashcard machine—Some of the software touted for preschoolers does little more than show them a series of flashcard images that can be matched or moved around by punching keys on a keyboard or moving a joystick or used for a simple drill-and-practice exercise. The programs usually reward correct answers with smiling faces or dancing cartoon figures or electronic sound effects.

These programs do give young children a chance to begin using a computer—with all of its powerful fascination and mystique. They can make youngsters feel important, successful, and competent and give them the learning satisfaction of being the cause of an electronic effect. Preschoolers can learn about shapes by manipulating them on the screen. They can match, compare, and contrast colors and sizes, drill on number facts, and learn letter shapes.

But except for the fun and learning experience of working the computer itself, most of this kind of learning can be done as well, or better, by manipulating real things directly. Preschoolers can understand concepts like "bigger" and "smaller," "under" and "over" much better by lifting and shifting concrete objects rather than electronic symbols. Some of the software programs suffer by being cutesy and so gimmicky it distracts from what they intend to teach.

235

Electronic teacher—Most programs used in schools provide what is known as "computer-assisted instruction" or CAI. These programs are designed to take a learner step by step toward a specific educational objective, providing drill and practice in the process.

A good computer teaching program offers a child several happy advantages. It can help him learn at his own speed. It can give him encouraging praise as happy feedback and reinforcement when he's right. It can let him move ahead to fresh challenges as soon as he's ready, so that he isn't bored.

A computer can correct a child's mistakes gently and in private, so that he need not fear being embarrassed or ridiculed by trying and failing in public. And if he's making a pattern of errors that suggests he's missed an element in a learning sequence, it can back up and try another way to teach the same point.

Another big advantage of using a computer for drill and practice and learning tasks that require memorization is that it's much more fun. The best of this software comes with several different skill levels, so that children can test their own knowledge and control the pace of their own learning.

But these programs give youngsters what are essentially electronic workbooks. They aim to move children more efficiently and happily toward traditional educational goals imposed on the learner by a teacher-programmer. And, said one critic, they have no more influence on student achievement than changing the truck that delivers the groceries improves children's nutrition.

"Much of the available software is poorly designed and deadly dull," said another. "That's a lot of junk out there."

"Drill and practice programs are occasionally useful for learning something like arithmetic," said Dr. Radia Perlman, in a report on research at the Artificial Intelligence Laboratory at the Massachusetts Institute of Technology. "However, it is more fun to use such a program if one writes it oneself.[4]

"Drill and practice programs are easy to write, and the child will certainly play with any program he writes. In ordinary computer-aided instruction, the child has little control over the environment, and any of the worthwhile aspects of the CAI environment can be duplicated by the child in an environment the child controls."

Computer enthusiasts and educators tuned in to the ideas of early learning see a much more creative role for this powerful new machine that holds such enormous fascination for children. Instead of shaping computer programs to simulate traditional classroom learning, they want to key youngsters in right from the beginning to the new kinds of thinking and symbol manipulation a computer makes possible. They see computers playing these kinds of roles with children:

Electronic playground—People who use and program computers often talk about "playing" with them and wanting to create software that encourages a sense of "playfulness" in young children. They aren't talking about "play" in the sense that teenagers stand in front of *Star Wars* games in video arcades playing to run up points. They are using the word as do inventive and creative adults who talk about "playing" with ideas and discoveries.

"A computer is a toy that never runs out of capabilities," pointed out Dr. Perlman.

One reason why it's important to help children see a computer as a playground and not just a drill-and-practice machine is explained by Dr. Perlman.

"The most important thing the child learns in an imaginative computer environment is a fearless, joyful attitude toward learning," said Dr. Perlman. "Very few programs run correctly the first time. One of the most enjoyable activities one engages in when communicating with a computer is debugging, finding out why the computer misunderstands what you want it to do.

"An answer on a multiple-choice test is either right or wrong, but the word 'wrong' is meaningless when applied to a computer program. The word 'right' is almost meaningless, too, since most programs can be improved or made fancier. The concept of debugging can be applied to any skill the child wishes to learn. Eventually, the concept of 'failing' at an activity will be meaningless to the child. If he is not doing the activity as he wants, he will try to discover where the bugs are and correct them, instead of ever giving up."

You can buy software games for your preschooler that teach as well as delight. Many inventive and joyful games help children learn a variety of important concepts, like, for example, a lemonade-stand game that lets youngsters play with the basic ideas of free enterprise and profit-and-loss.

Computer programs can let young children play at building monsters, killing dragons, solving puzzles, manipulating characters in a story, managing a railroad, getting power for a peanut-butter machine, and, of course, flying missions into outer space. The best of them can be played at several different levels of skill and difficulty that a child can choose for himself.

But the most "playful" programs, in the sense that computer programmers mean, are those a child can write himself and use to explore his own ideas.

Electronic sketchbook—Some of the first things young children discover about computers is how to create bright visual effects with programs that let them wash color over the screen, create rainbows, fill a garden with flowers, and direct shapes and patterns to dance across the screen. What a youngster is learning is not only another way to create art, but how to manipulate a marvelously responsive medium.

But critics point out that producing art by pushing keys is a pale imitation of the richer creative experiences children get when they use even such simple art materials as crayons or fingerpaint. And with basic art materials, children can be much freer in mixing colors and using their imagination than when they are limited by the need to program a machine.

Electronic pencil—Four- and five-year-olds have been taught to write and read by computer programs ever since Dr. Moore developed an elaborate system for doing so in the mid-1960s. Today, several programs are available that teach preschoolers simple writing and reading skills—some of them building on the theory of Dr. Montessori that writing comes first and easiest to a young child, who then discovers he can not only read his own material but other written words as well.

Writing with a simple word-processing program is ideal for young children for several reasons. Punching a keyboard is easier mechanically than printing out letters or using script, and freed from this painstaking labor, children can much more easily turn out sentences and little stories that have substance and hold their interest.

A computer makes it easy to correct and erase mistakes and to polish their creations, so that children can take great pride in the results. Experimental programs with five-year-olds in kindergartens show they can turn out logical, coherent stories of three and four paragraphs, with a little help with spelling. Pilot programs have been so successful that some educators are predicting that computers—perhaps with supplemental electronic typewriters—will be standard equipment in kindergartens.

Electronic hearth—A home computer can replace the television set as the focal point of the family room, the hearth around which parents and children gather to learn, socialize, and have fun together, computer enthusiasts say. Most youngsters say they prefer using a computer to watching television because they can have control over it, informal surveys show.

But an electronic hearth isn't a home atmosphere children can build by themselves. Parents must be willing to share their own enthusiasm for computers with their offspring. And one programmer told a *Wall Street Journal* reporter he thinks the greatest value a computer can provide for very young children is to give them time on the laps of parents who are computer addicts.

Electronic mudpie—The "mudpie" metaphor is Dr. Papert's. An associate of Dr. Piaget at the University of Geneva in Switzerland for six years, Dr. Papert sees the computer as giving children access to a whole new world of abstract ideas that they can manipulate as a natural part of their environment, as they might make a mudpie.

He also sees the computer as a way to embed basic mathematical ideas in children's environments in such a natural way that they will learn them as easily as they now acquire their native language. Youngsters will grow up speaking mathematics naturally, just as they now learn English, he envisions.

"The importance of the computer is that a whole range of abstract entities which could not physically be manipulated before can be now. They can become concrete. One can play with them, push them around," he said.[5]

"Now, putting the computer in the hands of the child and allowing the child . . . to play with the computer like a mudpie could mean that the child will learn certain concepts in a natural way. He or she wouldn't need to be 'taught' it . . .

"You can make a mudpie when you want to and play with it as your personal desires direct you. You do not practice mudpie ten minutes a day, because your schedule says that now it is mudpie time. In other words, I am talking about a world in which children have free access to a computer. They can decide where to go with it and what they want to do with it. They can play with it without adults standing over their shoulders. They can take possession of it, rather than be possessed by it."

Dr. Papert invented the computer programming language called LOGO especially for the use of young children. Using LOGO, youngsters can direct a little "turtle" symbol to draw all kinds of geometric patterns on the screen and in the process develop their ability to think logically and in mathematical concepts.

"Using the computer to concretize learning that is ordinarily abstract, the child absorbs it more quickly and easily, more thoroughly and at an earlier age," pointed out Dr. Papert. "The child can enter a personal relationship with mathematical material.

"Drill and practice might be a good thing," said Dr. Papert. "There are some statistics to show that drill and practice will produce some significant improvement in standardized achievement scores, and I don't want to deny that. But if we think of computers in terms of five or ten years from now, is drill and practice going to be a typical use? I think not.

"Giving to children microworlds that have—whether through LOGO or word processing or access to the computer in a more creative way—a more child-centered, freeflowing, intuitive approach, that style of using the computer is what we need to learn about now, because that's what the future needs."

Will you handicap your child for his twenty-first-century future unless you buy him a computer and an assortment of software for his third birthday? Not yet, say the researchers most enthusiastic about preschoolers' ability to use computers. But there are growing concerns that the opportunity to use a home computer that affluent parents can give their children may widen the gap between these youngsters and those from poor families who don't get this early boost.

It's worth remembering that the extraordinary computer geniuses who sparked the explosive growth of the computer industry in the 1970s and 1980s didn't learn their calling as young children; instead they brought a sense of playfulness, creativity, intelligence, and openness to discovery to a marvelous new kind of machine with unlimited capabilities.

This book gives you a wealth of good ways to foster your child's mental development at little or no direct cost. It isn't necessary to provide an expensive computer and software to help your child's mind grow well. You can do an extraordinary job of increasing your child's intelligence and learning abilities with much simpler methods and materials.

Moreover, you can't just buy a computer and some software, bring it home, plug it in, and plop your youngster in front of it like a kind of electronic baby-sitter, the way some parents use television. While a child can rather quickly become independent in using a computer, he does need adult guidance in getting started.

But if you do have a home computer you enjoy using, it will benefit your youngster if you can share some of your enthusiasm with him and get him started on good learning software and, more important, simple programming of his own.

Computers are changing much too fast for this book to be able to recommend any particular model. Software programs for young children are multiplying like dandelions in the spring; some are excellent, but many are little better than overly gimmicked coloring books. Some manufacturers are experimenting with ways to make keyboards easier for preschoolers to use, such as arranging them in alphabetical order and refitting them with larger keys. Such gimmicks probably aren't necessary and may be handicapping because they will require some relearning later on.

But if you've been following the ideas in this book and observing the ways in which your child learns, you will be able to tell whether a particular machine or a specific program will hold his attention and help his mind to grow. If you can provide a good match between your child and a computer program, you can share his joy in discovering some of the potentialities of a marvelous invention. As a research assistant in a Stanford University preschool using computers in an experimental program commented, "You can see learning happening."

11. How to Safeguard Your Child's Brain

Kevin was four on the wintry day that his father bundled him up and took him for a ride on the new sled he'd gotten for Christmas. The afternoon was brisk and bright and a fresh fall of snow covered the nearby beach where Kevin had enjoyed playing the previous summer. But the temperature was falling. And a chilly wind was rising off the lake.

Suddenly the sled hit a hidden bump and flipped on its side. Kevin spilled out and, before his horrified father could catch him, tumbled into the water. His bulky snowsuit quickly filled with water and the boy quickly sank out of sight into the dark, icy lake.

Kevin's father screamed for help and ran into the water, searching desperately for the child he could no longer see. A passerby dashed to help. Another flagged down a police car that radioed for paramedics and an ambulance. Frantic minutes went by—perhaps twenty in all—before Kevin's body was found and pulled to the surface. Even though the child was obviously dead, the policemen began cardiopulmonary resuscitation.

Just a minute or two later, the paramedics arrived. They began pouring oxygen into the boy's lungs, while continuing to pump on his chest in an effort to restart his heart. They, too, detected no sign of possible life, no pulse, no heartbeat, no movement of the eyes, no response. Still, they worked on in the chilling cold, hating to give up, hating to lose a child.

Frantically, they rushed Kevin into the ambulance and continued their efforts on the way to a children's hospital nearby.

At the hospital, a team of dedicated physicians took up the seemingly lost battle to save Kevin. They were hoping that two factors might tip the deadly odds against the child: The bitter cold might have quickly lowered the demands of Kevin's body for oxygen so that his brain might have survived. And the "diving reflex" might have channeled whatever oxygen the body had to the brain in a desperate strategy to survive.

Then the impossible happened. Kevin's pulse began to flutter. His heart started to beat on its own. And his breathing resumed, first in gasps and then with more regularity. For days, physicians kept the little boy sedated, using every medical means to minimize damage to his brain and to make his recovery as complete as possible.

But when Kevin at last regained consciousness, it was apparent that some brain damage had occurred. He had forgotten most of his four-year-old's explosive vocabulary. He had difficulty walking. And he had to relearn most of the skills he had acquired in the last two or three years of his short life.

With months of extensive therapy—at the hospital, at a rehabilitation center and at home—Kevin has been improving steadily. His motor skills have returned. So has his speech. He started school in a class for children with learning disabilities, but eventually, physicians hope, most of the traces of his tragic accident will disappear.

Just how much intellectual ability a child has at any given time is the result of three interacting factors, according to Dr. Richard Masland, former director of the National Institute of Neurological Diseases and Blindness.[1] These factors are:

1. The basic, genetic quality of the youngster's brain and the rest of his central nervous system, which he inherits.

2. Changes in or damage to this central nervous system by injury or disease, either before or after birth.

3. The impact upon the child's brain of his environment and his experiences.

You can't change the first factor—the quality of the brain

244

that your youngster possesses. This is determined by the complex of genes carried within the egg and sperm that joined at his conception. These in turn reflect his biological heritage from both his father's and his mother's families for innumerable preceding generations. The third factor has already been discussed at length in this book.

This chapter is concerned with the second of Dr. Masland's factors—what you can do to protect from injury and disease the brain your child has inherited, so that it will develop optimally and function effectively. Chapter 12 details more than a dozen steps that you can take during pregnancy to increase the likelihood that any future baby you have will be born with the best uninjured, healthy brain possible.

In the United States today there are at least five million individuals who have been diagnosed at some time in their lives as being mentally retarded. Probably an even larger number of people function inadequately throughout their lives because of a lesser degree of mental retardation or slight, unidentified brain damage or dysfunction.

In recent years, medical researchers have discovered that a substantial percentage of boys and girls who have behavior problems, who have trouble learning in school, who are overactive, hard to discipline, poorly coordinated, easily distracted, and who have specific learning disabilities may suffer from minor brain damage or dysfunction. Often this damage is so subtle that it can't be detected by the limited diagnostic techniques doctors now have. But it can sometimes be assumed because the child's symptoms match those of youngsters with proven brain injury and because the case history indicates when the damage probably occurred.

Children with minor brain damage are usually average, or above, in overall intelligence. But because of their difficulties and distortions in perception and because of other problems, they usually have a struggle learning to read and aren't able to make full use of their intelligence. Often these learning disabilities trigger secondary emotional problems, too.

At least 50 percent of all mental retardation can be prevented, even with the limited knowledge now available, the American Medical Association has estimated. So can much of the learning disability caused by brain injury. Many of the known ways to prevent brain damage lie chiefly within the control of parents—either before a child's birth or after. That's why it's important for you to learn about possible dangers to your child's brain and the ways in which you can protect him from learning disabilities and mental retardation—just as you guard his physical health from injury and disease as much as possible.

Odds are excellent that your child will be born with a normal, healthy brain, which will continue to grow and develop throughout childhood without injury. But a youngster's mental abilities are not something to leave to chance. You owe it to your offspring to learn all you can about the preventable causes of mental retardation and learning disabilities and to give him all the protection you can.

Here are some of the most important ways:

—Arrange to have your child in the care of a skilled and up-to-date physician who will give him regular medical checkups and all recommended immunizations.

It's becoming tempting, in recent years, for parents to be casual about immunizing their children to what used to be common diseases of childhood, like measles, whooping cough, and mumps. Widespread immunization programs have drastically reduced the incidence of these illnesses so that parents can easily assume that their youngsters simply will not be exposed to them. Some mothers and fathers also worry about the possibility their child could have an adverse reaction to the vaccine.

But measles (the regular, "red," two-week variety which doctors call rubeola), in particular, has not yet been eradicated by the vaccine that became available in 1963, despite widespread hopes that it could be. Although the number of reported cases has been reduced by 99 percent, it still occurs in the United States in localized epidemics—occasionally on college campuses and, particularly worrisome, even in hospitals.

Measles used to be considered a childhood nuisance, a necessary but rather minor evil. But measles can kill and is also the most serious cause of mental retardation of all the common childhood diseases. About one in every one thousand measles victims suffers a serious complication, such as pneumonia or encephalitis, and one third of these are left with severe, permanent brain damage. Researchers also report that measles, even in a mild form, may be a cause of less severe degrees of mental retardation, learning difficulties, and personality or behavior changes. Measles "can knock the edge off children's I.Q.s," warned Dr. James L. Goddard, when he was commissioner of the Food and Drug Administration. And the danger of brain damage from measles is greatest among preschoolers, researchers point out.

Today there is no need to risk even the most remote chance that measles could take the edge off your child's intellectual abilities. Effective measles vaccine is available, and your baby should be vaccinated against the disease as a routine part of his well-baby care during the first year of his life. The vaccine gives long-lasting, apparently permanent protection against the disease.[2]

Health experts still hope that with the cooperation of parents—and the United Nations and governments worldwide—measles can eventually be eliminated, as has smallpox. But it won't happen if the level of immunization falls. And until it does, you owe your child protection against what can turn into a tragic or deadly disease.

Besides measles, there are other infectious diseases and disorders which can damage the brain of a child who was born healthy and normal, and thereby limit his intelligence. Most of these, fortunately, are rare. Others are uncommon complications of diseases as ordinary as mumps and chickenpox. Some of these afflictions, like cretinism, can be corrected rather easily if diagnosed and treated early in life. Some can be prevented completely by routine shots on standard schedules. Some come on insidiously, slowly; others start with convulsions and fever and fear in the night.

No layperson can hope to know enough about all of these brain-damaging hazards to children. You don't need to. But it is important that your child be under the regular, routine care of a good physician who keeps informed of new research and who is as close as your telephone.

It is safer today to raise a child in the United States than ever before in history. Good, routine care and preventive medicine are two major reasons why. But it is still up to parents to take the initiative to make sure these are available to their children.

—Take reasonable precautions to prevent accidents which can injure your child's brain.

Sometimes you feel as if only a wrestler could keep your seven-month-old squirmer from wiggling off the table while he's being diapered. Or only a professional athlete could supervise a two-year-old explorer closely enough to stop him from tumbling down the stairs or off the top of the bookcase. Or only a Marine sergeant could bellow emphatically enough to make a four-year-old sit safely still in the car while you're driving.

But you must protect your child against accidents. For injuries involving the head can cause brain damage, which is reflected in loss of intellectual ability.

"If parents could see what happens to a child's electroencephalogram when he's hit on the head or falls down stairs and is knocked out for a minute or two, they wouldn't take accidents so casually," commented Dr. Frederic Gibbs, a neurologist and pioneer in the use of the EEG for brain research.

Accidental injuries cause about half of all deaths among children between the ages of one and fourteen. At least a hundred times that many youngsters suffer nonfatal injuries.[3]

Almost all head injuries can be prevented. In fact, many safety experts are urging that the word "accident" be replaced by "injury," to avoid even suggesting that what happened was a chance event that could not have been prevented.

Two cardinal principles to remember in protecting your baby or toddler from falls are these: He's stronger and quicker than you think. And every day he can do more than he did yesterday.

Starting the day you bring your infant home from the hospital, you should make it a habit not to leave him alone on a table or counter or in a bathinette, even for the second it takes to turn around for a fresh diaper. Even before he learns to roll over, a baby can dig his heels into a tabletop and shove himself off.

248

Never leave your baby alone in a high chair, either, even for the minute it takes to answer the phone. The day your baby crawls the first inch—or even before—put up gates at the top and bottom of every staircase. Police other members of your family to make sure that everyone locks the gate behind him. And be ready to get new locks or safety catches the minute your baby learns to pick the old ones. As soon as he can learn, teach him to go up and down stairs safely, holding on or sliding down on his padded bottom.

Train yourself to put up the sides of your baby's crib without fail. And when your toddler is old enough to begin climbing out by himself, keep an old mattress beside the crib to cushion tumbles. Or promote him to a youth bed. He may get up and inconvenience you sometimes when he's supposed to be sleeping. But he will be safer from falls. Be sure, too, that your windows are safely screened, especially above the first floor.

When your youngster reaches the jungle-gym-tree-climbing stage, teach him how to maneuver safely. It's better strategy to find safe, secure spots for him to do his climbing than to issue blanket orders against it.

The dangers of head injuries are greatest, of course, in cars. Auto accidents are the leading cause of death and serious, permanent, physical and mental disability among children. Typically, young children who are killed or badly injured in cars are in vehicles driven by a parent, usually during the day and within a few miles of their home; the accidents are usually not the fault of the driver of the car in which the children are riding. Children who are not wearing safety restraints when an accident occurs continue moving in the original direction of the car like flying missiles until they strike something solid or are thrown out of the car. Consumer Product Safety Commission data shows that 85 percent of children younger than age five who are hurt in car accidents have head injuries which can cause permanent neurologic disability.

Crash tests carried out by traffic experts show that it is not possible for an adult—even wearing a lap and shoulder restraint—to prevent a small child on her lap from smashing into the dashboard and windshield if an accident occurs, even at low or moderate speed. If the adult isn't wearing a seat belt, the force of her body also crushes against the youngster from behind. Yet most babies and young children ride in exactly this way in cars—a practice traffic researchers call "potentially lethal."

So many youngsters have been killed or suffered such tragic damage to their brains in auto accidents that the American Academy of Pediatrics conducts a major, ongoing campaign to educate parents how best to protect their offspring.

Car seats and seat belts are the quickest and most effective way to reduce the number and severity of car-accident injuries. Correct use of car seats by all youngsters could prevent 90 percent of the deaths and 60 percent of injuries, it's estimated by transportation experts. But parents are often careless about buckling their children in every trip, especially when they're tired and rushed and only going a short distance. And parents sometimes feel that car safety is just one more thing—one thing too many—to nag children about.

To counter this dangerous kind of parental negligence, many states have passed laws requiring drivers to buckle all youngsters younger than four or five—depending on the state—into approved types of safety seats. The penalty, usually, is a substantial fine.

The American Academy of Pediatrics is pushing a "First Ride/Safe Ride" campaign to educate parents that they must begin taking auto safety precautions from the very first time they bring their newborn home from the hospital. The organization also distributes "A Family Shopping Guide to Infant/Child Automobile Restraints" that lists and evaluates safety devices that meet federal standards and are commercially available. Several service groups, hospitals, and other health organizations provide car seats that parents can rent, if they prefer.

The academy points out that "the 'best' car seat is the one in which your child will be most comfortable, that you can anchor correctly in your car and that you are willing to use every time you travel. Try the seat in your car and with your child, if possible, before you buy." It recommends car seats for an infant that face backward and are best used in the rear seat, secured by the safety belt. Seats for toddlers and preschoolers usually face forward, involve a safety harness or padded shield for the child and are held down by a seat belt and, in some designs, by a top anchor strap that is bolted to the car's interior. Some safety seats can be converted from an infant's to a toddler's use.

Studies show that if parents are quietly insistent on using a car seat, right from the beginning and without allowing any exceptions, small children usually do not object to the restraints if they can see out of a window. And they tend to be better behaved than youngsters permitted to roam freely about a moving car or held in an adult's lap.

The American Academy of Pediatrics is also concerned about the possibility of brain damage occurring when children get involved in amateur boxing—as some do even when they are as young as three and four. Brain studies made using computed tomography (CT) scanning have found subtle brain injuries caused by blows to the head that previously had not been discovered by EEG and other neurologic testing.[4]

The pediatricians' organization warns that protective headgear may increase the risk of brain injury, rather than prevent it. It urges all doctors to become "vigorous opponents of boxing as a sport for any child or young adult." The American Medical Association is also working to ban boxing because of the dangers of brain injury.[5]

—Protect your child from brain-damaging poisons.

Of all the substances that can accidentally poison a small child, the one most likely to leave permanent brain damage is lead.

Two thousand years of human history—and a batch of worrisome new studies—all confirm that lead hurts the human brain and erodes the intelligence. It accumulates in the body, especially in young children, causing irreversible brain damage, harming other organs, leading sometimes to death. We know enough now to avoid poisoning from the lead water pipes and wine containers that did so much damage to the ancient Romans that historians say it may have contributed to the fall of the Roman Empire. But so much lead is now being put into the atmosphere from burning leaded gasoline and from industrial sources that all of us eat it, drink it, and breathe it every day.

Airborne lead from industry and from car and truck emissions settles on crops, soil, water, and urban streets and playgrounds. Studies show our diets today have a hundred times as much lead as those of our prehistoric ancestors and that our bodies have accumulated a thousand times as much lead as theirs. Studies show that 90 percent of the lead in the atmosphere comes from burning leaded gasoline, although exposure from paint containing lead continues to be a problem, according to federal government studies.

For most of us, the level of lead piling up in our bodies isn't known to be dangerous. But hundreds of thousands of young children, especially those living in what are called "urban lead belts" in large cities, are suffering from what worried physicians describe as a silent epidemic of lead poisoning. As a result, they are growing up with impaired intelligence and health. And the adverse consequences will last a lifetime.

Lead poisoning usually develops slowly, over several weeks or months, as the damaging substance accumulates in the body, especially in the brain. First symptoms are unusual irritability, followed by digestive upsets and tiredness and often by convulsions and death. Even when a child recovers, the chances of permanent brain damage are high—inevitable, according to some doctors.

Medical care and special education for lead-damaged children and their lost productivity as adults cost the nation nearly $1 billion a year, a University of Illinois study estimated. Lead poisoning is also linked to birth defects.

Until recently, most concern about lead poisoning in young children focused on old housing, where some toddlers and preschoolers habitually nibble on peeling, sweet-tasting, lead-based paint. Tacitly, the problem was blamed on greedy, neglectful landlords and mothers who didn't supervise their toddlers well.

But new studies suggest that much of the burden of lead accumulated in the bodies of young children really comes from environmental pollution, particularly from car and truck emissions.

The level of lead in the blood usually used to diagnose lead poisoning—80 micrograms per 100 milliliters of blood—was too high, researchers now say. Evidence of brain damage has been found in children with much lower blood levels and the standard has now been set at 30 micrograms. One study reports that as little as 10 to 15 micrograms can result in mental impairment and behavioral disorders.

In a recent year, out of 535,000 children screened in a government-financed program, 22,000 were found to have lead poisoning. It's estimated that 4 percent of all American children between six months and five years old have lead poisoning—a total of about 675,000, according to a survey by the National Center for Health Statistics. The youngsters most likely to have worrisomely high levels of lead in their bodies are black children living in the central-city sections of large, urban areas, the study reported.

Only part of this damage is done by lead in gasoline; lead poisoning is a complicated medical and technological problem. But there's considerable evidence that reducing the level of lead in gas is the least expensive and quickest way to reduce brain damage and other devastations of lead poisoning. For example, between 1976 and 1980, federal regulations cut the lead in the nation's gasoline from about 200,000 tons to 100,000 tons with a corresponding drop of about 37 percent in lead poisoning among young children.

So clear is this evidence that the Environmental Protection Agency issued rules intended to cut 90 percent of the lead in gasoline by 1986. The regulation forces owners of older cars that can use leaded gasoline to switch to unleaded gas that is slightly more expensive. But evidence is so clear that leaded gasoline is a major contributor to the burden of lead in the bodies of little children that the cost arguments are easily pushed aside.

By contrast, it's estimated that it would cost more than $28 billion to get rid of all the lead-based paint in buildings in the United States—probably with less effect on the lead poisoning toll.

What can parents do to reduce the hazards of lead poisoning—and its insidious brain damage—for their children? Those who live in an older home, regardless of its cost, should make sure there is no peeling paint, especially around windowsills, that a child could chew or lick unobtrusively.

Paints designed for indoor use now contain only a minimal amount of lead; but parents should check the labels on any paint they buy for use inside their home and in repainting toys and not let a teething toddler chew on anything that has been coated with paint intended for exterior use.

Dirt and dust in some urban areas where truck and auto traffic is high may be contaminated with dangerous amounts of lead, studies show. This airborne lead pollution may be a major reason why so many children in these areas show indications of lead poisoning and why the incidence of learning disabilities among them is so unusually high.

Researchers who have made studies of the levels of lead-contaminated dust in homes where small children live recommend extra effort be made to keep the dust cleaned up, especially around windowsills and floors near windows. They also emphasize the importance of keeping children's hands clean, to lessen the risk that they will get lead-contaminated dirt in their mouths.

12. How to Care for Your Baby Before Birth

"Is my baby all right?" The suspense of the question hangs over every hospital delivery room, intrudes into the mind of every prospective parent, haunts every pregnancy.

Most parents receive a happily reassuring "He's just perfect" from the doctor. But more than 100,000 babies are born every year in the United States with defects so obvious that they can be identified as mentally retarded at birth. And an "overwhelmingly larger number" of children have slight brain injury or malfunction that is not identified until later, according to the American Medical Association—until they are slow to talk or unable to keep up with their classmates in school. At least one infant in every sixteen in the United States has a birth defect of some kind.

Prospective mothers and fathers have worried about the possibility of birth defects in their children for at least as long as there has been recorded history.

Detecting the causes of these birth defects (factors which may also be responsible for millions of miscarriages) has become one of the most exciting and promising fields of medical research. Discoveries in recent years have drastically changed the recommendations doctors are giving pregnant women to follow to improve the likelihood that their baby will be healthy and normal with a good, undamaged brain.

If you plan to have another baby, there's much you can do

before and during pregnancy to help your child be born with a good brain capable of learning well. The care you take of your developing infant in the nine months before he is born is as important—perhaps even more so—as the care you give him at any other time in his life.

Much still remains to be learned about the causes of birth defects. Many of the known causes are still beyond medical prevention, resulting from inherited disorders that still can not be detected or prevented before birth or from mistakes in cell division just before or at the time of conception. Some disorders may be the result of the interaction of genes and factors in the environment, reflecting, perhaps, the genetic susceptibility of an individual unborn infant to an environmental circumstance that would not harm another developing infant.

But based on current knowledge, you can improve your chances—already great—of having a baby with a good-quality, healthy brain, by following these general rules:

1. Choose a good doctor who keeps up to date on new medical research and is affiliated with a reputable hospital, and begin your prenatal care as early in pregnancy as possible—preferably even before your baby's conception.

Whether it's your first or second or fifth baby, you need medical supervision all during the nine months your baby is growing within you—ideally beginning even before you become pregnant so you can make sure you are in good health, your immunizations are up to date, and any possible problems are corrected. Even if you've skated through having a baby happily before without a complication, even if your budget is tight, even if you have to wait an hour for a brief checkup with your doctor, it is important for your baby.

The reason is that you not only provide half of your baby's heredity, you also furnish his total environment during the fast-growing first nine months of his life. His environment—you—must be as healthy as possible. And the environment—you—is not ever quite the same with each baby that you have.

In recent years, doctors have learned an enormous amount about how an unborn baby grows. They have tracked the miraculous process by which a single, infinitesimal sperm, out of hundreds of millions, approaches and penetrates the ovum as it floats down a fallopian tube toward the uterus. They know that almost instantly, then, the ovum changes in ways that make it impossible for another sperm to enter, even though it reaches the ovum only a second or two too late. Quickly the nucleus of the sperm, bearing its unique load of chromosomes—the father's contribution to his offspring's genetic heritage—moves toward the nucleus of the ovum with its distinctive package of chromosomes and combines with it to form a new life. Already your baby's sex is determined. Already your child's lifelong genetic biological inheritance is decided. Never before, never again, will the biological instructions for the development of a human being be written in quite the same way in a genetic blueprint.

The fertilized ovum floats gently down the fallopian tube into the uterus, dividing and redividing into new cells as it drifts and implants itself into the lining of the uterus about the seventh day after conception. The next few weeks are particularly critical. All of your baby's major organs and basic bodily structures are formed during the next two months. And because they grow from just a small cluster of cells present in the earliest days of pregnancy, the injury or death of only a few cells can cause major damage.

Your baby's brain begins to form about the second week after conception—before you even experience any symptoms that suggest you could be pregnant. The brain's most critical period of development lasts until about the eleventh week. That's why factors which cause birth defects during the critical first few months of pregnancy so often harm the brain, causing mental retardation or other learning problems that affect a child's intelligence.

Because of the new knowledge about the relationship of prenatal care to mental retardation and birth defects, major efforts are made by both private and public agencies to be sure that good prenatal care is available to all women, particularly pregnant teenagers and those considered to be "high risk" mothers for any reason. In most cities, the local health department sponsors free prenatal clinics and so do most county hospitals and many teaching hospitals connected with medical colleges. Federal government programs also provide nutritious food to pregnant women, infants, and young children. Not only are these programs essential for humanitarian reasons, but they have also been proven to be cost-effective because they reduce the amount of costly neonatal care that must be given to endangered newborns and by reducing prematurity and birth defects, cut down on the amount of special education that disabled children need.

The March of Dimes Birth Defects Foundation has taken a lead in sponsoring programs that encourage prenatal care and help to educate women about how they can care effectively for a baby for the nine months before birth.

2. If you have any concerns about the possibility your baby could inherit a genetic disorder, get genetic counseling—before you become pregnant, if possible.

It's easy to worry that your child might inherit a genetic disease. The list of disorders that are caused by abnormalities in the chromosomes or in the genes they contain is long and continues to lengthen as researchers learn more about these exquisitely complex blueprints for individual human lives. Thousands of genetic disorders have now been identified—some as common as diabetes, others so rare that only a few cases have ever been identified. Some occur largely in certain ethnic or racial groups, such as Tay-Sachs among Jewish people with East European ancestry or sickle-cell anemia among blacks and Mediterranean populations. (The presence of these specific, defective genes can be a way of tracing the migrations of peoples across continents and through history, scientists have learned.) Some can be controlled with medical help. A few are inevitably fatal. Many include brain abnormalities and mental retardation among their symptoms.

If you belong to a population group which is known to be at risk for a particular genetic disorder or if you think someone in your family may have a disease linked to a defective gene or an abnormal chromosome, you should seek information and advice from a genetic counselor. Chances are good your worries can be resolved. If there is reason to believe that your unborn child—or the baby you are planning—could be at risk, the counselor can spell out the odds you face and can often show you how to increase the likelihood you can have healthy, normal children.

A genetic counselor will sort through your family's medical history and that of your spouse to determine if the disorders that concern you are, in fact, genetic. You may discover, for example, that the uncle who spent years in a mental institution had measles encephalitis as a child, not a genetic abnormality that could affect your offspring, and that the cousin with cerebral palsy suffered from a lack of oxygen at birth, not from a genetic disorder.

If there is a possibility that your child could inherit a defective gene or a damaged chromosome, a genetic counselor can explain to you which pattern of inheritance is involved and what the odds are that each of your offspring could inherit the defect. These odds differ, depending on whether the genetic mistake occurs on a dominant or a recessive gene, on an X or an autosomal chromosome, or whether part or all of an entire chromosome is abnormal. (Whatever the odds, it's essential to remember that, as in throwing dice, these odds operate independently in each pregnancy. For example, if the odds are one in four your child will inherit cystic fibrosis and your first baby has the disease, the odds are still one in four that your second youngster will have the defect.)

Even if you and your spouse are at risk of giving birth to a baby with a genetic disorder, a counselor may be able to tell you how you can increase the odds of having normal and healthy children. For example, abnormalities involving an entire chromosome or part of one can be detected by examining cells taken from an unborn infant by a process called amniocentesis, which is done about the fifteenth or sixteenth week of pregnancy. Tests can also be made on such cells that will identify unborn infants who have one of several dozen genetic disorders about which parents are worried, such as Tay-Sachs disease or sickle-cell anemia. If a test indicates an unborn infant suffers from a serious genetic disorder, parents may decide to terminate the pregnancy and try again for a normal, healthy infant.

The easiest way to find a genetic counselor is through your physician or by contacting the nearest medical school or medical center with a teaching hospital. The directory of genetic services published by the March of Dimes Birth Defects Foundation can be obtained from its headquarters at 1275 Mamaroneck Avenue, White Plains, N.Y., 10605.

3. If possible, plan to have your children when you are between the ages of eighteen and forty.

Teenage mothers and those over forty have more complications of pregnancy, such as toxemia, than do women in the optimal childbearing years between eighteen and forty, and their babies are more likely to be premature or have low birth weight. They run more risk of having a difficult delivery, with possible injury to the baby at birth. All of these factors can be linked to minimum brain damage and learning difficulties.

This doesn't mean that you can't bear a normal, intelligent, healthy baby if you are seventeen or forty-three. Countless women have and many women will in the future. But the odds are better for your baby when you are at least eighteen and not yet forty.

The major problem with getting pregnant in early adolescence is that a young teen's body is still in the process of maturing. Physical growth may not yet be complete. Although pregnancy is physiologically possible, chances of something going wrong are just a little greater. Infants born to mothers younger than age eighteen have a 35 percent greater chance of dying from the complications of pregnancy and birth than do those born to older mothers and run twice the risk of having a low birth weight.

Girls younger than eighteen have usually not finished school or built a stable marriage. They aren't ready financially, emotionally, or educationally to take optimal care of a baby. And because of the circumstances in which they become pregnant, many do not seek prenatal care as early as desirable. Because of the worrisomely high rate of teenage pregnancy in recent years, many junior high and high schools are offering sex education classes aimed at making young people more informed about the responsibilities that pregnancy and parenthood impose and how premature pregnancy can be avoided. Community health programs make extra efforts to reach out to teens who do become pregnant in hopes of minimizing the extra risks they are imposing on their offspring both before and after birth.

In recent years, several trends have combined to increase the interest of many women in postponing pregnancy until their mid-thirties or even later. They may have been caught up in the demanding work and excitement of developing a career or professional competence. They may not have established a stable marriage. Or they may simply not have felt a compelling interest in having children at a younger age. Now, they will find that medical science has new safeguards and new expertise to help them through pregnancy.

One of the biggest risks that a baby runs when his mother is older than forty is being born with an abnormal number of chromosomes, the rod-shaped structures within each cell which carry the genes that determine hereditary characteristics and direct the body's growth and functioning. Each human cell normally contains 46 chromosomes. New laboratory techniques now make it possible to photograph and identify these forty-six chromosomes, which are paired and numbered from 1 to 22, with two sex-determining chromosomes identified separately. Researchers can even map the location of some specific genes on particular chromosomes.

For reasons not yet understood fully, the presence of an extra chromosome, or part of one, causes abnormal development, which usually includes mental retardation. It's now known that several different types of birth defects can result when a baby's cells contain more or fewer than 46 chromosomes. Medical journals continue to report on relationships between chromosome abnormalities and disorders in physical and mental development.

Best known of these chromosomal defects is Down (formerly called Down's) syndrome, a condition characterized by short stature, a somewhat oriental look about the eyes, abnormalities in internal organs, stubby fingers, and mental retardation. Down syndrome is the most common single cause of mental retardation and accounts for 5 to 6 percent of all mentally retarded individuals. Most people with Down syndrome have 47 chromosomes instead of 46, with an extra one matching the pair numbered 21.

In most cases, the extra chromosome occurs because of a mistake in cell division, probably during the production of the ovum in the mother's body before conception. During the process of cell division, the two chromosomes in pair 21 fail to separate properly, resulting in an egg cell with an extra particle—enough to condemn the about-to-be-conceived infant to lifelong mental and physical abnormalities.

Why the mistake in cell division occurs is not yet known. There is some evidence suggesting that it might be triggered by radiation or chemical factors or even by viruses. But it is a fact that the risk of having a baby with Down syndrome increases from 1 in 270 for mothers who are between the ages of thirty-five and forty, to 1 in 80 for mothers older than forty, and to even worse odds for women who are already beginning menopause and have what is called a "change-of-life" baby.

There is evidence in a small percentage of cases that the extra chromosome which resulted in the birth of a child with Down syndrome came from the father's sperm.

When a baby with Down syndrome is born to a mother younger than thirty-five, doctors suspect a hereditary factor may be responsible. Many Down syndrome infants born to young mothers have a chromosome count of 46, which appears normal at first. But further study reveals that one chromosome is unusually large and contains extra genetic material.

Chromosome counts made of parents of these babies usually show that one parent has only 45 chromosomes, one of which is a combination of a number 21 with another, most often a number 15, giving that father or mother the correct total complement of genetic material. But when a sperm or an ovum containing the combined chromosome unites with a normal sperm or ovum at conception, the fertilized egg contains the disastrous extra number 21 particle and a child with Down syndrome results. Young parents who have a Down syndrome baby are now advised to have chromosome studies made and to seek genetic counseling before they plan to have another child.

A chromosome abnormality can be detected in an unborn baby by a test called amniocentesis. In this procedure, the position of the baby in the uterus is first determined by ultrasound. Then the mother's abdomen is numbed by a local anesthetic and a hollow needle is inserted into an area of the uterus away from the baby and a bit of the amniotic fluid surrounding the child is withdrawn. Amniotic fluid contains cells from the infant, which can be grown in the laboratory and tested for chromosome abnormalities and for many other genetic errors.

Amniocentesis cannot be done until about the fifteenth or sixteenth week of pregnancy. The laboratory tests on the cells in the fluid take about three weeks. No way is yet known to correct the chromosome abnormalities and genetic errors that can now be detected by these means. But couples may decide to terminate the pregnancy if the unborn baby is found to have serious abnormalities.

In most cases, those who have amniocentesis done get good news; in 97 percent of cases, the test shows that the unborn infant does not have the disorder about which parents are worried. The procedure appears to be completely safe for the mothers involved, and there have been no reports of injuries to them. But the risk of miscarriage following amniocentesis is increased by about one-half of one percent, studies show, although it appears to be declining. Most prospective parents who are concerned about a serious abnormality that can be detected by amniocentesis decide the very small extra risk is worth taking. But there is reason not to use the procedure routinely or out of curiosity, because it can be used to detect the sex of the baby.

The most common reason for having amniocentesis done is because a pregnant woman is older than thirty-five, when the risks of having a baby with Down syndrome begin to mount. But because of the safety of the test and the reassurances it can give prospective parents, amniocentesis is being used increasingly for younger women.

The American Academy of Pediatrics also recommends the procedure when either parent or a previous child has a chromosome abnormality, when there is a risk of a genetic abnormality that can be diagnosed by testing fetal cells before birth or that is linked to the X chromosome, when there are indications that the unborn infant could have spina bifida or a related defect, or when there is a risk of certain genetic disorders involving the blood.

Even "maternal anxiety" is now recognized as a reason for having amniocentesis, commented a geneticist in a hospital where the tests are given. "Husband anxiety" is another indicator one pregnant woman added to the list. But a few physicians have expressed concern that the test is used unnecessarily often. And it may be replaced, at least in many cases, by a newer technique, chorionic villi sampling, in which a tiny bit of the tissue surrounding the unborn infant is obtained through the mother's cervix for study. Chorionic villi sampling can be done as early as the eighth week of pregnancy and results known in a day or two, much earlier and faster than in amniocentesis.

Research on chromosome abnormalities is still only in its beginning stages. It's known, for example, that at least half of the babies who are miscarried very early in pregnancy, or who die before birth, have an abnormal chromosome count. Researchers hope that some day they will be able not only to detect chromosomal abnormalities before birth, but also to develop means of correcting these mistakes.

4. Plan to space your children at least two or three years apart.

There are two good reasons for this advice. Obstetricians know that a woman's body needs time to recover fully from one pregnancy before another begins. Having babies too close together increases the risks of birth defects and complications at birth, studies show.

If women in developing countries followed the safest pattern of family planning—having their children when they are between the ages of eighteen and thirty-five, having no more than four youngsters, and spacing births at least two years apart—the number of infant and maternal deaths could be cut more than half, according to a study by the Population Information Program at the Johns Hopkins School of Public Health.

"Births too young, too old, too close, or too many create extra dangers for mothers and their children," the report said. "Spacing births at least two years apart is even more important to a child's health than the mother's age or number of children. In developing countries, a child born less than two years after an older brother or sister is two to four times more likely to die than if the older child was born between two and six years before." One reason infant and maternal death rates are lower in developed countries is that women there are more likely to follow these child-bearing patterns, the study pointed out.

The other big reason for not having children too close together is that it's difficult to give the second baby as much time and attention as the first. Both youngsters must compete for the mothering and fathering they urgently need—a situation that increases sibling rivalry and adds stress to family life.

Children born close in age to an older brother or sister generally have a slightly lower intelligence than other youngsters in their family, several large, long-term studies show. The inability of a mother's body to do an optimal job of nourishing another pregnancy right away is one factor. Another is simply that parents lack the time and energy to give the second baby as much mental stimulation and attention as they did the first.

5. Be sure you are protected against rubella (German measles) and other contagious diseases for which immunization is now possible before you become pregnant.

Enormously successful immunization programs have markedly decreased the incidence of several infectious diseases that used to cause widespread illness, especially among children, and did considerable permanent damage to unborn infants. Smallpox has been totally eliminated from the entire world. The incidence of rubeola ("regular" or "red" measles) is now so low that some epidemiologists anticipate that it, too, can be wiped out. Polio, mumps, and whooping cough are also rare. But none of these diseases has been completely eliminated. Outbreaks still occur. And there is danger that as the incidence of these illnesses decreases, carelessness about immunization may grow, leaving substantial numbers of people—including pregnant women and their vulnerable unborn infants—at terrible risk.

The hazards an unborn baby faces from an infectious disease suffered by his mother can best be seen in the case of rubella. For generations, German measles was considered a mild and minor disease of childhood, commonly called "three-day measles" because its symptoms rarely lasted any longer. Typically, its victims suffer from a slight rash, a mild sore throat, and swollen glands in the back of the neck—nothing more. If they have a fever at all, it is seldom higher than 100 or 101 degrees, and it almost never lasts more than two or three days. Doctors used to think there were almost never any serious complications.

The first hint that German measles was a serious threat to an unborn baby, when contracted by a mother during pregnancy, came from Australia, in 1941. There, a brilliant bit of medical detective work by an eye specialist, Dr. Norman McAlister Gregg, ferreted out the first link between a virus disease in a pregnant woman and a birth defect in her baby.

Dr. Gregg noticed a sudden and sharp increase in the number of babies brought to him with cataracts. Many of these infants also had congenital malformations and were deaf. Questioning their mothers at length, he learned that almost all of them had had German measles early in pregnancy.

During the next two decades, doctors established that rubella occurring in the first three months of pregnancy could indeed damage a mother's unborn infant. When the disease strikes during the first month of pregnancy, about 50 percent of babies are born with defects, which can include brain damage, deafness, eye damage, and heart abnormalities.

Twenty-two percent of babies whose mothers have rubella in the second month of pregnancy and 7 percent in the third month are born with malformations. There is some evidence that rubella just before conception or in the fourth month can also trigger birth defects. In addition, at least 15 to 36 percent of the pregnancies in which German measles occurs end in miscarriage.

But not until the great German measles epidemic of 1964–65 in the United States did doctors learn the full extent of the damage that rubella can do during pregnancy. More than thirty thousand babies with serious defects resulted from that epidemic, despite the fact that doctors in many major hospitals performed abortions on mothers who had rubella in early pregnancy. Some of these babies had severe and different symptoms never before recognized as being due to the German measles virus.

It is now known that many babies whose mothers have

German measles early in pregnancy don't get over the disease quickly, as their mothers do. They may continue to be actively infected with rubella all during the seven or eight months of pregnancy remaining and are born with active, severe, and contagious illness. This fact was not realized, or confirmed, until new techniques for identifying the rubella virus became available in 1963.

About 30 percent of babies born to mothers who have German measles in early pregnancy are now known to be born with chronic infections. These babies may have extensive hemorrhages into the skin, enlarged liver and spleen, lung disorders, jaundice, bone abnormalities, and infections of the liver, heart, or brain. They may—or may not—also have malformations. These babies have been called "the Typhoid Marys of rubella" because they can continue to spread the disease to other people for at least six months, sometimes longer.

Rubella can be such a mild disease that many individuals have it without any symptoms at all. In one large study, only one case in every three detected by lab tests was recognized by symptoms.

But even an undetected case without symptoms can cause severe damage to an unborn infant if it occurs while his mother is pregnant. Babies have been born with chronic rubella—with or without birth defects—to mothers who were not ill during pregnancy and were not even aware of being exposed.

There's still another complication to the rubella problem. Other viruses can cause a mild, rashy disease which imitates German measles. Some women who think that they are immune to rubella may not actually have had the disease. Laboratory tests for antibodies prove that a substantial number of women are mistaken about whether or not they have had rubella.

Fortunately, there is a test to determine whether or not an individual has had German measles. It is simple, reliable, inexpensive, and can tell within hours whether an individual has antibody protection against rubella.

An effective vaccine against rubella has been available since 1969 and large-scale immunization programs have been carried out ever since. Young children have been the primary targets of these campaigns, on the theory that such youngsters are the chief sources of infection among pregnant women. Rubella immunization has also become a routine part of well-baby medical care. But the problem still has not been completely eliminated.

To safeguard any future baby you might have, it's essential that you make absolutely sure you cannot have rubella during pregnancy. Your doctor or the nearest hospital can arrange for the simple blood test that can tell you for sure whether you are protected against the disease, either by immunization or because you have had the illness itself. If you are not already protected, you should be immunized at least two or three months before you plan to become pregnant. Because the vaccine does contain live rubella virus, although in a greatly weakened form, it is theoretically possible that the vaccine could cause congenital rubella in an unborn baby if his mother were immunized early in pregnancy. So doctors have been advised not to give the vaccine to any woman of childbearing age unless it is certain that she is not pregnant, is using a reliable contraceptive, and will not become pregnant for at least two months.

6. Do everything you can to keep yourself well during pregnancy and to avoid exposure to contagious diseases.

If a mild disease such as German measles can do so much damage to an unborn infant, what about other viruses and bacteria? All of the answers aren't yet clear. But as techniques improve for identifying viruses and the antibodies a woman's body produces to fight them, it becomes increasingly evident that they are linked to a wide range of birth defects, miscarriages, and stillbirths.

As with rubella, how much damage is done to an unborn child depends more on the stage of pregnancy when the infection occurs than on how ill the mother herself becomes. Any illness caused by a virus within the first three months of pregnancy—especially in the first eight weeks—may possibly injure the unborn infant, according to the American Medical Association. In the last three months of pregnancy, a severe virus infection may trigger premature birth, which is sometimes related to learning difficulties later on in childhood.

Mothers who have influenza during early pregnancy seem to run a higher risk of having a baby born with defects or subsequent learning difficulties, some studies are showing. Polio has also been implicated as a possible cause of birth defects, miscarriage, stillbirth, and prematurity. Rubeola ("two-week" measles) is also. You should be protected against both, and against whooping cough and mumps, before you become pregnant.

Coxsackie and ECHO viruses, which cause an illness most people call "some kind of flu" or "that bug that's going around this month" can also produce birth defects in babies whose mothers are infected during pregnancy.

Strong evidence also exists that birth defects and mental retardation can be caused by cytomegalovirus (one of the herpes group), which produces a disease in adults that is usually so mild that there are no symptoms whatsoever. Yet it is associated with a variety of birth defects including deafness, seizures, spasticity, brain malformations or hemorrhage, and jaundice. Some physicians are concerned about a study showing that cytomegalovirus can spread rapidly among young children in a day-care center and even though they have few or no symptoms themselves, the children can pass the infection to mothers or teachers who happen to be pregnant.

Syphilis, tuberculosis, and infectious hepatitis in a pregnant woman can also be harmful to her unborn infant and require a doctor's careful supervision and treatment.

Mild virus infections during pregnancy may also be linked with learning disabilities, many doctors now suspect. This subtle brain damage may not become obvious until the age of five or six or even later, when the youngster experiences difficulties learning normally in the classroom.

Among all of the children born each year with birth defects and with damaged brains, there is no known cause, no explanation, in at least half of the cases. Viruses are a logical suspect in many of these situations, researchers theorize.

Much more remains to be learned about the effects of infectious diseases on unborn infants. With the current state of knowledge, doctors' advice can be summed up like this: Before you become pregnant, establish immunity to as many infectious diseases as possible by vaccination. During pregnancy, avoid exposure to disease if you can. And should you become ill, contact your doctor immediately.

7. If you have ever had a genital herpes infection, or if you have a sex partner who has, you should inform your physician so he can take precautions to safeguard your infant.

Genital herpes has become one of the most common sexually transmitted diseases since its incidence began increasing rapidly in the early 1970s. It holds one known danger to unborn infants, and researchers are theorizing it could also cause a second kind of damage.

Almost everyone is familiar with the "cold sores" or "fever blisters" caused by the herpes simplex I virus. These itchy, watery little blisters are just a minor annoyance and clear up without treatment. But they tend to reappear occasionally, usually following a fever or illness.

A related virus, herpes simplex II, is spread by sexual contact with an infected person and produces the same kind of itchy, watery little blisters in the pubic and genital areas. Outbreaks may be accompanied by swollen glands, fever, and a general feeling of malaise and achiness. Just as in the case of herpes I, the body doesn't seem able to destroy the herpes II virus completely. After the initial sores heal up, the virus retreats to nerves in the lower body near the spinal cord, becomes dormant and remains there for the rest of the individual's life, occasionally causing new bouts of blisters and illness.

Subsequent flare-ups of genital herpes can be triggered by sexual intercourse, stress, fatigue, other illness, menstruation, or other unknown factors. But generally, symptoms are milder during recurrences than in the initial infection. The drug acyclovir is useful in helping to speed the healing of herpes sores. But it does not destroy the latent virus and/or prevent repeat attacks.

Doctors know that a baby born to a woman when she has an active illness can become infected during passage through the birth canal. The disease can be devastating to a newborn. Herpes virus can do severe damage to his brain, spinal cord, liver, or kidneys. Half or more of these babies die.

Two-thirds of those who survive have permanent brain damage. Most of these neonatal infections are caused by the herpes II virus. But the increase in oral-genital sex activity has resulted in genital infections with herpes I, and this virus accounts for almost one-third of the damage in infants.

To guard a baby from coming in contact with herpes sores during the process of birth, physicians monitor a pregnant woman who has herpes carefully during the last weeks of pregnancy. If there are any signs that the disease is active when labor begins or when the end of pregnancy nears, the baby is delivered by cesarean section.

One problem is that about 70 percent of newborns who have herpes are born to women with no signs of active disease. Doctors can use weekly blood tests to check for recurring infections in high-risk women. But there is some medical debate about whether this extra cost is justified for all women who have ever had herpes.

Because herpes can do so much harm to a baby during the process of birth, the American Academy of Pediatrics now advises that a pregnant woman should not have any sexual contact with a partner who has a genital infection during the last several months of pregnancy.

Researchers are also learning more about another way herpes virus can endanger an unborn infant. It is known that women who have herpes infections—especially an initial attack—run an increased risk of having a miscarriage. Now, new techniques are turning up evidence that herpes virus can cause a persistent, symptomless infection of endometrial cells in the lining of the uterus, then cross the placenta and harm the unborn baby. This prenatal infection—what one researcher, Dr. James A. Robb, a pathologist at the University of California, called a "cold sore of the embryo"—can result in a miscarriage, a stillborn infant, or a baby with abnormalities. He and his colleagues suggest that such persistent, inapparent herpes infections may account for as many as 30 percent of the miscarriages which can not be attributed to other causes.[1]

The discovery that the drug acyclovir could help heal herpes sores has spurred hopes that a permanent cure for the infection will someday be found and that perhaps some kind of immunization against the virus can be developed. Until then, a woman who is pregnant, or ever hopes to be, should try to avoid acquiring the infection by not having sexual contact with a partner who has an active infection. Women who do have herpes should work closely with their doctor to protect their unborn offspring.

8. While you are pregnant, don't eat any undercooked meat or handle any cat that might be a source of toxoplasmosis infection.

Tennis star Martina Navratilova made headlines all around the world when her game slipped briefly late in 1982. She wasn't feeling well, she told the press. Her doctor diagnosed her illness as a toxoplasmosis infection and traced its origins to her pet cat. The champion recovered quickly and soon was consistently beating all of her opponents on the court, as usual. But her illness helped to call attention to a disease that can be a major threat to an unborn infant.

Normally, in adults, the comma-shaped toxoplasma organism causes a mild disease that may include a brief rash, cough, swollen glands, and other coldlike symptoms. Sometimes the infection is so slight it goes unnoticed, especially in a woman who is not required to be at the peak of physical conditioning all of the time. A woman who has toxoplasmosis during pregnancy recovers quickly from the disease. But, as with rubella, an infected unborn infant may continue to have active infection all the rest of his prenatal life and after birth. About 20 percent of these infected babies are born with major defects, such as mental retardation, epilepsy, eye damage, hearing loss, and hydrocephalus.

The chief sources of human infection by toxoplasma organisms seem to be raw or undercooked red meat and the feces of cats. The organisms can be killed by heating meat to at least 140 degrees—the "rare" reading on a cooking thermometer. So it's safe to eat rare lamb and beef, if you can be sure all of it has actually reached this temperature. In a restaurant, it's safer to order meat well-done to avoid the possibility that some of it may be dangerously undercooked. Raw meat, such as steak tartare, should be avoided all during pregnancy. And if you handle red meat in the process of cooking it at home, you should make sure your hands are thoroughly washed immediately.

Toxoplasma organisms also live in the digestive tracts of cats, where they produce oocysts, another infectious stage of the organisms; these are then excreted in the feces. The usual disinfectants aren't effective against these oocysts, and they can remain hazardous for as long as a year, especially in moist soil or water. Cats acquire the organisms by eating raw meat, mice, or other animals or by coming in contact with infected cats.

You can guard against the possibility of toxoplasmosis by taking these steps: Don't bring any new cat into your home while you are pregnant. Any cat you already have should not be fed raw or undercooked red meat or allowed to hunt or come in contact with other cats that might be infected. (Commercial or canned cat food is safe because the canning or drying process destroys the organisms.) Don't empty your cat's litter box if you are pregnant; it should be cleaned daily, however, by someone who wears rubber gloves, and the litter should be burned or dumped away from any area where you could come in contact with it. You should not garden in any place where cat litter has been deposited, and if you have a backyard sandbox, it should be covered at all times it's not in use.

A cat that isn't allowed to hunt and has been in your family for several months should be safe. But if there's any possibility of infection, you can ask a veterinarian to test your cat for toxoplasmosis infection. Your doctor can also give you a blood test to determine whether you have had the disease and are immune, or whether you are still at risk of getting it.

9. Do not take any drug or any medicine, not even aspirin, during pregnancy—and especially during the first three months—unless absolutely necessary and then only under doctor's orders.

Along with the traditional photographs of exuberant college graduates in cap and gown, several newspapers recently ran a picture of a remarkable, pretty young woman sitting on the floor writing with a pen grasped between her toes. She had only small stumps of arms. But she had managed to complete her college work, using her toes as fingers whenever she could.

She was one of hundreds of "thalidomide babies," survivors of a major medical tragedy that alerted the medical world to a new and then unsuspected kind of danger to unborn children.

It took a unique and lucky combination of circumstances to identify thalidomide as the cause of the epidemic of serious birth defects that shocked German physicians in 1961 and 1962. The damage was easy to spot immediately at birth, unlike much brain injury which doesn't become obvious for many months or even years; these infants lacked legs or arms or ears. It was widespread, because the drug became popular so quickly and was taken in such large quantities by millions of people who did not need a doctor's prescription to get it. And it occurred over a relatively short period of time.

Another clue was that not even one of the thirty-two thousand babies born to United States military personnel stationed in Germany during this period had similar defects. The drug was not given to armed forces families because it had not yet been approved for sale in the United States. This sparing of American babies made it possible for medical researchers to rule out quickly such possible causes as a disease epidemic or an environmental chemical or pollutant.

News that the drug thalidomide had caused thousands of infants in Germany, Great Britain, and Australia to be born with deformed limbs and other defects in 1961 and 1962 rang a loud alarm in the medical profession. Doctors were as shocked and as grieved as the rest of the world about the plight of the crippled babies. They were also stunned that such a tragedy could be caused by thalidomide, a sedative so mild and so apparently safe that it was sold without prescription.

Immediately, the fearful question arose: If one tablet of a drug as mild as thalidomide taken at a critical time during early pregnancy could deprive a baby of his arms or legs, how many other drugs taken by pregnant women might also be responsible for miscarriage, stillbirth, mental retardation, and malformation?

Doctors still don't know the answer to this question. They probably never will, precisely and completely, despite urgent and continuing efforts.

But the thalidomide tragedy did help researchers learn much more about how unborn infants develop and how hazards affect them as they grow. Doctors now know, almost to the day, when each organ is being developed during the early weeks of pregnancy. From the type of defect existing at birth, they can often deduce just when damage to the unborn infant took place.

Germany's Dr. Wido Lenz, who studied the thalidomide-damaged babies, reported that when an infant was born with a complete absence of arms, it was then discovered that his mother had taken the drug between the thirty-ninth and forty-first days after menstruation. Those who had no legs were born to mothers who had used thalidomide between the forty-first and forty-fourth days. Interference with development on the thirty-fifth day resulted in a child without ears. After the fifty-second day, thalidomide could apparently have been taken every day for the rest of the pregnancy without harming the unborn infant.

For example, one German mother of a boy with shortened arms and bent hands is certain she took only two thalidomide tablets. She could pinpoint the day precisely, even months later, because she was trying to calm her nerves after her father died of a heart attack. Another mother took only half of one tablet. But because it was a critical day in the development of her baby, he was born deformed months later.

Usually, in medical detective work, it's much more difficult to link precisely cause and effect, drug and defect.

One problem is that a drug may only harm an unborn child during certain, specific days of his prenatal life. Or it may only affect his ability to survive on his own without his mother's support system immediately following birth. Its damage may not even show up for years, as in the case of diethylstilbestrol (DES), which was taken by millions of women during the 1940s and 1950s in hopes it would prevent threatened miscarriage. It was not until almost two decades later that DES was linked to abnormal cells and cancerous tissues in some of the teenage and adult daughters of these mothers. Another problem for researchers is that a drug may do damage only to unborn infants who have a specific genetic susceptibility to it.

The fact that a woman is exposed to so many different substances in so many forms during the long nine months of pregnancy also complicates research. It is almost impossible for a mother who has given birth to an infant with a birth defect to remember everything that could have affected her child in the months previous.

Researchers have also learned that unborn animals do not always react to drugs and other substances in precisely the same way as human babies. While laboratory tests are useful in alerting scientists—and pregnant women—to drugs that could harm unborn children, they can not be relied on to provide all of the answers.

The Food and Drug Administration is now aware of the need to establish the safety of specific drugs for unborn infants as well as for children and adults. But this can sometimes be tricky. Recently a well-known prescription remedy for nausea in pregnancy, which had apparently been used by hundreds of thousands of women without any known adverse effects on their unborn children, was withdrawn from the market because of a few reports suggesting it might be linked to birth defects in a small number of infants. Many physicians still think that the drug is safe. There is simply no infallible way of knowing for sure.

Many of the prescription medications now on the market carry the cautionary note, "The safety of this drug for use in pregnancy has not been established."

Because of these problems, there is no safe alternative except to issue the broad and stringent rule for all women who are pregnant or think it is possible that they could be: Do not take any medicine at all during pregnancy, unless it is absolutely necessary and unless it is ordered by a physician who knows you are pregnant.

To spell out the warning even more clearly, to underline it and emphasize it, doctors add:

—Don't continue to take medicine prescribed for you before you became pregnant, unless you tell your doctor that you think you might be going to have a baby and he again says that the drug is essential.

—Do remember that some of the most crucial weeks of your baby's existence occur before you ever make your first prenatal visit to your physician. That's why the responsibility for safeguarding your unborn infant lies primarily with you. Some doctors even advise that every sexually active woman of childbearing age should refrain from taking any medicines, without strict supervision by a doctor, because injury to a baby could take place before she even suspects she might be pregnant.

—Avoid a general anesthetic during pregnancy, if at all possible. It comes under the heading of "medicine," too. If you need to have dental work done during pregnancy, be sure that your dentist knows about the baby, so he will give you only a local anesthetic, if it's necessary, and will take proper protective steps in taking X-rays.

—Do be sure you realize how much that word "medicine" includes. It means not only pills, but every type of medicinal spray, ointment, salve, and liquid—even aspirin. It includes fizzing powders, baking soda, and home remedies for "heartburn." Digestive "aids," nose drops and sprays, laxatives, sedatives, tranquilizers, wake-up pills, mineral oil, "nerve tonics," reducing medicines, and even vitamin supplements are also on the list. Some doctors even warn against spraying insecticides around a room because you might inhale small quantities.

—The warning against using drugs during pregnancy includes street drugs or "recreational drugs," too, even though the evidence linking them to specific damage to unborn infants is not complete. Marijuana, for example, may increase the risk of miscarriage and stillbirth, some studies show, and because substances in pot can cross through the placenta and accumulate in the fatty tissues of the unborn baby—and in his brain—it's considered possible that abnormalities in development could occur. The National Institute of Drug Abuse warns that using marijuana during pregnancy is "very unwise" and "should be especially discouraged," in its eighth annual report to the U.S. Congress, "Marijuana and Health."

If a pregnant woman is addicted to a drug while she is pregnant, it's likely that her unborn infant will be addicted, too. After birth, he will have to go through a painful and risky withdrawal period. And follow-up studies show that some children of addicted mothers, particularly those using heroin, may suffer from neurological and psychological problems and growth abnormalities even years later. So devastating is the effect of a mother's heroin addiction on her unborn infant that in one instance, the Illinois Department of Children and Family Services tried the legally uncertain ploy of charging a pregnant addict with child abuse and announcing it was taking custody of her unborn child so it could order the mother into medical care.

Almost nothing is known about the possibility that drugs taken by a father prior to conception could have an adverse effect on his baby; almost all of the research that's been done so far concerns substances that cross the placenta and harm the developing baby after they have been taken by the mother. But some evidence has been found in research with experimental animals suggesting that perhaps exposure of males to substances such as alcohol, lead, morphine, methadone, and other chemicals could be linked to abnormal development in their offspring.

The male reproductive system is not fully understood, as scientists trying to develop an effective male contraceptive point out. No one knows whether a drug or chemical taken by a human male could damage the sperm, or the cells that produce the sperm, in some small way or affect the semen so slightly that fertilization could still occur but development would not be quite normal.

But research is probing into these questions, in part because of the insistent claims by some veterans of the fighting in Vietnam that their exposure to the dioxin in Agent Orange has resulted in birth defects in their children. Several long-term epidemiological studies are underway to test these concerns. Almost no evidence has been found so far, although a few researchers say there are enough small indications that the possibility should receive further study.

It's unfortunate that the warnings about using drugs and exposure to chemicals are so vague and extensive and worrisome. Tentative concerns about the role of male exposure to drugs prior to conception may turn out to be false alarms. And, of course, millions of women have taken tens of millions of drugs during pregnancy and still have given birth to healthy, normal babies.

But the list of drugs known to harm unborn infants is growing. Undoubtedly, not all of them have been found. Those which hurt only a few infants with specific genetic susceptibility, those which produce fairly common birth defects, and those responsible for learning problems and mental retardation that doesn't become obvious until long after birth may be particularly hard to detect. But because the risks to an unborn infant are so great, there is no alternative now except to warn pregnant women to avoid every unnecessary drug.

10. Don't drink anything alcoholic if you are pregnant, or think that you possibly could be.

There is no doubt that an unborn infant can be harmed if his mother drinks excessively during pregnancy. There is also no doubt that millions of women have had alcoholic drinks during pregnancy without doing any apparent damage to their unborn offspring. But no one knows for sure just where the damage level begins at a specific time in a particular pregnancy. So no one knows for sure just how strictly women should be warned to abstain from the use of alcohol for the sake of their unborn child.

Drinking during pregnancy is linked to miscarriage, stillbirth, low birth weight, hyperactivity, learning problems, and a cluster of marked physical and mental abnormalities called fetal alcohol syndrome (FAS). It's curious that the connection between a pregnant woman's drinking and damage to her children has been reported many times over the last three centuries. But it wasn't until two research papers were published in 1973 that contemporary physicians began to pay attention to the problem and to warn their pregnant patients about it.

Once physicians were alerted to watch for fetal alcohol syndrome, they discovered that moderate drinking during pregnancy also did some damage to unborn children. Much hyperactivity, jitteriness, learning difficulties, and borderline mental retardation in children is now known to be due to moderate use of alcohol by their mothers during pregnancy.

Fetal alcohol syndrome, the most easily recognized birth defect caused by a mother's drinking, has now been reported by physicians all over the world. Children with FAS show a pattern of retarded growth, before or after birth or both. They have characteristic facial abnormalities that typically include a small head, small eyes and a short nose with a flattened bridge. They are also mentally retarded or behave abnormally. They tend to be hyperactive and jittery. Sometimes affected youngsters have other symptoms, too: an abnormal opening between the chambers of the heart, eye and ear defects, birthmarks, hernias, and abnormalities of the genitourinary tract.

Women who drink run twice the risk of losing a baby by miscarriage. Those who have two or more drinks a day run three times the risk of having their infant be born premature. And the more they drink, the smaller their infant is likely to be.

Babies born to mothers who drink don't sleep as long or as soundly as normal infants. As children, they tend to have a short attention span, be restless, are easily distractable, and need to be in special education classes. The more their mothers drink during pregnancy, the lower their I.Q. is likely to be.

Five percent of all birth defects may result from a mother's drinking during pregnancy, one study suggests. In fact, the use of alcohol during pregnancy may be the single biggest cause of mental retardation in the Western world, two other researchers estimate, after surveying the incidence of alcohol-related problems all over the world.

But exactly what is meant by "moderate" drinking and whether any level of alcohol use during pregnancy is safe for an unborn infant isn't known. There are several reasons for the uncertainty. It is difficult for researchers to get accurate reports of precisely how much alcohol a woman consumes at exactly what stage in pregnancy, especially if attempts are made to collect this information after she has given birth to an affected infant. Some unborn babies may be genetically more susceptible to damage from alcohol than others. And it may be difficult to separate out the effects of alcohol from other factors that could hurt an unborn baby, such as a mother's inadequate nutrition and lack of good prenatal care.

How quickly a woman consumes the alcoholic drinks also

seems to make a difference in how badly affected her unborn infant may be. So does her individual metabolism. Concentrated, binge drinking on a rare Saturday night probably does more damage than the same amount of alcohol spread out over days or weeks. There are even some reports that drinking just before conception can contribute to the risk of miscarriage early in pregnancy.

Because of these uncertainties, there are some differences of opinion about how urgently pregnant women should be warned about drinking. A strict caution that a pregnant woman should drink absolutely no alcohol at all was issued by the U.S. Surgeon General in 1981. The ban, the Surgeon General's report said, was based on research showing that when a mother drinks as little as one ounce of alcohol a day—equal to two cans of beer, two glasses of wine or two mixed drinks—there is increased risk her baby could be born with an abnormally low weight and that the risk of miscarriages goes up when a pregnant woman drinks as little as one ounce of alcohol twice a week.

An unborn infant whose mother drinks three or four ounces of alcohol a day—the equivalent of six or more glasses of wine or cans of beer or mixed drinks—is at major risk of developing some or all of the symptoms of fetal alcohol syndrome, most researchers agree. If his mother consumes two or more ounces of alcohol daily, his chances seem to be about one in five of being born with some abnormalities. And even if she drinks only one or two ounces a day, odds are at least one in ten that he will show some adverse effects after birth.

Even so, the March of Dimes Birth Defects Foundation has backed away a step or two from the stern warning it used to issue against all drinking during pregnancy. ("If you're pregnant, don't drink. If you drink heavily, don't become pregnant. If you can't stop drinking on your own, seek help before you become pregnant. Alcohol and pregnancy don't mix.")

What made the March of Dimes modify its stand was the fact that women who had inadvertently had a glass or two of wine or beer or a gin and tonic before they realized they were pregnant were telephoning in a panic, worrying that they might have hurt their unborn infant, and in a few cases, even considering having an abortion. Now the organization simply spells out the dangers of drinking during pregnancy and reminds women that they have it in their individual power to protect their unborn infant completely from this particular, real danger.

A more specific recommendation was issued by the American Council on Science and Health in 1981: "For those women who choose to drink during pregnancy, ACSH advises that they limit their daily intake to two drinks or less of beer, wine, or liquor. The alcoholic content of two 12-ounce glasses of beer, two four-ounce glasses of table wine, or two mixed drinks each containing one and one-half ounces of 80-proof liquor is approximately the same; each contains about one ounce of 100 percent alcohol.

"Although no absolutely safe level of alcohol ingestion has been defined or probably ever will be, the health risks associated with the above level of consumption are apparently low, if they exist at all. These recommendations are intended only as guidelines, as there are substantial differences among women in their ability to tolerate alcohol."

In making your own decision about drinking during pregnancy, it may help to remember that when you drink, you force your unborn infant to drink, too. And the effects on him could well last a lifetime.

11. Don't smoke cigarettes during pregnancy.

The more researchers look for links between what happens to a woman during pregnancy and the health of her infant at birth, the more evidence turns up about the dangers of smoking cigarettes. The warning that a smoking mother forces her unborn baby to live in a smoke-filled womb isn't literally true, but it vividly emphasizes the very real hazards.

For example, several long-term studies are underway to determine whether there would possibly be any link between exposure of American servicemen to Agent Orange in Vietnam and birth defects in their children who were conceived after their return to the United States—a fear many veterans have. The first report to be issued as a result of this research came from the Ranch Hand study, which carefully compared the medical records and reproductive histories of the Air

Force "Ranch Hand" personnel who handled Agent Orange and had the most exposure to it during the Vietnam spraying operations with similar air force veterans who had no contact with the herbicide.

The first Ranch Hand report finds no significant difference in the incidence of birth defects and in the health of the children born to the two groups of veterans. What is strongly linked with birth defects and learning disabilities in Ranch Hander families and those in the control group of other veterans is smoking by the mother during pregnancy. Drinking during pregnancy is also strongly associated with physical handicaps in children in both groups.

So many other studies have confirmed the dangers of a mother's smoking during pregnancy that no doubts can remain about it.

For example, the U.S. Surgeon General's report to Congress in 1980 says that smoking increases a mother's risk of losing a baby in miscarriage by 70 percent and of having a stillborn infant by 25 percent. A woman who smokes runs a 36 percent greater chance of having a baby who is born prematurely and a 98 percent greater danger that her offspring will have low birth weight, with all of the associated hazards.

Babies of smokers average about one-half pound less in birth weight than infants of nonsmokers. The more a mother smokes, the less her baby is apt to weigh at birth.

It isn't just a lack of fatty tissue that makes infants of smoking mothers weigh less, investigators have found. These babies also tend to be shorter in length, indicating that their overall growth and development have been retarded during pregnancy. The damage seems to be done, primarily, by the nicotine which is known to pass through the placenta into the body of the growing baby before birth and because the high level of carbon monoxide in the mother's blood reduces the amount of oxygen carried to the unborn child.

A baby with low birth weight, whether it is caused by being born prematurely or because of growth retardation before birth, faces many extra risks and difficulties, at the time of birth and afterward. A big part of the efforts of groups concerned about helping children to be born healthy and normal, such as the March of Dimes Birth Defects Foundation, goes to trying to prevent low birth weight and prematurity.

There is also convincing evidence that mothers who smoke during pregnancy suffer a higher incidence of childbirth complications, including too-early separation of the placenta, bleeding, and premature rupture of the protective membranes surrounding the infant before birth.

Researchers have also found that the risks of a baby dying of sudden infant death syndrome are four times greater for the offspring of mothers who smoked during pregnancy.

Even long after birth, the effects of a mother's smoking can be traced in her children. The offspring of smokers tend to be more irritable than other babies. As children, they are more hyperactive and more likely to have emotional and behavioral problems and respiratory illnesses. They also continue to show some lag in physical development all through childhood and early adolescence, according to recent research.

You may find it easier to give up smoking during the early months of pregnancy than at any other time. The taste of cigarettes and the odor of cigarette smoke are high on the list of things that trigger nausea in a substantial percentage of pregnant women. You can consider it a lucky break for your baby—and for yourself—if you experience this powerful reaction to smoking and use it to help yourself stop.

12. Avoid X-ray examination or radiation treatment, especially in the abdominal area and particularly during the first three months of pregnancy.

The danger that radiation could deform an unborn infant and damage his sensitive brain during the first three months after conception was first detected in 1929. In that year, it was noted that some mothers who accidentally had been overexposed to X-rays during treatment for pelvic disease gave birth to babies who were brain-damaged. Studies of infants born after the atom-bombing of Hiroshima and Nagasaki confirmed this discovery. So has extensive research with laboratory animals.

Today, the precautions that are necessary to guard against

harming an unborn child by X-ray are well understood and routinely followed. It's a standard practice, for example, that X-rays of the abdomen in a woman of child-bearing age are made only during the first ten days following the start of a regular and normal menstrual period, except in serious emergency, to guard against accidental exposure to a young unborn infant. A woman who is having X-rays of any kind, even as part of a dental examination, should tell the doctor or dentist if she is pregnant or if there is any possibility that she could be, so that extra precautions can be taken.

In fact, it's now considered good medical practice to shield the reproductive organs of both women and men—including girls and boys—any time X-rays are made or radiation treatment used, to prevent any possible genetic damage that could be passed on to future offspring.

The development of ultrasound as a means to check on the size, position, and condition of an unborn infant has largely replaced the use of X-ray for this purpose. So doctors no longer must weigh the possible hazards to an unborn infant of brief exposure to radiation against the need for more information about his health and growth. There is no evidence that ultrasound can harm either a pregnant woman or her unborn infant in any way. But physicians have learned to be supercautious about protecting the unborn. And it's now recommended that ultrasound be used only when medical information is necessary and not just out of curiosity about the baby or as part of a routine checkup.

The enormous increase in the use of computers with video display terminals in offices and elsewhere has generated considerable concern that they might emit enough radiation to damage an unborn child, especially if a mother spends most of a forty-hour work week sitting before the screen. There have been several reports that clusters of miscarriages, stillbirths, and birth defects have occurred among the offspring of mothers who use computers extensively at work. But these clusters seem to be part of a normal statistical variance. Radiation experts say the amount of radiation from a computer terminal is well under any minimum level associated with damage to humans or unborn babies. There appears to be no reason for worry or for pregnant women to take special precautions in using a computer.

13. Make sure your workplace is safe for your unborn child.

Concerns that a mother who holds a job while she is pregnant might damage her unborn child have largely disappeared with the abundant evidence that millions of women have done so and their infants have flourished. But a few workplaces could be harmful to an unborn baby—a problem that has caused considerable angry controversy among working women, unions, employers, and government agencies such as the Occupational Safety and Health Administration (OSHA) and the Equal Employment Opportunity Commission (EEOC).

The chief problem is that there is no firm list of substances in workplaces that could do damage to an unborn infant if his mother were exposed. Lead is considered to be highly suspect. So is organic mercury. Questions have also been raised about the anesthetics in operating rooms to which surgical nurses are exposed (some studies show that they have more miscarriages and babies with birth defects than nurses who work elsewhere in hospitals). Other possible hazards are carbon tetrachloride, vinyl chloride, some substances in pharmaceuticals, and pesticides.[2]

But it is difficult to prove that such danger exists, if it does. To protect unborn infants—and to guard against the possibility of lawsuits—some employers have tried to ban all women of childbearing age from jobs that involve exposure to possible teratogens. But some feminists and unions have angrily charged that such bans can be turned into an excuse to keep women out of well-paying jobs. They argue that employers must make workplaces safe for all employees—men, women, and unborn infants. Their argument is bolstered by the fact that most substances which cause birth defects (teratogens) may also cause cancer (carcinogens).

Until that ideal is reached, however, much of the responsibility for protecting an unborn child from danger in the workplace belongs to pregnant women. It won't be easy, because often possible dangers are not understood or documented. Sources of information that might be useful include union leaders, the employer's medical director, your own doctor, and the OSHA office in your area or at 200 Constitution Avenue, N.W., Washington, D.C. 20001. Some states have passed laws requiring employers to post notices of any substances that could possibly be hazardous to which workers are exposed.

14. You should plan to have a normal or near-normal weight before you become pregnant and maintain a nourishing, well-balanced diet during pregnancy.

Because you are your baby's total environment during the first crucial nine months of his existence, you must make sure that you are as healthy and as nourishing an environment as possible. This means that your diet must contain all the essential building blocks your baby needs to lay the foundation of a strong and healthy body, plus all the foods essential to keep your own body functioning well.

Women who have an inadequate diet do have more miscarriages, more stillborn babies, and more infants with low birth weight than those who are well nourished, many studies have shown. And there are many links between poor nutrition during pregnancy, low birth weight, and less-than-optimal mental and physical development after birth.

Experiments with laboratory animals demonstrate that depriving them of certain essential food elements will cause their offspring to be born with malformations and damaged brains. A shortage of protein, for example, is linked with abnormalities in brain development in animals. Although evidence is not so specific with humans—in part because research cannot be done in the same controlled way—there is good scientific reason for making sure your body is well nourished so that it, in turn, can be optimally nourishing for your unborn infant.

Women who can afford to eat an adequate diet during pregnancy may still not get sufficient nourishment for the health of their unborn infant, simply because they try to limit their weight gain too drastically. A three-year study by the National Research Council concludes that cutting calories too much during pregnancy may hurt the unborn baby's neurological development and make his birth weight danger-ously low. The council says that the ideal increase in weight during pregnancy should be about 24 pounds, or within the range of 20 to 25 pounds.

The American Medical Association sets the recommended gain for women during pregnancy at 22 to 26.4 pounds, added at a steady rate of a little less than one pound a week after the first trimester. Some physicians even consider an optimal weight gain to be as much as 30 pounds and are not concerned if the increase begins during the first months of pregnancy.

It is unusual now for a physician to recommend that a pregnant woman try to lose weight. It's much safer for the baby to wait to diet until after his birth.

Your baby should weigh at least five pounds and, ideally, closer to seven and a half pounds at birth for the safest, healthiest start in life. You will probably have to add about three hundred calories to your daily food intake to nourish him well in the months before he is born. You will also need extra protein, calcium, phosphorus, iron, and folic acid to provide for him adequately. The March of Dimes Birth Defects Foundation recommends this kind of a daily eating plan during pregnancy:

- Milk—Three cups daily for the first three months; four cups for the remaining six months.
- Protein—Three servings daily for the first trimester; four thereafter. Two to three ounces of cooked lean meat, poultry or fish, or 1/4 cup of peanut butter, or one ounce of nuts, or one egg equals one serving.
- Leafy green vegetable—Two servings.
- Fruits and vegetables rich in Vitamin C—One serving.
- Other fruits and vegetables—One serving.
- Whole grain cereals and enriched bread—Three servings a day, counting one slice of bread, 1/4 cup of rice or cereal or cooked pasta, or one muffin, pancake, waffle, or biscuit, or 3/4 cup of ready-to-eat cereal as a serving.

288

You may also need a vitamin supplement or additional iron. But you should take it only at your doctor's direction.

15. You should have good, regular prenatal care all during pregnancy supervised by a physician who is up-to-date on new medical research, the prevention of birth defects, and advances in childbirth and newborn care and who is associated with an excellent hospital.

Good prenatal care, for example, can help protect your baby from being born weighing less than a normal five pounds or more, with all the associated risks of less-than-normal mental and physical development. Advances in neonatal and perinatal care in recent years have saved the lives of a substantial percentage of low-birth-weight babies who previously would have died and have improved the likelihood that they will flourish well after leaving the hospital.

But starting life weighing abnormally little does impose extra risks on an infant that should be avoided if possible. For example, low-birth-weight babies have a much higher infant mortality rate than other infants. They are more likely to suffer injuries during childbirth. And being born too small is linked with a higher incidence of many other childhood problems, such as learning difficulties, mental retardation, and impairments of vision and hearing.

The term "low birth weight" covers two major groups of babies who are born weighing less than five pounds. Some babies are truly "premature." They are born three or more weeks before the end of the normal 266-day pregnancy and usually weigh about what a normal baby would be expected to weigh at that time in pregnancy. The other group are sometimes called "small-for-date" infants and, even if they are born at about the expected time, weigh considerably less than normal. Both groups of infants are "high risk" babies.

Babies can be born too small and/or too soon for any of several reasons, some of which may be interrelated. Often the baby's mother simply does not provide an optimal environment for her infant's development. She may be ill, malnourished herself (even during her own prenatal life), smoke during pregnancy, or be too old or too young or too often pregnant for her body to nourish a baby optimally. She may be carrying twins, who are likely to be born weighing less than single-born infants. Or the baby may be a tough survivor of abnormal development that would usually have resulted in miscarriage earlier in pregnancy.

It has long been known that low-birth-weight babies require extra care, that they need more frequent feedings, better protection from infections, and more careful control of temperature and humidity, and that they are more likely to suffer from medical problems than full-term, full-size infants. Doctors have also discovered that such babies are especially susceptible to medications, that even oxygen in excess can cause damage.

Low birth weight is also associated with neurological impairment later on in life, especially for the small-for-date babies. Intelligence among children who weighed markedly less than normal at birth is distributed on a curve, just as that of youngsters born with normal weight. But the whole curve is slightly lower than the one for other children, with a larger percentage of youngsters clustered in the lower-than-average part. Some research shows that children born too small are more vulnerable to their environment than other youngsters and that ample opportunities for early learning are particularly important for them.

In recent years, enormous medical progress has been made in safeguarding low-birth-weight babies. A new medical subspecialty—neonatology—is now devoted to the care of these infants and other high-risk babies. Most large teaching hospitals have developed complex neonatal intensive care units where arsenals of sophisticated equipment and specially trained nursing staffs concentrate on monitoring and treating these endangered children.

As a result, the mortality rate among low-birth-weight babies has been dropping steadily. Some infants weighing as little as two pounds or less now survive. And studies suggest that the long-term outlook for these children is now considerably brighter than it was when this book was first written.

Even so, it's important to protect your baby from the risk of low birth weight by all possible means. Regular prenatal care is one of the most important things you can do for your unborn infant. The March of Dimes Birth Defects Foundation made a study of 1.5 million full-term live births which showed that the more prenatal visits a pregnant woman made to her physician or to a health clinic, the greater the chances that her infant would be born full-term and of normal weight. Only 2 percent of the women who had the recommended thirteen to fourteen checkups had low-birth-weight babies, while 9 percent of those who had no prenatal care had high-risk infants.

You can also increase the chances that your baby will be born with normal weight by not smoking during pregnancy. By eating a proper diet. By getting sufficient rest. By avoiding exposure to infectious diseases. And by taking extra good care of yourself if you are older than forty, are pregnant with twins, or if you have already had a baby born too small or too soon.

Many conditions in a mother which can harm her unborn infant are now known and can be prevented or detected and treated by a doctor. For example, if a mother's thyroid gland is over—or under—active, her baby can be damaged, even if she isn't affected. Another mother whose baby may be in danger without her realizing it is the prediabetic. Her baby may be born ill, even though she herself may not develop actual diabetes for many more years.

In studying the case histories of mentally retarded children, it is frequently found that their mothers suffered complications of pregnancy, such as bleeding or toxemia. When these complications are associated with low birth weight, the baby runs a high risk of cerebral palsy, epilepsy, or mental retardation. If the baby is not born premature, he still has a greater-than-usual chance of having minor types of brain damage that can result in learning disabilities and behavior problems. One major purpose of prenatal care is to check for the possibility of toxemia and other complications and to prevent them or treat them quickly if they occur.

One technique researchers have developed to monitor a pregnancy is aimed at early detection of spina bifida, a crippling defect of the spinal column and spinal cord that often occurs in association with hydrocephalus, an abnormal amount of fluid in the brain which can cause brain damage and mental retardation. A test of the mother's blood can show if an abnormal amount of a substance called alphafeto-protein (AFP) is leaking from the baby's open spine into the amniotic fluid and into the mother's bloodstream. If the test is positive, the physician then orders further tests: another check of AFP levels, ultrasound, and amniocentesis.

Many physicians are reluctant to use these tests for spina bifida routinely on all patients for several reasons: The disorder is rare. The test must be so sensitive to AFP in the mother's blood to detect the substance at all that it picks up an enormous number of false positives. Out of all the pregnancies where the initial AFP test suggests the baby could have the abnormality, further tests eliminate all but about two percent. Detecting this small number of cases may not justify widespread screening of pregnant women, many of whom will be unnecessarily worried because of the initial report that something could be wrong. And as yet there is no treatment that can be started before birth. Parents of an unborn infant who is definitely diagnosed as having spina bifida have only two options: to terminate the pregnancy or to arrange for the infant to be delivered in a hospital equipped to give him the special care he will need.

Another reason for prenatal care is so your physician can detect whether you are at risk for having an infant with Rh disease and to protect him—and any future children you may have—from this disorder. Once a dreaded cause of brain damage and death before birth, Rh disease can almost always be prevented now, provided women whose unborn children are at risk of having this genetic problem get good medical care.

Basically, the Rh factor is present in the blood of about 85 percent of the population. It is an inherited trait, with the Rh-positive gene dominant and the Rh-negative gene recessive. Problems are possible only when an Rh-negative woman, married to an Rh-positive man, is carrying a baby whose blood is Rh-positive, like his father's.

Sometimes, as the Rh-positive baby is being born, as the placenta pulls away from the lining of the uterus, some of the infant's blood may seep into the mother's body through the uterine vein. The Rh-negative mother's body reacts to the Rh-factor in the baby's blood as if it were an invading foreign substance and begins to manufacture antibodies to destroy it. The antibodies don't harm the mother, because they are only directed at invading Rh-positive blood cells, not her own Rh-negative ones.

But the next time the mother becomes pregnant with an Rh-positive infant, these antibodies in her body can seep back across the placenta into the bloodstream of the growing baby and because they are produced specifically to attack Rh-positive blood cells, they do exactly that. If there are enough antibodies, they can destroy so many of the baby's red blood cells that he becomes anemic. A by-product of the destruction of the red blood cells is a pigment that causes jaundice. This substance can stain and kill brain cells and cause irreparable damage to the baby's central nervous system.

The damage may be so great that the growing baby dies in the fifth or sixth month of pregnancy or between that time and birth. In other cases, he may be born alive, but severely damaged. Or he may appear normal at birth, but may suffer from jaundice which develops rapidly in the first days after birth.

Amniocentesis was first developed—by Dr. A.W. Liley, of the University of Auckland in New Zealand—to diagnose unborn infants suffering from Rh disease. The first instances of unborn babies being given medical treatment were the blood transfusions Dr. Liley gave his severely ill Rh victims.

That method of fetal transfusion did save the lives of some endangered, unborn infants. But much better protection has now been developed which makes such complicated and risky treatment unnecessary in most cases. Now the blood of offspring of Rh-negative mothers is tested immediately after birth. If the baby is Rh-positive, the mother is given an injection of Rho-Gam, a gamma globulin substance with a high concentration of anti-Rh antibodies.

The antibodies in the Rh vaccine quickly go to work in the bloodstream of the Rh-negative mother, seeking out the baby's Rh-positive blood cells, coating them and destroying them before the mother's immune system can be turned on to produce antibodies against the invading blood cells. The antibodies in the vaccine last only about four months in the mother's body and will be gone before they could do damage to an unborn child in a future pregnancy.

The injection of Rh vaccine must be given to an Rh-negative woman within seventy-two hours after every birth of an Rh-positive baby, if Rh disease is to be prevented in her next infant. It must also be given following every miscarriage and abortion.

Unfortunately, Rh vaccine won't help women who became sensitized to Rh-positive blood before the vaccine became available, either because of a pregnancy or, in rare instances, because of a mismatched blood transfusion. But with the vaccine, Rh disease is becoming much more rare and once a generation of women has gone through their child-bearing years with this protection, Rh disease should become a rarity.

A good physician who has kept careful medical checks on a woman throughout pregnancy can do much to prevent any possible danger to her baby during the process of birth. New techniques for monitoring the well-being of the infant during labor and delivery can do much to prevent the possibility of brain damage and are responsible for substantial cuts in the incidence of infant mortality.

The hazards of being born are real, despite the exhilaration and sentiment that surround the entrance of a new life into the world and despite this country's comparatively low and decreasing infant mortality rate. You don't need to know all of the complications that can endanger your baby at birth. But you do want a doctor who knows.

Studies that trace the case histories of children who have learning problems in school, who can't read at grade level, and who have behavior difficulties often turn up records of difficult birth, birth injury, or delay in breathing. The normal process of labor and birth, even without anesthetics, cuts down markedly on a baby's supply of oxygen. Anesthetics, given in too large a quantity or at the wrong time during labor, can slice this slim margin of safety too thin, resulting in the possibility of brain damage or even death.

Drugs, such as muscle relaxants and depressants given to a mother in labor, can be a problem for a baby after birth. These medications don't wear off as quickly in a newborn as they do in the mother. When the infant is suddenly forced to survive on his own, the lingering effects of these drugs can prove more than he can handle, particularly if he has other problems. One reason you want a skilled and knowledgeable physician caring for you is to make any necessary medical decisions in a way that balances your welfare with that of your infant.

Learning all you can about pregnancy, labor, and birth and preparing your body for the process of childbirth can often reduce your need for pain-relieving drugs that might not be in your baby's best interests.

You should also make arrangements before your baby's birth for a pediatrician or family doctor who keeps up to date professionally to take over the medical care of your newborn. Your doctor should make sure your baby is given the simple blood test that can detect the devastating genetic disease phenylketonuria (PKU) and any other screening test for inborn metabolic disorders that your state requires or that your medical history suggests could be useful. If such a disorder is detected soon after birth and treatment—usually including a special diet—is begun, much of the worst damage can often be prevented.

Learning about the known hazards to an unborn infant can be uncomfortable and depressing, especially when they are all lumped together in a chapter like this. But it should be encouraging and hopeful, instead of frightening. When you understand some of the reasons why birth defects and mental retardation occur, then it's possible for you to take steps to prevent them from happening to your baby. With this knowledge, you can increase the odds—already tremendously in your favor—that the doctor will say of your next newborn infant, "He's just perfect!"

13. The Joys of Having a Bright Child

If you surround your youngster with the sort of mentally stimulating, encouraging home environment described in this book, will he become a "bright" child? Will he be classed as "highly intelligent" when he goes to school and will he be placed in top reading groups and in fast-track programs?

That's too sweeping a promise to make about a specific child at this point in the research about the development of intelligence in children and the effects of early learning. But it's a likelihood that many behavioral scientists and educators are studying seriously.

You can raise the intelligence level of almost every youngster a substantial degree by a stimulating, warm, early home environment. That much seems certain. Whether your child was born with a poor, average, or superior brain, an enriched environment will raise his eventual level of intellectual functioning, regardless of the genes he has inherited. If your youngster has been lucky enough to inherit an average or above-average brain to start with, chances are great that a warm, loving, mentally stimulating environment from infancy will help him develop into a bright or gifted youngster.

"Bright" and "gifted" are terms often used interchangeably to describe the kind of boys and girls who have superior ability and who consistently do better, develop sooner, or learn more and faster than children generally in any area of significance. Dr. Paul Witty, who spent most of his career at Northwestern University studying bright youngsters, defined giftedness as "consistently remarkable performance in any worthwhile line of endeavor."

Others who have studied highly talented youngsters define giftedness as the "ability to think, generalize, and to see connections and to use alternatives" and as "ability to think in the abstract, to perceive cause and effect relationships, and to project ideas into the future."

In a report to Congress in 1972, U.S. Commissioner of Education Sidney P. Marland used a broad definition of gifted and talented children as those capable of high performance in "any of the following areas: (a) general intellectual ability, (b) specific academic aptitude, (c) creative or productive thinking, (d) leadership ability, (e) visual and performing arts, (f) psychomotor ability."

The Gifted and Talented Children's Education Act of 1978 defined "gifted and talented" children as those "possessing demonstrated or potential abilities that give evidence of high performance capabilities, in areas such as intellectual, creative, specific academic or leadership ability, or in the performing and visual arts." (Many state education departments also use this definition or Dr. Marland's. With cutbacks in federal involvement in education, states now have much of the responsibility for developing programs for the gifted.)

Sometimes schools identify bright and gifted children by I.Q. test alone. Most prefer to add teacher evaluation, grades, and other criteria. Most programs use a broad definition that includes children who are highly capable not only in academic work but also in the creative arts and who show unusual leadership abilities.

A stimulating home environment in early childhood has played a part in the lives of an impressive number of highly intelligent and highly gifted individuals of great achievement. And when researchers probe into the background of school-age children rated as gifted or mentally superior by I.Q. tests, they typically find a stimulating home life and often deliberate planning by parents to help their children learn to use their brain.

For example, in collecting information about twenty-five

youngsters with superior I.Q.s, all of whom could read by the time they were three years old, Dr. Fowler discovered that 72 percent had "definitely enjoyed a great deal of unusually early and intensive" mental stimulation. Information wasn't available on the early childhood of the others.[1]

"The association between cognitive precocity and the application of intensive stimulation from infancy has always been impressively high," emphasized Dr. Fowler.

Dr. Robert J. Havighurst, of the University of Chicago, put it this way: "Boys and girls who are mentally superior have become so because of (1) a home and school environment which stimulated them to learn and to enjoy learning; (2) parents and other significant persons who set examples of interest and attainment in education which the children unconsciously imitated; and (3) early family training which produced a desire for achievement in the child. When these influences act upon a child with average or better biological equipment for learning, the child will become mentally superior."[2]

On the other hand, if a youngster who is born with superior biological endowment does not receive adequate early stimulation, he will not develop into a bright or gifted individual, researchers point out. It has been estimated that at least half of our potentially gifted children are wasted for lack of early opportunity to learn at a sufficiently fast and enriched rate.

But even if it is possible that you can help your youngster become mentally superior, is it desirable? Do you want a bright child in your family?

"I couldn't care less about a high I.Q. I just hope my kids turn out to be nice, average, normal youngsters," you occasionally hear a parent say. Some fathers and mothers—and even a few teachers—still picture a highly intelligent child as being a pale, puny prig who wears glasses and is just as inferior socially, emotionally, and physically as he is superior mentally. But they're just as mistaken as those who used to argue that genius is only a thin line away from insanity.

Another widely held—and mistaken—idea about gifted children is that they are pouring energy and effort into intellectual activities to cover up a painful inadequacy in another area of their life. No such evidence exists in dozens of excellent studies about the gifted. For much research has been done about what bright youngsters are really like—if not enough about precisely how and why they develop.

Researchers have learned that, as a group, bright youngsters are better adjusted emotionally than average children. They have fewer emotional problems and are better able to cope with the ones they do have. They are more emotionally stable and more emotionally mature than classmates of the same age.

Gifted children not only learn faster and easier than other youngsters, but sometimes seem to be learning in different ways. Often they don't need the step-by-step learning process that other children do; instead, they seem to acquire information in great jumps.

Gifted boys and girls are usually well liked and popular with other young people of all ability levels. They are elected to school offices more frequently and hold more leadership posts in extracurricular activities than their classmates. In the special tests that psychologists sometimes use to measure popularity among children, most gifted youngsters rank high, and they are usually chosen by many others as friends.

Studies of the very few children who have I.Q.s above 180 suggest that it's more difficult for these genius-level youngsters to find common interests and make friends with classmates of the same age who have average abilities. But they do get along easily and happily, generally, with high-ability classmates whose I.Q. may be 40 or 50 points lower.

Bright boys and girls aren't grinds who do nothing but study. They participate in extracurricular activities, including sports, as much or more than average-ability classmates. They have more hobbies and wider interests. They make more collections—larger and more scientific—than other children. They belong to more clubs. They know more games at a younger age. They write well, often with surprisingly mature insights. They are better able to amuse themselves when friends aren't available.

Nor are gifted youngsters stodgy and dull. They have a

more active sense of humor than other youngsters, research shows. They know, tell, and appreciate more jokes. And they are rated by researchers as happier and more enthusiastic about life in general than other youngsters.

In height, weight, coordination, and physical endurance, bright children as a group also tend to be above average. They have fewer illnesses and better-than-average health.

(These findings seem to point up the inherited aspects of high ability in children. But experiments with laboratory animals show clearly that early stimulation and learning experiences not only make the animals more intelligent than others born in the same litter, but also result in larger, stronger animals that are more resistant to diseases.)

Many educators have worried that gifted children, particularly if grouped in special high-ability classes, would become conceited, feel superior, and develop into an intellectual elite. Not so, research points up. Bright young people tend to underestimate their abilities and accomplishments, studies make clear. They boast less than other youngsters. They are more self-critical. And they usually rate the achievements and abilities of average classmates higher than they really are.

Bright children usually score high on measures of creativity and originality, although these are considered different factors in overall intelligence from those measured by the I.Q. test alone. Groups of high-I.Q. children, as a whole, do better in music and art than average youngsters.

Research shows that bright youngsters cause fewer problems for their parents than average youngsters. They are more self-sufficient and self-directing than others of the same age. They are less likely to have undesirable personality traits. They are dependable and self-starting; they have superior ability to adjust to problems and stress. They are responsible, conscientious, truthful, and trustworthy. They cheat less in school and cause fewer discipline problems than other children.

Contrary to some fears that gifted young people would exploit others, especially if identified openly and grouped together in classes, they tend to be altruistic and have an active social conscience. Their sense of personal responsibility is keen, and they typically feel more disturbed about injustices than classmates. It's apt to be the bright boy or girl who tries to play competitive games according to the rules, who stands up for the underdog, who is aware of the feelings and emotions of others.

Because gifted children are better than most youngsters at applying what they know to new situations and in seeing relationships, they rate high in traits like common sense. They are also adept at finding good, but unusual ways in which to solve problems or to reach goals.

Most gifted youngsters like school—unless it pressures them too much to conform to limited levels of work. They learn quickly, without much repetition, make good grades, and often list difficult subjects as their favorites. They read widely—twice as many books as average students, according to one study.

Gifted young people are more likely than other youngsters to go to college, and they make better grades than classmates when they are in college. They're also more apt to take postgraduate work.

Increasingly, bright children are being viewed as a national asset, as a treasured resource that should be cherished and guarded and helped to flourish. In recent years many schools have started special programs for gifted youngsters, who are identified by a variety of means, such as I.Q. tests, teacher recommendations, and evidences of unusual talent. Bright children may be assigned to enrichment programs, given opportunities to participate in special art or music classes, allowed to take experimental science courses, or invited to join Saturday programs for the gifted.

In some schools, bright children are grouped together in special fast tracks that whiz through an enriched curriculum at a speed more comfortable for them than the pace in a regular classroom. A typical program puts youngsters at least a year ahead of grade level by the time they finish junior high school, then allows them to take advanced college placement courses in high school. It's not unusual for such students to earn a year or more of college credits before high school graduation. They can then finish undergraduate requirements in three years, cutting college costs substantially, and get an earlier start on professional training or a job.

As interest in finding and stimulating the minds of gifted children grows, an increasing number of colleges, universities, and private schools are now offering summer enrichment programs for bright elementary and high school students. Organizations of parents and teachers devoted to the best interests of gifted children are at work in almost every state, making sure that bright youngsters are discovered and helped wherever they can be found. Most state departments of education also push for programs and special resources for the gifted. There are even periodic international conferences held to explore and promote better education for bright and gifted children.

As adults, the gifted typically fulfill the promise of their early youth and become productive, happy, contributing gifted men and women. There is no indication in any scientific research that the old adage of "early ripe, early rot" applies to bright youngsters.

Individuals who were identified as gifted in childhood and who have been followed into middle age have done well in high-level occupations, with earnings and achievements well above not only the general population, but above the average college graduate. Most are highly satisfied with their occupations. They read widely, particularly biography, history, and current drama. They are active in community affairs and organizations; they enjoy sports and have the same superior physical status and health records as they did in childhood. They report their marriages, generally, to be stable and their own lives to be happy to a greater degree than do individuals of average intelligence.

The long-term study begun by Lewis Terman, who followed the lives of a large group of gifted children beginning in 1922, has been continued by associates since his death in 1956. It has confirmed that these bright children generally do grow up to be superior to average individuals in general health, mental health, adult intelligence, income, careers, publications, patents and other evidences of high achievement and even in contentment with their lives and accomplishments.

Research like this sometimes makes gifted children sound almost too good to be true. Of course, not every bright child has all of these characteristics. Some with superior abilities

302

who aren't challenged enough in school turn into mischievous troublemakers or unhappy introverts. A few are exploited by parents who don't understand that their social and emotional needs are still those of children generally.

But on the whole, bright children are happy, productive, well liked, and have fewer problems than other youngsters. They are a joy to know and to rear. You will be glad if your offspring turns out to be gifted. You will undoubtedly feel that it has been worth the effort to give him a mentally stimulating first six years of life.

REFERENCES

CHAPTER 1

1. Seymour Papert, *Mindstorms: Children, Computers and Powerful Ideas,* New York, Basic Books, Inc., 1980.
2. Burton L. White, *The Origins of Human Competence,* Lexington, Massachusetts, D. C. Heath and Company, 1979.
3. J. McV. Hunt, *Intelligence and Experience,* New York, The Ronald Press Company, 1961.
4. Dolores Durkin, "Children Who Learned to Read at Home," *Elementary School Journal,* Vol. 62, October, 1961; and Dolores Durkin, "An Earlier Start in Reading?" *Elementary School Journal,* Vol. 63, December, 1962; and Dolores Durkin, "Children Who Read Before Grade 1: A Second Study," *Elementary School Journal,* Vol. 64, December, 1963; and Dolores Durkin, *Children Who Read Early,* New York, Teachers College Press, 1966.
5. Benjamin S. Bloom, Allison Davis, and Robert Hess, *Compensatory Education for Cultural Deprivation,* New York, Holt, Rinehart and Winston, Inc., 1965.
6. P. Berrueta-Clement and others, *Changed Lives: The Effects of the Perry Preschool Program on Youths*

Through Age 19, Ypsilanti, Michigan, High/Scope Press, 1984.

7. Judy C. Pfannenstiel and Dianne A. Seltzer, *Evaluation Report: New Parents as Teachers Project,* Missouri Department of Elementary & Secondary Education, Jefferson City, Missouri, 1985; "Parents as First Teachers," a series of guides for parents, Ferguson-Florissant School District, Florissant, Missouri, 1985.

8. William Fowler, "Longitudinal Study of Early Stimulation in the Emergence of Cognitive Processes," a paper sponsored by the Social Science Research Council, University of Chicago, February, 1966.

9. Richard Lynn, "I.Q. in Japan and the United States Shows a Growing Disparity," *Nature,* Vol. 297, 1982.

10. Harold W. Stevenson, "Making the Grade: School Achievement in Japan, Taiwan, and the United States," from the Annual Report of the Center for Advanced Study in the Behavioral Sciences, Ann Arbor, Michigan, 1984.

CHAPTER 2

1. Hunt, *op. cit.*

2. Wayne Dennis, "Causes of Retardation Among Institutional Children: Iran," *The Journal of Genetic Psychology,* Vol. 96, 1960.

3. Wayne Dennis and Yvonne Sayegh, "The Effect of Supplementary Experience Upon the Behavioral Development of Infants in Institutions," *Child Development,* Vol. 36, March, 1965.

4. Hunt, *op. cit.*

5. Mark R. Rosenzweig, David Krech, Edward L. Bennett, and Marian C. Diamond, "Heredity, Environment, Learning, and the Brain," a paper presented at annual meeting of the American Association for the Advancement of Science, Berkeley, California, December, 1965.

6. Lewis P. Lipsitt and John S. Werner, "The Infancy of Human Learning Processes," *Developmental Plasticity,* E. S. Gollin, editor, New York, Academic Press, Inc., 1981.

7. Hunt, *op. cit.*

8. Benjamin S. Bloom, *Stability and Change in Human Characteristics*, New York, John Wiley and Sons, Inc., 1964.

9. *Ibid.*

10. Wilder Penfield, "The Uncommitted Cortex," *The Atlantic Monthly*, Vol. 214, July, 1964.

11. Maria Montessori, *The Montessori Method*, new edition, Cambridge, Massachusetts, Robert Bentley, Inc., 1964.

12. George Stevens, "Reading for Young Children," in *Building the Foundations for Creative Learning*, Urban K. Fleege, editor, New York, American Montessori Society, 1964.

13. Wilder Penfield and Lamar Roberts, *Speech and Brain-Mechanisms*, Princeton, New Jersey, Princeton University Press, 1959.

14. Wilder Penfield, *The Second Career*, Boston, Little, Brown and Company, 1963.

15. Papert, *op. cit.*

16. Charles D. Smock and Bess Gene Holt, "Children's Reactions to Novelty: An Experimental Study of Curiosity Motivation," *Child Development*, Vol. 33, September, 1962.

17. Jean Piaget, *The Origin of Intelligence in Children*, New York, International Universities Press, 1952.

18. Robert W. White, "Motivation Reconsidered: The Concept of Competence," *The Psychological Review*, Vol. 66, 1959.

19. Piaget, *op. cit.*

CHAPTER 3

1. Kenneth D. Wann, Miriam Selchen Dorn, and Elizbeth Ann Liddle, *Fostering Intellectual Development in Young Children*, New York, Teachers College Press, 1962.

2. Rita Dunn, "Learning Style and Its Relation to Exceptionality at Both Ends of the Spectrum," *Exceptional Children*, April, 1983.

3. Robert D. Hess, "Social Class Influences Upon Pre-school Early Cognitive Development," an address to the American Montessori Society Seminar, New York, June, 1965; and Robert D. Hess and Virginia Shipman, "Early Blocks to Children's Learning," *Children*, Vol. 12, September–October, 1965.

4. Ellen Sheiner Moss, "Mothers and Gifted Preschoolers: Teaching and Learning Strategies," a paper presented at the annual meeting of the American Educational Research Association, Montreal, Canada, April, 1983.

5. Wann, *op. cit.*

6. Victor Goertzel and Mildred G. Goertzel, *Cradles of Eminence*, Boston, Little, Brown and Company, 1962.

7. Merle B. Karnes, Allan M. Shwedel, and Susan A. Linnemeyer, "The Young Gifted/Talented Child: Programs at the University of Illinois," *The Elementary School Journal*, Vol. 82, January, 1982.

8. Benjamin S. Bloom, "The Role of Gifts and Markers in the Development of Talent," *Exceptional Children*, Vol. 48, April, 1982.

9. Margie Kitano, "Young Gifted Children: Strategies for Preschool Teachers," *Young Children*, Vol. 37, May, 1982.

CHAPTER 4

1. Lewis P. Lipsitt, "Critical Conditions in Infancy," *American Psychologist*, Vol. 34, October, 1979.

2. Leon Eisenberg, "Reading Retardation: Psychiatric and Sociologic Aspects," *Pediatrics*, Vol. 37, February, 1966.

3. Anneliese F. Korner and Rose Grobstein, "Visual Alertness As Related to Soothing in Neonates: Implications for Maternal Stimulation and Early Deprivation," *Children Development*, Vol. 37, December, 1966.

4. Hunt, *op. cit.*

5. Newell C. Kephart, "Teaching the Child With Learning Disabilities," an address given to the West Suburban Association for the Other Child, Glen Ellyn, Illinois, January, 1968.

CHAPTER 5

1. Ernst L. Moerk, "The Mother of Eve—As a First Language Teacher," a paper given at a meeting of the Society for Research in Child Development, San Francisco, March, 1979.
2. Committee on Accident Prevention, "Responsibility Means Safety for Your Child," American Academy of Pediatrics, 1964.
3. Dorothy Aldis, *All Together,* New York, G. P. Putnam's Sons, New York, 1952.
4. Aileen Fisher, *Up the Windy Hill,* New York, Abelard-Schuman Limited, 1953.

CHAPTER 6

1. Wann, *op. cit.*

CHAPTER 7

1. Mabel Morphett and Carleton Washburne, "When Should Children Begin to Read?" *Elementary School Journal,* Vol. 31, March, 1931.
2. Arthur I. Gates, "Unsolved Problems in Reading: A Symposium, *Elementary English,* Vol. 31, October, 1954.
3. Montessori, *op. cit.*
4. Durkin, *op. cit.,* 1966.
5. *Chicago Tribune,* "Short Cuts to Reading You Can Teach Your Child," adapted by Joan Beck and Becky, from "Listen and Learn with Phonics," by Dorothy Taft Watson, *Chicago Tribune,* August–November, 1964.
6. Siegfried Engelman, Phyllis Haddox, and Elaine Bruner, *Teach Your Child to Read in 100 Easy Lessons,* New York, Cornerstone Library, Simon and Schuster, 1983.
7. Gates, *op. cit.*
8. Arthur W. Staats and Carolyn K. Staats, *Complex Hu-*

man Behavior, New York, Holt, Rinehart and Winston, Inc., 1964.

9. Joseph E. Brzeinski and John L. Hayman, Jr., Denver Public Schools, "The Effectiveness of Parents in Helping Their Preschool Children to Begin to Read," Denver, Denver Public Schools, September, 1962.

10. William H. Teale, "Positive Environments for Learning to Read: What Studies of Early Readers Tell Us," *Language Arts,* Vol. 55, November/December, 1978.

11. Dolores Durkin, "A Fifth Year Report on the Achievement of Early Readers," *Elementary School Journal,* Vol. 65, November, 1964.

12. Paul McKee and Joseph E. Brzeinski, "The Effectiveness of Teaching Reading in Kindergarten," Denver, Denver Public Schools, 1966.

CHAPTER 8

1. E. Paul Torrance, "Education and Creativity," in *Creativity: Progress and Potential,* Calvin W. Taylor, ed., New York, McGraw-Hill Book Company, Inc., 1964.

2. E. Paul Torrance, *Guiding Creative Talent,* Englewood Cliffs, N.J., Prentice-Hall, Inc., 1962.

3. Torrance, *op. cit.,* 1964.

CHAPTER 9

1. Montessori, *op. cit.*

CHAPTER 10

1. Ann McCormick Piestrup, "A Computer in the Nursery School," in *Intelligent Schoolhouse: Readings on Computers and Learning,* Dale Peterson, editor, Reston, Virginia, Reston Publishing Company, Inc., 1984.

2. Fred D'Ignazio, "Can Toddlers Tackle Computers?" *Compute!'s PC & PC jr,* Vol. 1, August, 1984.

3. Mina Spencer and Linda Baskin, "Microcomputers in

Early Childhood Education," a report for the National Institute of Education, Washington, D. C., 1983.

4. Radia Perlman, "Using Computer Technology to Provide a Creative Learning Environment for Preschool Children," a report for the National Science Foundation, Washington, D. C., 1976.

5. Seymour Papert, "Computer as Mudpie," in *Intelligent Schoolhouse: Readings on Computers and Learning,* Dale Peterson, *op. cit.*

CHAPTER 11

1. Richard L. Masland, "Mental Retardation," in *Birth Defects,* Morris Fishbein, editor, Philadelphia, J. B. Lippincott Company, 1963.

2. Samuel L. Katz, "International Symposium on Measles Immunization: Summary and Recommendations," in *Pediatrics,* Vol. 71, April, 1983.

3. American Academy of Pediatrics, Committee on Research and Committee on Accident and Poison Prevention, "Reducing the Toll of Injuries in Childhood Requires Support for a Focused Research Effort," *Pediatrics,* Vol. 72, November, 1983.

4. American Academy of Pediatrics, Committee on Sports Medicine, "Participation in Boxing Among Children and Young Adults," *Pediatrics,* Vol. 74, August, 1984.

5. Robert Glenn Morrison, "Medical and Public Health Aspects of Boxing," *Journal of the American Medical Association,* Vol. 255, May 9, 1986.

CHAPTER 12

1. Marsha F. Goldsmith, "Possible Herpesvirus Role in Abortion Studied," *Journal of the American Medical Association,* Vol. 251, June 15, 1984.

2. Lisa J. Raines and Stephen P. Push, "Protecting Pregnant Workers," *Harvard Business Review, Vol. 64, May–June, 1986.*

CHAPTER 13

1. William Fowler, "Cognitive Learning in Infancy and Early Childhood," *The Psychological Bulletin,* Vol. 59, March, 1962.
2. Robert J. Havighurst, "Conditions Productive of Superior Children," *Teachers College Record,* Vol. 62, April, 1961.

Bibliography

Aase, Jon M., "The Fetal Alcohol Syndrome, 1984," a paper presented at the annual meeting of the American Association for the Advancement of Science, New York, May, 1984.

Adams, Judith, and Craig R. Ramey, "Structural Aspects of Maternal Speech to Infants Reared in Poverty," *Child Development,* Vol. 51, December, 1980.

Albert, Robert S., "Exceptionally Gifted Boys and Their Parents," *Gifted Child Quarterly,* Vol. 24, Fall, 1980.

Alcohol, Drug Abuse, and Mental Health Administration, *The Fifth Special Report to the U.S. Congress on Alcohol and Health,* Rockville, Maryland, U.S. Department of Health and Human Services, 1983.

Almay, Millie, Edward Chittenden, and Paula Miller, *Young Children's Thinking,* New York, Teachers College Press, 1966.

American Academy of Pediatrics, Committee on Fetus and Newborn and Committee on Infectious Diseases, "Perinatal Herpes Simplex Virus Infections," *Pediatrics,* Vol. 66, July, 1980.

———, Committee on Genetics, "Prenatal Diagnosis for Pediatricians," *Pediatrics,* Vol. 65, June, 1980.

———, Committee on Research and Committee on Accident

and Poison Prevention, "Reducing the Toll of Injuries in Childhood Requires Support for a Focused Research Effort," *Pediatrics*, Vol. 72, November, 1983.

American Council on Science and Health, "Health and Safety Aspects of Video Display Terminals," September, 1983.

Anger, W. Kent, "Neurobehavioral Testing in the Workplace," a paper presented at the annual meeting of the American Association for the Advancement of Science, Washington, D.C., January, 1982.

Annest, Joseph L., and others, "Chronological Trend in Blood Lead Levels Between 1976 and 1980," *The New England Journal of Medicine*, Vol. 308, June 9, 1983.

Anthony, Sylvia, "Suggestions to 'Turn On' Bright Children at Home," *G/C/T*, November/December, 1982.

Apgar, Virginia, and Joan Beck, *Is My Baby All Right?* New York, Simon and Schuster, 1972.

Backman, Joan, "The Role of Psycholinguistic Skills in Reading Acquisition: A Look at Early Readers," *Reading Research Quarterly*, Vol. 18, Summer, 1983.

Bakeman, Roger, and Josephine V. Brown, "Early Interaction: Consequences for Social and Mental Development at Three Years," *Child Development*, Vol. 51, June, 1980.

Banks, Martin S., "The Development of Visual Accommodation During Early Infancy," *Child Development*, Vol. 51, September, 1980.

Barrera, Maria E., and Daphne Maurer, "Discrimination of Strangers by the Three-Month-Old," *Child Development*, Vol. 52, June, 1981.

Bates, John E., and others, "Dimensions of Individuality in the Mother-Infant Relationship at Six Months of Age," *Child Development*, Vol. 53, April, 1982.

Beck, Joan, *Best Beginnings*, New York, G. P. Putnam's Sons, 1983.

———, *Effective Parenting*, New York, Simon and Schuster, 1975.

Belsky, Jay, "The Determinants of Parenting: A Process Model," *Child Development*, Vol. 55, February, 1984.

———, Mary Kay Goode and Robert K. Most, "Maternal Stimulation and Infant Exploratory Competence:

Cross-Sectional, Correlational and Experimental Analyses," *Child Development*, Vol. 51, December, 1980.

Benbow, Camilla P., and Julian C. Stanley, "Intellectually Talented Students: Family Profiles," *Gifted Child Quarterly*, Vol. 24, Summer, 1980.

Benbow, Camilla P., and Julian C. Stanley, editors, *Academic Precocity: Aspects of Its Development*, Baltimore, The Johns Hopkins University Press, 1983.

Berger, Lawrence R., and others, "Promoting the Use of Car Safety Devices for Infants: An Intensive Health Education Approach," *Pediatrics*, Vol. 74, July, 1984.

Berrueta, Clement P. and others, *Changed Lives*, Ypsilanti, Michigan, The High/Scope Press, 1984.

Binkin, Nancy J., Jeffrey P. Koplan, and Willard Cates Jr., "Preventing Neonatal Herpes," *The Journal of the American Medical Association*, Vol. 251, June 1, 1984.

Blanton, William E., "Preschool Reading Instruction: A Literature Search, Evaluation and Interpretation," National Center for Educational Communication, Department of Health, Education, and Welfare, Washington, D.C., June, 1972.

Bloom, Benjamin, editor, *Developing Talent in Young People*, New York, Ballantine, 1985.

———, "The Role of Gifts and Markers in the Development of Talent," *Exceptional Children*, Vol. 48, April, 1982.

———, *Stability and Change in Human Characteristics*, New York, John Wiley & Sons, 1964.

Boegehold, Betty D., and others, *Education Before Five: A Handbook on Preschool Education*, New York, Bank Street College of Education, 1977.

Bowlby, John, *Attachment*, New York, Basic Books, 1969.

———, *Separation*, New York, Basic Books, 1973.

Bowman, Barbara T., "Do Computers Have a Place in Preschools?" a paper presented at a meeting of the New Mexico Association for the Education of Young Children, Albuquerque, February, 1983.

Bradley, Robert H., and Bettye M. Caldwell, "Early Home Environment and Changes in Mental Test Performances in Children from Six to 36 Months," a paper presented at the American Educational Research Association meeting, Washington, D.C., 1975.

————, "The Relation of Home Environment, Cognitive Competence, and I.Q. Among Males and Females," *Child Development*, Vol. 51, December, 1980.

Braude, Monique C., and Jacqueline P. Ludford, *Marijuana Effects on the Endocrine and Reproductive Systems*, National Institute on Drug Abuse, Department of Health and Human Services, Rockville, Maryland, 1984.

Brazelton, T. Berry, "The Joint Regulation of Infant-Adult Interaction," a paper presented at the annual meeting of the American Association for the Advancement of Science, Denver, February, 1977.

————, *On Becoming a Family: The Growth of Attachment*, New York, Delacorte Press/Seymour Lawrence, 1981.

Brenner, Barbara, and Mari Endreweit, *Bank Street's Family Computer Book*, New York, Ballantine Books, 1984.

Brock, William M., "The Effects of Day Care: A Review of the Literature," Southwest Regional Laboratory for Educational Research and Development, Los Alamitos, California, 1980.

Brunell, Philip A., "Prevention and Treatment of Neonatal Herpes," *Pediatrics*, Vol. 66, November, 1980.

Brzeinski, Joseph E., and John L. Hayman, *The Effectiveness of Parents in Helping Their Preschool Children to Begin to Read*, Denver, Denver Public Schools, September, 1962.

Brzeinski, Joseph E., and Will Howard, "Early Reading— How, Not When!" *The Reading Teacher*, Vol. 25, 1971.

Bureau, M. A., and others, "Carboxyhemoglobin Concentration in Fetal Cord Blood and in Blood of Mothers Who Smoked During Labor," *Pediatrics*, Vol. 69, March, 1982.

————, "Maternal Cigarette Smoking and Fetal Oxygen Transport," *Pediatrics*, Vol. 72, July, 1983.

Burton, Barbara K., and Henry L. Nadler, "Antenatal Diagnosis of Metabolic Disorders," *Clinical Obstetrics and Gynecology*, Vol. 24, December, 1981.

Carew, Jean V., "Experience and the Development of Intelligence in Young Children at Home and in Day Care," *Monographs of the Society for Research in Child Development*, Vol. 45, 1980.

————, "Predicting I.Q. from the Young Child's Everyday Experience," a paper presented at the symposium "Soziale Bedingungen fur die Entwicklung der Lernfahigkeit," Bad Homburg, West Germany, October, 1975.

————, and others, "Observed Intellectual Competence and Tested Intelligence: Their Roots in the Young Child's Transactions with His Environment," a paper presented at the Eastern Psychological Association meeting, New York, April, 1975.

Carrelli, Anne O'Brien, "Sex Equity and the Gifted," *G/C/T*, November/December, 1982.

Chall, Jeanne, *Learning to Read: The Great Debate*, New York, McGraw-Hill, 1967.

Charney, Evan, and others, "Childhood Lead Poisoning," *The New England Journal of Medicine*, Vol. 309, November 3, 1983.

Chattin-McNichols, John P., "The Effects of Montessori School Experience," *Young Children*, Vol. 36, July, 1981.

"Children in Crashes," Insurance Institute for Highway Safety, Washington, D.C., December, 1980.

Children's Defense Fund, "Give More Children a Head Start," Washington, D.C., CDF Publications, 1983.

Clarke-Stewart, Alison, *Child Care in the Family: A Review of Research and Some Propositions for Policy*, New York, Academic Press, 1977.

Clarren, Sterling, and David W. Smith, "The Fetal Alcohol Syndrome," *The New England Journal of Medicine*, Vol. 298, May 11, 1978.

Cohen, Leslie B., "Our Developing Knowledge of Infant Perception and Cognition," *American Psychologist*, Vol. 34, October, 1979.

Cohen, Sarale E., and Leila Beckwith, "Preterm Infant Interaction with the Caregiver in the First Year of Life and Competence at Age Two," *Child Development*, Vol. 50, September, 1979.

Coleman, Dona, "Parenting the Gifted: Is This a Job for Superparent?" *G/C/T*, March–April, 1982.

Colletti, Richard B., "Hospital-Based Rental Programs to Increase Car Seat Usage," *Pediatrics*, Vol. 71, May, 1983.

Consortium on Developmental Continuity, "The Persistence of Preschool Effects: A Long-Term Follow-Up of 14 Infant and Preschool Experiments," Washington, D.C., Department of Health, Education, and Welfare, September, 1977.

Cuffaro, Harriet K., "Microcomputers in Education: Why Is Earlier Better?" *Teachers College Record,* Vol. 85, Summer, 1984.

Davidson, Jane, "Wasted Time: The Ignored Dilemma," *Young Children,* Vol. 35, May, 1980.

Day, David E., *Early Childhood Education: A Human Ecological Approach,* Glenview, Illinois, Scott, Foresman, and Company, 1983.

Day, Mary Carol, and Ronald K. Parker, editors, *The Preschool in Action: Exploring Early Childhood Programs,* Boston, Allyn and Bacon, Inc., 1977.

D'Ignazio, Fred, "Can Toddlers Tackle Computers? *Compute!'s PC and PC jr,* Vol. 1, August, 1984.

Douglas, Jane T., "Dollars and Sense: Employer-Supported Child Care: A Study of Child Care Needs and the Realities of Employer-Support," Washington, D.C., Office of Child Development, Department of Health, Education, and Welfare, 1976.

Drash, Philip W., and Arnold L. Stolberg, "Acceleration of Cognitive, Linguistic and Social Development in the Normal Infant," Tallahassee, Florida, Florida State Department of Health and Rehabilitative Services, 1977.

Dunn, Rita, "Learning Style and Its Relation to Exceptionality at Both Ends of the Spectrum," *Exceptional Children,* April, 1983.

Durkin, Dolores, "Children Who Learned to Read at Home," *Elementary School Journal,* Vol. 62, October, 1961.

———, "Children Who Read Before Grade 1: A Second Study," *Elementary School Journal,* Vol. 63, December, 1962.

———, *Children Who Read Early,* New York, Teachers College Press, 1966.

———, "An Earlier Start in Reading?" *Elementary School Journal,* Vol. 63, December, 1962.

————, *Getting Reading Started,* Boston, Allyn, and Bacon, Inc., 1982.

————, "A Six Year Study of Children Who Learned To Read in School at the Age of Four," *Reading Research Quarterly,* Vol. 10, 1974.

Earls, Felton, "The Fathers (Not the Mothers): Their Importance and Influence with Infants and Young Children," in *Annual Progress in Child Psychiatry and Child Development,* edited by Sella Chess and Alexander Thomas, New York, Brunner Mazel, 1977.

Eisenberg, "Social Context of Child Development," *Pediatrics,* Vol. 68, November, 1981.

Elardo, Richard, and others, "A Longitudinal Study of the Relation of Infants' Home Environments to Language Development at Age Three," Center for Early Development and Education, Department of Health, Education and Welfare, Washington, D.C.

Elardo, Richard, Robert Bradley, and Bettye M. Caldwell, "The Relation of Infants' Home Environment to Mental Test Performance from Six to 36 Months: A Longitudinal Analysis," *Child Development,* Vol. 46, March, 1975.

Eliason, Claudia Furiman, and Loa Thomson Jenkins, *A Practical Guide to Early Childhood Curriculum,* St. Louis, C. V. Mosby Company, 1981.

Emery, Donald G., *Teach Your Preschooler To Read,* New York, Simon and Schuster, 1975.

Engelmann, Siegfried, Phyllis Haddox, and Elaine Bruner, *Teach Your Child To Read in 100 Easy Lessons,* New York, Cornerstone Library, Simon and Schuster, 1983.

Epstein, Carol B., "The Gifted and Talented: Programs that Work," National School Public Relations Association, Arlington, Virginia, 1979.

Eveloff, Herbert H., "Some Cognitive and Affective Aspects of Early Learning Development," *Child Development,* Vol. 42, December, 1971.

Family Policy Panel of the Economic Policy Council of UNA–USA, "Work and Family in the United States: A Policy Initiative," New York, 1985.

Fantz, Robert L., and Joseph F. Fagan III, "Visual Attention to Size and Number of Pattern Details by Term and Preterm Infants During the First Six Months," *Child Development,* Vol. 46, March, 1975.

Fehrle, Carl C., and others, "The Most-Asked Questions about Gifted Children: Answers for Parents and Educators," Extension Publications, University of Missouri/Columbia, 1982.

Ferguson, Patricia, Thomas Lennox, and Dan J. Lettieri, editors, *Drugs and Pregnancy,* Rockville, Maryland, National Institute on Drug Abuse, Department of Health, Education, and Welfare, November, 1974.

Field, Jeffrey, and others, "Infants' Orientation to Lateral Sounds from Birth to Three Months," *Child Development,* Vol. 51, March, 1980.

Field, Tiffany, and Reena Greenberg, "Temperament Ratings by Parents and Teachers of Infants, Toddlers, and Preschool Children," *Child Development,* Vol. 53, February, 1982.

Flank, Sandra, "Little Hands on the Computer," *G/C/T,* November/December, 1982.

Flavell, John H., *Cognitive Development,* Englewood Cliffs, N.J., Prentice-Hall, 1977.

Fowler, William, "Structural Dimensions of the Learning Process in Early Reading," *Child Development,* Vol. 35, December, 1964.

————, "Teaching a Two-Year-Old to Read: An Experiment in Early Childhood Learning," *Genetic Psychology Monographs,* Vol. 66, 1962.

Fox, Lynn H., "Preparing Gifted Girls for Future Leadership Roles," *G/C/T,* March/April, 1981.

Furey, Eileen M., "The Effects of Alcohol on the Fetus," *Exceptional Children,* Vol. 49, 1982.

Gallas, Howard B., and Michael Lewis, "Mother-Infant Interaction and Cognitive Development in the 12-Week-Old Infant," a paper presented at the Society for Research in Child Development, New Orleans, March, 1977.

Gelman, Rochel, "Preschool Thought," *American Psychologist,* Vol. 34, October, 1979.

Geschwind, Norman, "Neurological Foundations of Hemispheric Functional Asymmetry," a paper presented at the annual meeting of the American Association for the Advancement of Science, Houston, January, 1979.

Ginsberg-Riggs, Gina, "Being Comfortable with Gifted Children," *G/C/T*, March/April, 1981.

Gladieux, Rosemary, "How to Help Your Gifted Child: It's as Easy as ABC," *G/C/T*, September/October, 1981.

Goldsmith, Marsha F., "Possible Herpesvirus Role in Abortion Studied," *The Journal of the American Medical Association*, Vol. 251, June 15, 1984.

Goodman, Norman, and Joseph Andrews, "Cognitive Development of Children in Family and Group Day Care," *American Journal of Orthopsychiatry*, Vol. 51, April, 1981.

Gordon, Ira, "Parent Oriented Home-Based Early Childhood Education Program: Research Report," Gainesville, Florida, Florida University, Institute for Development of Human Resources, May, 1975.

Gould, Toni S., *Home Guide to Early Reading*, New York, Walker and Company, 1976.

Green, James A., Gwen E. Gustofson, and Meredith J. West, "Effects of Infant Development on Mother-Infant Interactions," *Child Development*, Vol. 51, March, 1980.

Greenberg, David J., and William J. O'Donnell, "Infancy and the Optimal Level of Stimulation," *Child Development*, Vol. 43, June, 1972.

Greenfield, Patricia Marks, *Minds and Media: The Effects of Television, Video Games, and Computers*, Cambridge, Massachusetts, Harvard University Press, 1984.

Grotberg, Edith H., and Bernard Brown, "Research on Child Care," a paper presented at the Research Forum on Children and Youth, Washington, D.C., May, 1981.

Guilford, Arthur M., Jane Scheuerie, and Susan Shonburn, "Aspects of Language Development in the Gifted," *Gifted Child Quarterly*, Vol. 25, Fall, 1981.

Guillory, Andrea, "The First Four Months: Development of Affect, Cognition, and Synchrony," a paper presented at the American Psychological Association meeting, Washington, D.C., August, 1982.

Gurren, Louise, and Ann Hughes, "Intensive Phonics vs. Gradual Phonics in Beginning Reading: A Review," *The Journal of Educational Research,* Vol. 58, April, 1965.

Hanson, James W., Ann Pytkowicz Steissguth, and David W. Smith, "The Effects of Moderate Alcohol Consumption During Pregnancy on Fetal Growth and Morphogenesis," a paper presented at the Fifth International Conference on Birth Defects, Montreal, August, 1977.

Harvey, Mary Ann Sedgwick, Marcella J. McRorie, and David W. Smith, "Suggested Limits to the Use of Hot Tub and Sauna by Pregnant Women," *Obstetrical and Gynecological Survey,* Vol. 37, 1982.

Hertz, Thomas H., "The Impact of Federal Early Childhood Programs on Children," Washington, D.C., Department of Health, Education, and Welfare, July, 1977.

Hess, Robert D., "The Effects of Parent Training Programs on Child Performance and Parent Behavior," a paper presented at the annual meeting of the American Association for the Advancement of Science, Denver, February, 1977.

Hock, Ellen, "Alternative Approaches to Child Rearing and Their Effects on the Mother-Infant Relationship: Final Report," Washington, D.C., Department of Health, Education, and Welfare, 1976.

————, "Working and Nonworking Mothers and Their Infants: A Comparative Study of Maternal Caregiving Characteristics and Infant Social Behavior," *Merrill-Palmer Quarterly,* Vol. 26, April, 1980.

Holden, George W., "Avoiding Conflict: Mothers as Tacticians in the Supermarket," *Child Development,* Vol. 54, 1983.

Holton, Felicia Antonelli, *CompuKids: A Parents' Guide to Computers and Learning,* New York, New American Library, 1985.

Holtzman, Mathilda, "The Verbal Environment Provided by Mothers for Their Very Young Children," *Merrill-Palmer Quarterly,* Vol. 20, January, 1974.

Holtzman, Neil A., and others, "Effect of Informed Parental Consent on Mothers' Knowledge of Newborn Screening," *Pediatrics,* Vol. 72, December, 1983.

Hunt, J. McV., *Intelligence and Experience*, New York, Ronald Press, 1961.

Jennings, Kay D., and Robin E. Conners, "Children's Cognitive Development and Free Play: Relations to Maternal Behavior," paper presented at the Society for Research in Child Development meeting, Detroit, April, 1983.

Jensen, Rita A., and John Wedman, "The Computer's Role in Gifted Education," *G/C/T*, November/December, 1983.

Joffe, S., R. Childiaeva, and V. Chernick, "Prolonged Effects of Maternal Alcohol Ingestion on the Neonatal Electroencephalogram," *Pediatrics*, Vol. 74, September, 1984.

Kagan, Jerome, "The Effect of Day Care on the Infant," a paper prepared for the Department of Health, Education, and Welfare, Washington, D.C., June, 1976.

——, "The Effects of Infant Day Care on Psychological Development," a paper presented at the annual meeting of the American Association for the Advancement of Science, Boston, February, 1976.

——, and Margaret Hamburg, "The Enhancement of Memory in the First Year," *The Journal of Genetic Psychology*, Vol. 138, 1981.

——, Richard B. Kearsley, and Philip R. Zelazo, *Infancy: Its Place in Human Development*, Cambridge, Massachusetts, Harvard University Press, 1978.

Kalter, Harold, and Josef Warkany, "Congenital Malformations: Etiologic Factors and Their Role in Prevention," *The New England Journal of Medicine*, Vol. 308, February 24, 1983.

Karger, Rex H., "Synchrony in Mother-Infant Interaction," *Child Development*, Vol. 50, September, 1979.

Karnes, Frances A., and M. Ray Karnes, "Parents and Schools: Educating Gifted and Talented Children," *The Elementary School Journal*, Vol. 82, January, 1982.

Karnes, Merle B., Allan M. Shwedel, and Susan A. Linnemeyer, "The Young Gifted/Talented Child: Programs at the University of Illinois," *The Elementary School Journal*, Vol. 82, January, 1982.

Katz, Samuel L., "International Symposium on Measles Immunization: Summary and Recommendations," *Pediatrics*, Vol. 71, 1983.

Kierscht, Marcia, "Correlates of Early Infant Competence: A Multivariate Approach, Final Report, Part I," Washington, D.C., Department of Health, Education, and Welfare, August, 1975.

Kilmer, Sally, "Infant-Toddler Group Day Care: A Review of Research," a paper sponsored by the National Institute of Education, Washington, D.C., December, 1977.

Kitano, Margie, "Young Gifted Children: Strategies for Preschool Teachers," *Young Children*, Vol. 37, May, 1982.

Klein, Ronald D., "An Inquiry into the Factors Related to Creativity," *The Elementary School Journal*, Vol. 82, January, 1982.

Krekel, Sylvia, "Placement of Women in High Risk Areas," a paper given at the Conference on Women and the Workplace, Washington, D.C., June, 1976.

Lamb, Michael E., "Development and Function of Parent-Infant Relationships in the First Two Years of Life," a paper given at the Society for Research in Child Development meeting, New Orleans, March, 1977.

Laosa, Luis M., "Maternal Teaching Strategies and Cognitive Styles in Chicano Families," *Journal of Educational Psychology*, Vol. 72, 1980.

Lavine, Mary P., "Biology in the Workplace: Ethical and Policy Problems," a paper presented at the annual meeting of the American Association for the Advancement of Science, New York, May, 1984.

Ledson, Sidney, *Teach Your Child To Read in 60 Days*, New York, W. W. Norton and Company, Inc., 1975.

Levin, Stephen R., Thomas V. Petros, and Florence W. Petrella, "Preschoolers' Awareness of Television Advertising," *Child Development*, Vol. 53, August, 1982.

Lewkowicz, David J., and Gerald Turkewitz, "Intersensory Interaction in Newborns: Modifications of Visual Preferences Following Exposure to Sounds," *Child Development*, Vol. 52, September, 1981.

Lipper, Evelyn, and others, "Determinants of Neurobehavioral Outcomes in Low-Birth-Weight Infants," *Pediatrics*, Vol. 67, April, 1981.

Lipsitt, Lewis P., "Critical Conditions in Infancy," *American Psychologist,* Vol. 34, October, 1979.

————, and John S. Werner, "The Infancy of Human Learning Processes," *Developmental Plasticity,* E. S. Gollin, editor, New York, Academic Press, Inc., 1981.

Longo, Lawrence D., "Maternal Smoking: Effects on the Fetus and Newborn Infant," a paper given at the annual meeting of the American Association for the Advancement of Science, San Francisco, January, 1980.

Lowman, Kaye, *Of Cradles and Careers,* Franklin Park, Illinois, La Leche League International, 1984.

Lynn, Richard, "I.Q. in Japan and the United States Shows a Growing Disparity," *Nature,* Vol. 297, May 20, 1982.

Lytton, Hugh, and Denise Watts, "Continuities and Discontinuities in Cognitive and Social Characteristics from Age 2 to Age 9," a paper presented at the Society for Research in Child Development meeting, Boston, April, 1981.

Macri, James N., David A. Baker, and Roger S. Baim, "Diagnosis of Neural Tube Defects by Evaluation of Amniotic Fluid," *Clinical Obstetrics and Gynecology,* Vol. 24, December, 1981.

Mactutus, Charles F., and Laurence D. Fechter, "Prenatal Exposure to Carbon Monoxide: Learning and Memory Deficits," *Science,* Vol. 223, January 27, 1984.

Malone, Thomas W., "Guidelines for Designing Educational Computer Programs," *Childhood Education,* March/April, 1983.

March of Dimes Science News Information File, *Radiation and Birth Defects,* March of Dimes Birth Defects Foundation, August, 1979.

Marland, Sidney P., Jr., "Education of the Gifted and Talented," report to the Congress of the United States by the U.S. Commissioner of Education, Washington, D.C., U.S. Government Printing Office, 1972.

Mass, Leslie Noyes, "Developing Concepts of Literacy in Young Children," *The Reading Teacher,* Vol. 35, March, 1982.

McCall, Robert B., "Environmental Effects on Intelligence: The Forgotten Realm of Discontinuous Nonshared

Within-in Family Factors," *Child Development,* Vol. 44, April, 1983.

McHardy, Roberta, "Planning for Preschool Gifted Education," *G/C/T,* September/October, 1983.

McKee, Paul, and Joseph Brzeinski, *The Effectiveness of Teaching Reading in Kindergarten,* Denver, Denver Public Schools, 1966.

McQuilkin, Charlette E., "Parents of the Gifted—Look Homeward," *G/C/T,* March/April, 1981.

Meltzoff, Andrew N., and M. Keith Moore, "Newborn Infants Imitate Adult Facial Gestures," *Child Development,* Vol. 54, June, 1983.

Metzl, Marilyn Newman, "Teaching Parents a Strategy for Enhancing Infant Development," *Child Development,* Vol. 51, June, 1980.

Meyer, Mary B., "Smoking and the Developing Fetus," a paper presented at the annual meeting of the American Association for the Advancement of Science, San Francisco, January, 1980.

Miller, Bernard S., and Merle Price, editors, *The Gifted Child, the Family, and the Community,* New York, The American Association for Gifted Children, 1981.

Miller, Louise B., and Rondeall P. Bizzell, "Long-Term Effects of Four Preschool Programs: Sixth, Seventh and Eighth Grades," *Child Development,* Vol. 54, 1983.

Moerk, Ernst L., "The Mother of Eve—As a First Language Teacher," a paper given at the Society for Research in Child Development meeting, San Francisco, March, 1979.

Montessori, Maria, *The Absorbent Mind,* New York, Holt, Rinehart, and Winston, 1967.

———, *The Discovery of the Child,* New York, Ballantine Books, 1972.

———, *A Montessori Handbook,* edited by R. C. Orem, New York, G. P. Putnam's Sons, 1965.

———, *The Montessori Method,* Cambridge, Massachusetts, Robert Bentley, 1964.

———, *The Secret of Childhood,* New York, Ballantine Books, 1972.

Moore, Nancy Delano, "The Joys and Challenges in Raising a Gifted Child," *G/C/T,* November/December, 1982.

Moran, James D. III, Roberta M. Milgram, Janet K. Sawyers, and Victoria R. Fu, "Original Thinking in Preschool Children," *Child Development,* Vol. 54, August, 1983.

Moss, Ellen Sheiner, "Mothers and Gifted Preschoolers: Teaching and Learning Strategies," a paper presented at the annual meeting of the American Educational Research Association, Montreal, Canada, April, 1983.

Motz, Sister Mary, *Montessori Matters: A Language Manual,* Cincinnati, Ohio, Sisters of Notre Dame de Namur, 1980.

Moxley, Roy, *Writing and Reading in Early Childhood,* Englewood Cliffs, New Jersey, Educational Technology Publications, 1982.

Murray, Ann D., "Maternal Employment Reconsidered: Effects on Infants," *American Journal of Orthopsychiatry,* Vol. 45, October, 1975.

Naeye, Richard L., "Influence of Maternal Cigarette Smoking During Pregnancy on Fetal and Childhood Growth," *Obstetrics and Gynecology,* Vol. 57, January, 1981.

Ogbu, John U., "Origins of Human Competence: A Cultural-Ecological Perspective," *Child Development,* Vol. 52, June, 1981.

Omenn, Gilbert, "Eco-genetics: Human Variation in Susceptibility to Environmental Agents," a paper presented at the annual meeting of the American Association for the Advancement of Science meeting, Toronto, January, 1981.

Oviatt, Sharon, L., "Inferring What Words Mean: Early Development in Infants' Comprehension of Common Object Names," *Child Development,* Vol. 53, February, 1982.

Palmer, Francis H., "The Effects of Early Childhood Intervention," a paper presented at the annual meeting of the American Association for the Advancement of Science, Denver, February, 1977.

Papert, *Mindstorms: Children, Computers, and Powerful Ideas,* New York, Basic Books, Inc., 1980.

Pass, Robert F., and others, "Increased Frequency of Cytomegalovirus Infection in Children in Group Day Care," *Pediatrics,* Vol. 74, July, 1984.

————, "Outcome of Symptomatic Congenital Cytomegalovirus Infection: Results of Long-Term Longitudinal Follow-up," *Pediatrics,* Vol. 66, November, 1980.

Passow, A. Harry, "The Nature of Giftedness and Talent," *Gifted Child Quarterly,* Vol. 25, Winter, 1981.

Penfield, Wilder, *The Second Career,* Boston, Little Brown, 1963.

————, and Lamar Roberts, *Speech and Brain Mechanisms,* Princeton, New Jersey, Princeton University Press, 1959.

Perino, Sheila C., and Joseph Perino, *Parenting the Gifted: Developing the Promise,* New York, R. R. Bowker, 1981.

Peterson, Dale, editor, *Intelligent Schoolhouse: Readings on Computers and Learning,* Reston, Virginia, Reston Publishing Company, Inc., 1984.

Phillips, John L., *The Origins of Intellect: Piaget's Theory,* San Francisco, W. H. Freeman, 1969.

Piaget, Jean, *The Language and Thought of the Child,* Cleveland, World Book, 1955.

————, *The Origin of Intelligence in Children,* New York, International Universities Press, 1952.

————, *Psychology of Intelligence,* Paterson, New Jersey, Littlefield, Adams, 1963.

Pincus, Cynthia S., Leslie Elliott, and Trudy Schlachter, *The Roots of Success,* Englewood Cliffs, New Jersey, Prentice-Hall, 1980.

Pines, Maya, "Baby, You're Incredible," *Psychology Today,* Vol. 16, September, 1979.

Plomin, Robert, "Developmental Behavioral Genetics," *Child Development,* Vol. 54, April, 1983.

Portnoy, Fern C., and Carolyn H. Simmons, "Day Care and Attachment," *Child Development,* Vol. 49, March, 1978.

Price, Eunice H., "How Thirty-Seven Gifted Children Learned to Read," *The Reading Teacher,* Vol. 30, 1976.

Provence, Sally, Audrey Naylor, and June Patterson, *The Challenge of Daycare,* New Haven, Connecticut, Yale University Press, 1977.

Ramey, Craig T., Dale C. Farren, and Frances A. Campbell,

"Predicting I.Q. from Mother-Infant Interactions," *Child Development,* Vol. 50, June, 1979.

Ricciuti, Henry N., "Effects of Infant Day Care Experience on Behavior and Development: Research and Implications for Social Policy," Washington, D.C., a review prepared for the Department of Health, Education, and Welfare, 1976.

Rinehart, Ward, and Adrienne Kols, with Sidney H. Moore, "Healthier Mothers and Children Through Family Planning," *Population Reports,* May–June, 1984.

Rogan, Walter, "Intrauterine Exposure," a paper presented at the annual meeting of the American Academy of Pediatrics, Chicago, September, 1984.

Rosenzweig, Mark R., and others, "Heredity, Environment, Learning, and the Brain," a paper presented at annual meeting of the American Association for the Advancement of Science, Berkeley, California, December, 1965.

Rothbart, Mary Klevjord, "Measurement of Temperament in Infancy," *Child Development,* Vol. 52, June, 1981.

Rovee-Colliers, Carolyn K., and Lewis P. Lipsitt, "Learning, Adaptions, and Memory in the Newborn, *Psychobiology of the Human Newborn,* P. Stratton, editor, New York, John Wiley and Sons, Ltd., 1982.

Royster, Eugene C., and others, "A National Survey of Head Start Graduates and Their Peers," Cambridge, Massachusetts, Abt Associates, 1978.

Rubenstein, Judith L., and Carollee Howes, "Caregiving and Infant Behavior in Day Care and in Homes," *Developmental Psychology,* Vol. 12, January, 1979.

Ruddy, Margaret G., and Marc H. Bornstein, "Cognitive Correlates of Infant Attention and Maternal Stimulation over the First Year of Life," *Child Development,* Vol. 53, February, 1982.

Rutter, Michael, "Social-Emotional Consequences of Day Care for Preschool Children," *American Journal of Orthopsychiatry,* Vol. 51, January, 1981.

Sakamoto, Takahiko, "Preschool Reading in Japan," *The Reading Teacher,* Vol. 29, December, 1975.

Sameroff, Arnold J., Ronald Seifer, and Penelope Kelly Elias, "Sociocultural Variability in Infant Temperament Ratings," *Child Development*, Vol. 51, February, 1982.

Sawyer, Robert N., "By-Mail Options for Brilliant Middle School Youth," a paper presented at the annual meeting of the American Academy of Pediatrics, Chicago, September, 1984.

Schachter, Frances Fuchs, "Toddlers with Employed Mothers," *Child Development*, Vol. 52, September, 1981.

Schetky, Diane H., "The Emotional and Social Development of the Gifted Child," *G/C/T*, May/June, 1981.

Schubert, Jan Bascom, Sharon Bradley-Johnson, and James Nuttal, "Mother-Infant Communication and Maternal Employment," *Child Development*, Vol. 51, March, 1980.

Schwartz, Lita Linzer, "Are You a Gifted Parent of a Gifted Child?" *Gifted Child Quarterly*, Vol. 25, Winter, 1981.

Schwartz, Pamela, "Length of Day-Care Attendance and Attachment Behavior in Eighteen-Month-Old Infants," *Children Development*, Vol. 54, August, 1983.

Seitz, Victoria, "Long-Term Effects of Intervention: A Longitudinal Investigation," a paper presented at the annual meeting of the American Association for the Advancement of Science, Denver, February, 1977.

Shwedel, Allan, "A New Direction in the Identification of Children for a Preschool Gifted Program," a paper presented at the annual meeting of the American Educational Research Association, Boston, April, 1980.

Siegal, Linda A., "Infant Tests As Predictors of Cognitive and Language Development at Two Years," *Child Development*, Vol. 52, June, 1981.

Siegel, Linda S., "Reproductive, Perinatal, and Environmental Factors as Predictors of the Cognitive and Language Development of Preterm and Full-Term Infants," *Child Development*, Vol. 53, August, 1982.

Siegelbaum, Laura, and Rotner, Susan, "Ideas and Activities for Parents of Preschool Gifted Children," *G/C/T*, January/February, 1983.

Silva, P.A., and J. Bradshaw, "Some Factors Contributing to Intelligence at Age of School Entry," *British Journal of Educational Psychology*, Vol. 50, 1980.

Smith, Allen N., and Carl M. Spence, "National Day Care Study: Optimizing the Day Care Environment," American Journal of Orthopsychiatry, Vol. 50, October, 1980.

Snyder, Solomon H., "Neurosciences: An Integrative Discipline," *Science,* Vol. 225, September 21, 1984.

Spencer, Mina, and Linda Baskin, "Microcomputers in Early Childhood Education," a report for the National Institute of Education, Washington, D.C., 1983.

Spitzer, Dean R., *Concept Formation and Learning in Early Childhood,* Columbus, Ohio, Charles E. Merrill Publishing Company, 1977.

Stagno, Sergio, and others, "Congenital Cytomegalovirus Infection," *The New England Journal of Medicine,* Vol. 306, April 22, 1982.

————, "An Outbreak of Toxoplasmosis Linked to Cats," *Pediatrics,* Vol. 65, February, 1980.

Stein, Zena A., "Adverse Reproductive Outcomes and the Environment," a paper presented at the annual meeting of the American Association for the Advancement of Science, New York, May, 1984.

Stevenson, Harold W., "Making the Grade: School Achievement in Japan, Taiwan, and the United States," from the Annual Report of the Center for Advanced Study in the Behavioral Sciences, Ann Arbor, Michigan, 1984.

Stewig, John Warren, *Teaching Language Arts in Early Childhood,* New York, CBS College Publishing, Holt, Rinehart, and Winston, 1982.

Strobino, Barbara Reiber, Jennie Kline, and Zena Stein, "Chemical and Physical Exposures of Parents: Effects on Human Reproduction and Offspring," *Journal of Early Human Development,* Vol. 1, February, 1978.

Sutton, Marjorie Hunt, "Children Who Learned To Read in Kindergarten: A Longitudinal Study," *The Reading Teacher,* Vol. 22, April, 1969.

Teale, William H., *Early Reading: An Annotated Bibliography,* Newark, Delaware, International Reading Association, 1980.

Teale, William H., "Positive Environments for Learning to Read: What Studies of Early Readers Tell Us," *Language Arts,* Vol. 55, November/December, 1978.

Teale, William H., "Toward a Theory of How Children Learn to Read and Write Naturally," *Language Arts*, Vol. 59, September, 1982.

Thompson, Ross A., Michael E. Lamb, and David Estes, "Stability of Infant-Mother Attachment and Its Relationship to Changing Life Circumstances, in an Unselected Middle-Class Sample," *Child Development*, Vol. 53, February, 1982.

Tittle, Bess M., "Why Montessori for the Gifted?" *G/C/T*, May/June, 1984.

Torrance, E. Paul, *Guiding Creative Talent*, Englewood Cliffs, New Jersey, Prentice-Hall, 1962.

————, *Rewarding Creative Behavior*, Englewood Cliffs, New Jersey, Prentice-Hall, 1965.

Truss, Carroll V., and others, "Parent Training in Preprimary Competence," a paper presented at the American Psychological Association meeting, San Francisco, August, 1977.

Tulkin, Steven R., and Jerome Kagan, "Mother-Child Interaction in the First Year of Life," *Child Development*, Vol. 43, March, 1972.

Turkle, Sherry, *The Second Self: Computers and the Human Spirit*, New York, Simon and Schuster, 1984.

United States Air Force, Epidemiology Division, "An Epidemiologic Investigation of Health Effects in Air Force Personnel Following Exposure to Herbicides," February, 1984.

Uzgiris, Ina C., "Patterns of Cognitive Development in Infancy," *Merrill-Palmer Quarterly*, Vol. 19, October, 1973.

Verp, Marion S., and Albert B. Gerbie, "Amniocentesis for Prenatal Diagnosis," *Clinical Obstetrics and Gynecology*, Vol. 24, December, 1981.

Wagoner, Joseph K., Peter F. Infante, and David F. Brown, "Genetic Effects Associated with Industrial Chemicals," a paper presented at the Conference on Women and the Workplace, Washington, D.C., June, 1976.

Walbert, Herbert J., and others, "Childhood Traits and Environmental Conditions of Highly Eminent Adults," *Gifted Child Quarterly*, Vol. 25, Summer, 1981.

Wann, Kenneth D., Miriam Selchen Dorn, and Elizabeth Ann Liddie, *Fostering Intellectual Development in Young Children*, New York, Teachers College Press, 1962.

Watrin, Rita, and Paul Hanly Furfey, *Learning Activities for the Young Preschool Child*, New York, D. Van Nostrand Company, 1978.

Watt, Dan, "Teaching Turtles," *Popular Computing*, July, 1982.

Weissbourd, Bernice, and Judith Musick, editors, *Infants: Their Social Environments*, Washington, D.C., National Association for the Education of Young Children, 1981.

Werner, John S., and Lewis P. Lipsitt, "The Infancy of Human Sensory Systems," from *Developmental Plasticity*, E. S. Gollin, editor, New York, Academic Press, Inc., 1981.

Weyer, Stephen A., "Computers for Communication," *Childhood Education*, March/April, 1983.

Whelan, Elizabeth M., *A Smoking Gun*, Philadelphia, George F. Stickley Company, 1984.

White, Burton L., "Critical Influences in the Origins of Competence," *Merrill-Palmer Quarterly*, Vol. 21, October, 1975.

———, "Early Stimulation and Behavioral Development," in *Genetics, Environment and Intelligence*, edited by A. Oliverior, Elsevier/North Holland, Biomedical Press, 1977.

———, "Guidelines for Parent Education, 1977," a paper presented at the Planning Education Conference, Flint, Michigan, September, 1977.

———, *Human Infants: Experience and Psychological Development*, Englewood Cliffs, New Jersey, Prentice-Hall, 1971.

———, *The Origins of Human Competence*, Lexington, Massachusetts, D. C. Heath and Company, 1979.

———, "Should You Stay Home with Your Baby?" *Educational Horizons*, Fall, 1980.

———, and Peter Castle, "Visual Exploratory Behavior Following Postnatal Handling of Human Infants," *Perceptual and Motor Skills*, Vol. 18, 1964.

————, and Jean Carew Watts, *Experience and Environment*, Englewood Cliffs, New Jersey, Prentice-Hall, 1973.

————, and others, "Child Rearing Practices and the Development of Competence, Final Report," Cambridge, Massachusetts, Harvard University Graduate School of Education, 1974.

Whitley, Richard J., and Others, "The Natural History of Herpes Simplex Virus Infection of Mother and Newborn," *Pediatrics,* Vol. 66, October, 1980.

Willerman, Lee, "Effects of Families on Intellectual Development," *American Psychologist,* Vol. 34, October, 1979.

Williams, Frank E., "Developing Children's Creativity at Home and in School," *G/C/T,* September/October, 1982.

Wilson, Christopher B., and others, "Development of Adverse Sequelae in Children Born with Subclinical Congenital Toxoplasma Infection," *Pediatrics,* Vol. 66, November, 1980.

Wilson, James G., and Margery W. Shaw, editors, *Handbook of Teratology,* New York, Plenum Press, 1977.

Yaffe, Sumner J., "Drugs and Pregnancy," a paper presented at the annual meeting of the American Association for the Advancement of Science, San Francisco, January, 1980.

Young, Karl W., and Teri Young, "Putting Montessori and the Computer Together," The Constructive Triangle, Vol. 11, Summer, 1984.

Yurchak, Mary-Jane H., and others, *Infant-Toddler Curriculum of the Brookline, Early Education Project,* Brookline, Massachusetts, Brookline Early Education Project, November, 1975.

Yussen, Steven R., "Performance of Montessori and Traditionally Schooled Nursery Children on Social Cognitive Tasks and Memory Problems," *Contemporary Educational Psychology,* Vol. 5, April, 1980.

Ziajka, Alan, "Microcomputers in Early Childhood Education?" *Young Children,* July, 1983.

Zigler, Edward F., and Edmund W. Gordon, editors, *Day*

Care: Scientific and Social Policy Issues, Boston, Auburn House Publishing, 1982.

———, and Jeanette Valentine, editors, *Project Head Start: A Legacy of the War on Poverty,* New York, Free Press, 1979.